Employment and Technical Change in Europe

Work Organization, Skills and Training

Edited by Ken Ducatel
Lecturer
PREST
University of Manchester

Edward Elgar

Published by

Edward Elgar Publishing Limited
Gower House
Croft Road
Aldershot
Hants GU11 3HR
England

Edward Elgar Publishing Company
Old Post Road
Brookfield
Vermont 05036
USA

British Library Cataloguing in Publication Data

Employment and Technical Change in Europe:
Work Organization, Skills and Training
    I. Ducatel, Ken
    331.125094

Library of Congress Cataloguing in Publication Data

Employment and technical change n Europe : work organization, skills, and training / edited by Ken Ducatel.
    272 p.   23 cm.
    Includes bibliographical references and index.
    1. Employees—Effect of technological innovations on—Europe.
    2. Product planning—Europe.   3. Skilled labour—Europe.
    4. Occupational training—Europe.   I. Ducatel, Ken.
    HD6331.2.E85E47   1994
    331.25—dc20   94–15927
                                                        CIP

ISBN 1 85278 775 9

Printed in Great Britain at the University Press, Cambridge

Contents

Tables

Figures

List of Contributors

Lars Erik Andreasen is in DGV (Directorate-General Industrial Relations and Social Affairs) in the European Commission. Originally an agriculturalist, he worked for some years in the Danish Ministry of Agriculture before joining the European Commission. In DGV he has been particularly interested in fostering a climate of innovation in work organization. To this end he has facilitated numerous conferences, seminars and studies on organizational modernization, including the project from which the chapters in this book originally stemmed.

Ken Ducatel has been lecturer in PREST (Programme of Policy Research in Engineering Science and Technology) at the University of Manchester since 1989. His current research interests include the consequences of information technology on work, the emerging policy debate on transport telematics and urban information technology innovations. He is co-author of the recent book 'Transport in the Information Age' (Belhaven).

Chris Freeman is Professor at the Maastricht Economic Research Institute on Innovation and Technology (MERIT), the University of Limburg. He is also Emeritus Professor of Science Policy at the University of Sussex, where he was the first director of the Science Policy Research Unit (SPRU). He has published widely on the economics of technological change and is co-author, with Luc Soete, of the forthcoming book 'Work for All or Mass Unemployment?' (Pinter).

Ian Miles is Associate Director of the Programme of Policy Research in Engineering Science and Technology (PREST), the University of Manchester. Initially a social psychologist, he worked at SPRU, the University of Sussex for 14 years. He has made major contributions to the study of innovation in services and the development of telematics. His current interests include innovations in clean technology. He recently co-authored 'Development Flexibility and Technology' (Routledge).

Gareth Rees is Professor in the Department of Adult and Continuing Education at the University of Wales, Swansea. He has written extensively on vocational education and training and on the social impacts of industrial change. He has often advised government departments, local authorities and development agencies in Britain and elsewhere.

Teresa Rees is a Reader at the School for Advanced Urban Studies, the University of Bristol. She has considerable research experience in the areas of education, training and labour, which has resulted in her acting as consultant to many training bodies from local authorities to the European Commission. Her recent publications include 'Women and the Labour Market (Routledge) and 'Our Sisters' Land' (University of Wales Press).

Jacqueline Senker is Research Fellow at SPRU, the University of Sussex. Her research interests concern the links between industry and the public sector. These links are explored in her forthcoming book 'Knowledge Frontiers' (Oxford University Press).

Peter Senker is Senior Fellow at SPRU, the University of Sussex. He is a widely acknowledged authority on training policy and the implications of technological change for skill requirements. His recent publications include 'Industrial Training in a Cold Climate' (Avebury).

Luc Soete is Professor of International Economics and Director of MERIT at the University of Limburg. He has published extensively on the economics of technological change on both theoretical and empirical levels. He is co-author, with Chris Freeman, of 'Work for all or Mass Unemployment?' (Pinter).

Foreword

Lars Erik Andreasen

The modernization of the workplace is a major challenge to all the parties involved in industrial, technology and employment policy. For firms it means identifying and moving towards more effective work practices through the efficient deployment of new technologies. Technical innovation has often had a deeply disappointing payoff in terms of productivity, particularly if careful thought is not given to how new technologies are introduced in the workplace. For workers and their representatives there are the threats and opportunities of changing working practices. New technologies have long been associated with job losses and gains, changes in skills. But there are also new requirements of workers. The cycles of a working life are different now; no longer can someone assume that when they enter a craft or profession as a young person they will ply that trade for life. People will have to retrain not just once but several times during a working life. Workers are also more often expected to take responsibility for more of their work. A decentralization of control in work is taking place, partly through the deployment of new technology. The result is often that workers have to be willing to take greater self-responsibility than in the past. Workers' representatives are often in a weak position in respect of technological change. They want their industry to be successful, and investment in new technology is a sign that management is optimistic about the future. However, workers often have to accept radical changes in the nature and status of their work. New technologies often promote a blurring of skill categories, reorganization and the restructuring of the status of workers. It is often hard to secure the most advantageous conditions when new technology is introduced; the technologies are very complex and unpredictable and there is now so much uncertainty in labour markets, forcing them to be very pragmatic about what they can achieve.

Clearly, new information technologies form a key component of the future competitiveness of European industry. The policy actions needed to support the shift towards an information economy are very difficult to identify. For instance, a success in one region of the European Union cannot be directly imitated in another. It is hard to transfer experience from one situation to another. We need to learn considerably more about the relationships between technology and social factors than we know now before innovation becomes a reliable guarantor of economic growth and stable employment generation. The process we are embarking on is to define good practice in a new era of industrial and technological management - one that is relevant to the information age. It is not only necessary but urgent to conduct debate on work organization, skills and training policy from an informed standpoint, a debate for which the papers in this book provides food and fuel.

DGV,
European Commission,
Brussels, 1994

1. Introduction

Ken Ducatel

Ever faster change in economic and social life seems to be one of the few constant features of modern life. Among the strongest themes of such change in recent years have been increasingly pervasive effects of technology, changing patterns of employment relations and a heightened internationalism, in business, government and in the private lives of European citizens. The papers presented in this book address all three of these core features of the current context of change in the industrial environment of Europe. They arose out of a programme of work undertaken for the European Commission at the start of the 1990s. The aim, at that time, was to provide a documentary background, on the basis of existing knowledge, about the work environment, skill trajectories and training implications of new information and communication technologies (IT) up to the beginning of the 21st Century.

IT is particularly interesting as focus for the study of employment in Europe given both its pervasiveness and flexibility. Not only does it seem to affect all types of business, but nearly all types of work are being changed through contact with IT-based products and processes. At the same time, it differs from all previous forms of technology in that it is extremely malleable. The tendency of IT to become cheaper, more powerful, more robust and easier to use means that more and more opportunities for its application are presenting themselves all the time. The facility to reprogram IT means that the same capital equipment can perform a variety of functions, which if not reducing the rate of technological obsolescence at least means that the rate of innovation in processes is not so tied to a particular cycle of capital investment. Such changes increase the potential for productivity increases because of reduced retooling time, greater integration between functions and the opportunity to extract economies of scope, by integrating a number of activities into a single work process. In addition, IT directly deals with flows of information and transactions in a firm, thus many of the core business activities, such as much office work, are liable to transformation as the potential for direct data collection and control over information becomes greater.

1

COMMON THEMES

Given the defining features of IT, it is not surprising that we feel vindicated in advancing a claim for serious and specific attention to the employment implications of IT.   However, this is not to say that IT has a determinate role in defining employment outcomes.   On the contrary, a theme which consistently re-emerges throughout this book is that the flexibility of IT contributes to a wide range of potential outcomes in terms of skill, training and work organization.   Nevertheless, there are consistent features in the way that IT is being taken up by European industry, and in the sorts of trends which seem to be emerging which are affecting European managers and workers.   One obvious area for debate, therefore, is the extent to which it is possible to codify a set of best practice principles for the introduction and management of IT, which will be good for all European contexts.   Such a suggestion may appear to fly in the face of our empirical evidence - which underlines the complexity of interactions between industry, technology, training, culture and other contextual variables, thus reducing the chances of a single workable solution to IT management in Europe.   However, the emergence of pan-European actors, in the form of the legislative actions of the European Union (EU) and European Companies operating on a pan-European basis may indicate a future trend towards greater integration in European labour markets and employment practices.

For the moment, however, discussion will be confined to a number of areas of consistency across Europe, which repeatedly appear in the studies which this book contains.   These concern: the profile of adoption in terms of leading and lagging firms and industries; the overall trends in skills demands, which are remarkably consistent at the general level if not in the particular; institutional barriers which are as much inhibitors to the widespread adoption of IT as technical ones; and the uneven of receptiveness to IT in different countries which seems to relate to differences between national institutional structures.   Each will be briefly discussed in turn before turning to a direct consideration of the chapters which make up the book.

The Adoption of IT

The rate of adoption of IT in Europe has been rapid, but uneven in respect of region, sector and occupational group.   Large and wealthier countries such as Germany, France and the UK tend to lead overall, although more advanced smaller countries such as the Netherlands have a very high per capita rate of adoption of IT.   Within countries the leading regions tend to be around the administrative core of the country, the main cities where headquarters and the seats of government are located. That these sections of the economies of Europe, in which executive activities cluster, are leading the shift to IT is indicative of an important feature of IT adoption, which is that informational activities are earlier adopters of IT. Thus, industries such as the financial, telecommunication and business services have tended to lead in applying IT. This is true for all European countries, even those that tend to lag overall. For instance, in Greece banks are among the most vigorous adopters of IT. A slightly different process of adoption is seen in manufacturing industry where leadership is in industries which have a high level of technical competence to begin with, particularly those closely involved in the production of IT products, or where there is a good deal of large scale repetitive assembly work.

Geography and industrial specialization are not the only general determinants of adoption. The other main factors which seem to be common are firm size and the type of technology itself; although these are far from independent of sector and region. Slower adoption in both services and manufacturing seems to be related to small firm size and high levels of product variety, perhaps due to small batches or inconsistent raw materials. Industries characterized by small-scale craft production are more resistant to automation, perhaps because of the relatively low educational attainments of management and workforce. Again this tends to be a persistent feature of labour intensive industries in the poorer parts of Europe, for instance textile production in Greece and Portugal. Also, certain technologies tend to be adopted more slowly in manufacturing, particularly those which are more complex because they bring together a number of, previously separate work processes. Examples include flexible manufacturing systems and robots which are expensive to buy, install and implement, and as such tend to be limited to larger scale, more repetitive and predictable work operations such as paint spraying and welding operations in automobile production. Beyond this general picture of the scale of adoption, there are wide variations in the way that individual firms implement the technologies. A striking feature revealed in this book is that, whilst rates of adoption from place to place may be similar, the nature of the adoption process and the productivity gains achieved vary significantly from firm to firm and region to region.

Skills Structures and IT

The findings which emerge from the studies presented here indicate that overall there is an increase in the level of skills required from workers as a result of exposure to IT. There are exceptions to this general trend, and individual managements can find ways to pursue deskilling strategies, if they so desire. The indications are, however, that such strategies are likely to be sub-optimal in most cases. However, for some managers there may be no alternative to operating a low skill work environment. In effect, if the quality of the skills available to them in the labour market are insufficient they may be forced to implement new IT in ways which are sub-optimal.

Retailing is particularly notable as an area in which some of the traditional skills of staff and management are being reduced as result of the computer-mediated centralization of information process. For instance, the ordering of goods and the rostering of staff are more likely to take place centrally rather than being decided in-store. In a similar way, decisions about shop displays and appearance are likely to be decided more by central management. This industry has in any case rather low levels of training across the whole of Europe, although some countries have a consistently higher rate of qualified shop workers.   In other industries, routine maintenance and machine operator skills might be redistributed as a result of the digitalization of equipment. For instance, field engineers are reduced to operating diagnostic systems and replacing modules. Thus, the skill demands will increase only for the bench engineers who have to work on more demanding procedures such as resolving equipment failures, software errors and so forth.

Only where maintenance and operation tasks are fully computerized are there likely to be significant skill declines. In practice, many technicians will be expected to work on old and new generations of equipment simultaneously, requiring a broader range of skills and disciplines, covering perhaps mechatronics, pneumatics, and electronics as well as mechanical and electrical skills. In addition, there is strong evidence, from the range of studies reviewed here, that workers of all types are more often being required to work in a more collaborative manner in teams. The range of skills, therefore, is broadened to include communication skills and taking individual and group responsibility.

Finally, a message which occurs again and again is that the balance of skills is shifting from manual and craft skills to intellectual and cognitive abilities. Thus, there is a growth in the demand for abstract reasoning from all levels of workers. In part this is because workers now tend to work at one remove from the actual process. They are systems controllers rather than directly intervening in production. Thus, they need to be able to interpret read outs produced by machines, which in turn often requires a grasp of the theoretical concepts on which these messages are based. Because these machines are often very expensive to purchase and install, there is a strong trend for managers to see the benefits of having well trained workers, who can anticipate trouble, and perhaps shoot it before it halts production.

Institutional Barriers to IT

Confining the analysis to skill demands would lead one to overlook one of the key features of IT in the workplace, that the skills upgrading comes at a considerable cost in terms of the number of jobs, particularly amongst the unskilled, semi-skilled and many craft workers. There may be a case to argue that the overall upgrading occurs because the tail of lower skilled employment is being cut off. Moreover, it is not at all clear that the rate of generation of new opportunities from new product markets and industries based directly on IT will provide a sufficiently large substitute for the employment which is being lost.

It might, therefore, be a redeeming feature of institutional inertia in adoptive behaviour that it tends to slow the rate at which job loss might otherwise occur. However, such advantages are likely to be short-term and constrained in their impact. In general, organizational inertia has major negative consequences directly for the industry concerned, for a wider cross-section of industry which depends upon its productive efficiency and for individuals who suffer because of deeply embedded social practices. Examples of the first two negative consequences of inertia can be seen in industrial sectors which have had little direct experience with IT. A good example is the construction industry, which has been relatively slow to adopt IT compared to the rest of manufacturing. This lack of direct experience represents a major challenge because industry is increasingly expecting new buildings to offer high levels of automation. There are new demands for integrated security services, the automation of heating control, air conditioning and so forth mean that the construction industry now has to face the initial installation and retrofitting of such systems. Electronic related services in some complex buildings can amount to 50% of construction costs. The result is a significant and growing shortfall for IT expertise in construction both in specialist areas, and in broad multi-skilling for repair and maintenance.

From the point of view of development at the regional level in less advanced areas of Europe, such as Greece, attitudes of managers and workers are often not conducive to the adoption of IT. Few firms regard training of existing staff as a serious objective, preferring to recruit pre-skilled personnel where necessary. Similarly, the barriers to IT-related job opportunities which confront women and minorities are related to social inertia. Given the shift from the requirement of physical strength in automated environments one would expect there to be wider opportunities open to women. However, as Teresa Rees discusses in this volume, equality of access to training will not by itself overcome the social inertia of women's traditional roles and the strongly male gendered aura of new technologies.

Institutional Compatibilities with IT

Despite the complexity of outcomes which are possible when IT is introduced into the employment situation there do appear to be regularities in the way that some institutional structures in Europe match the characteristics of IT better than others. The potentialities of IT seem to be most effectively exploited in situations in which there are arrangements which make the most of its flexibility. Such institutional flexibility is achieved through a number of different interlocking structures. First, the skill structures which seem best adapted are those where workers, and managers, are not constrained by historical horizontal and vertical demarcations, this allows greater organizational adaptivity. Second, where workers, workers' representatives and management have a less conflicting approach to the introduction of new technologies it can improve not only the productivity of the new technology but also the quality of work. In turn, this may lead to improved industrial relations founded on trust. For instance, traditions and culture in Danish industry enhance the ability of workers to accept change and to move towards team working; in addition a history of good labour relations facilitates acceptance of the new technology and work organization. Similar conclusions might be made about German industrial structures.

However, although this might imply that widely celebrated employment best practice, such as the German dual training system, will remain a model for all of Europe, this is not necessarily the case. In fact, highly formalized institutional systems, such as Germany's dual training and industrial relations systems, are placed under pressure by the increasing breadth of skills necessary even in quite small scale enterprises, the rapid rate of obsolescence of the skills profile in local economies, and the difficulty of making decisions which are robust for all workplaces through centralized negotiating machinery. Perversely, the better structured systems create constraints on meeting demand, given existing administrative structures, recruitment channels and so on. Whilst on balance they currently produce more appropriately skilled workers and industrial relations than other regions of Europe, they may not meet medium term demands on European industry due to competitive pressures and the opportunities of new IT.

THE CONTRIBUTIONS

The book retains much of the original structure of the research project upon which it is based. The division of labour in the project was that: Jacky and Peter Senker were responsible for analysing skills demands; Teresa and Gareth Rees undertook an analysis of training structures; and Ian Miles and Ken Ducatel looked at work organization and industrial relations issues. Inevitably there were overlaps in the coverage of such interlocking issues, some of which is retained in this book. Fortunately, the areas of overlap showed remarkable consistency in findings, despite our natural differences in emphasis and perspective. The result is a consistency of message, which is reflected in the general features brought out above.

The first main chapter of the book (Chapter 2 by Ken Ducatel and Ian Miles) provides a backdrop to IT related innovation in European industry. It aims to give a sense of the importance of IT to industry and employment by outlining its unprecedented flexibility as a technology, which results from its reprogrammability, and its nature as an information processing tool. However, Ducatel and Miles are emphatic that the technology is not determining, but is subject to social forces in the way that it is employed. As the later chapters confirm, the overall picture of adoption of IT reflects both the general pattern of wealth and development across Europe, with the bigger, more advanced economies, such as Germany, France and the UK being significantly ahead of the others. Other countries, such as Spain, which are under-going rapid restructuring are, however, catching up in terms of overall investment levels. Some countries, such as Greece and Portugal show significant lags in investment levels and adoptive profile, which is revealed by later chapters to relate to a largely traditional industrial structure, the generally low level of the existing skills profile of the population and to institutions and cultures which are resistant to rapid transformations of the economy.

The section on skills (by Jacky and Peter Senker) considers in turn the implications of IT in the core IT industries, such as telecommunications and computer services (Chapter 3), manufacturing industry and construction (Chapter 4) and services (Chapter 5). Here the emphasis is upon the relationship between the overall effects on job numbers and the skills profiles of a series of industries. In overall terms, as noted above, the results indicate that there are increasing demands for highly skilled workers able to operate and repair highly complex systems of technology. On the other hand, many lower skill and traditional skill occupations are under threat as traditional manual and electro-mechanical operations are turned over to full computerization. Thus, even in the core-IT industries, particularly telecommunications, there may be an absolute decline in jobs for workers engaged in traditional craft and semi-skilled tasks. At the same time, there are persistent shortages of adequately skilled workers in most industries which have been extensively exposed to IT. This can be seen very clearly in the core-IT, engineering and automotive industries. The structure of skills seems to have shifted in these manufacturing industries, with the broadening of some skill areas, for instance the integration of tasks such as milling, drilling, cutting and grinding operations into one workstation. On the other hand, there has been a transfer of design and programming activities from operators to specialists in many instances. Thus, the overall upgrading effects on skill are mediated by a redistribution of responsibilities, with a considerable blurring of roles. As a result, many firms have engaged in internal training schemes, but problems such as poaching of trained workers and the high cost of retraining existing employees are consistent features across Europe.

A feature of the studies in this book is that, for once, consideration is given to industries which are ignored in studies of employment changes, such as the food industry and retailing. These two industries both show a tendency for the automation of mainly manual activities, such as the stacking and placing of packages and products. Similarly, bar coding of products reduces much of the work in tracking and tracing of inventory and sales. Once again, therefore, there is an overall replacement of lower skill categories. However, food processing is resistant to automation because of the variability of the basic raw material and because hygiene regulations and sterilization procedures make for a very hostile environment for IT. Thus a degree of manual intervention is likely to persist in these areas. In a similar way, the labour intensity of retailing, which is a large sector of employment, is likely to persist, for although jobs may be eroded by automation a considerable amount of shelf filling and (electronic) check out operation will remain for the foreseeable future.

Although store management in retailing seems to be undergoing deskilling, through the computer-mediated centralization of decision making, such managers may in time see a return to more devolved forms of control, if counter centralization trends elsewhere in services are duplicated. The examples of branch network reorganization in banking and the creation of typing pools in office work had unsatisfactory results both in terms of worker morale and the quality of the organization's performance. In both cases, there has been, with the emergence of distributed computer networks, a more recent turn towards decentralization of control, although central management seemed able to retain a considerable power of central direction.

The chapters on training begin with Gareth Rees' conceptualization of the much debated issue of the appropriateness of different Vocational and

Educational Training (VET) Systems (Chapter 6).   Rees argues that there will inevitably be a diversity of outcomes in terms of training practices, given the complexity of factors at play such as the local industrial structure and practices, structures of political decision making and the existing condition of the labour market in terms of appropriately skilled and trained labour. He makes the important point that the definition of a VET System to deliver what is needed is hampered in many ways, not the least that most of the time employers cannot define their individual skill needs.   He, therefore, maintains that there can be no direct relationship between the VET structure and national economic performance, because causal mechanisms are more deeply intertwined in other factors. Moreover, improvement in the VET System cannot be expected to pay off directly in increased competitiveness.

Even so, there is an issue as to the degree of congruence which exists between labour market demands, associated with competition in the Single European Market and new IT, and the ability of the VET System to supply them. Certainly there is wide variation in participation in post compulsory education across Europe: from 90 per cent in Germany down to 50 per cent in parts of Southern Europe. There is also wide variance in how vocational education is in character and also in the quality of training.   For instance, the UK only competes with France and Germany in output and quality at the higher degree level. One worrying feature across the whole of Europe is that enrolments in technical and scientific disciplines have declined in the past decade, which may inhibit the ability to provide technically skilled workers for the future.   This is of concern given that a higher level of initial training arguably makes it easier to provide retraining for new production techniques.   Thus, simple quantitative measures of output from the VET System are no reliable guide to the appropriateness of the training provided.   As Rees shows by examining school, intermediate and higher level education, there is very little consistency in approach to vocational education within or between these levels anywhere in Europe. Nor is there a clear articulation between the skill need as felt by industry and the outputs, or an easy way of remedying the situation. Where successful matching of VET output to demand has occurred it is arguably more by happy coincidence than careful planning. As already noted, these criticisms can even be levelled at the much vaunted German dual training system, which is being placed under pressure by the increasing breadth of training necessary even in quite small scale enterprises and the rapid rate of obsolescence of the skills profile of local economies.

Teresa Rees (Chapter 7) points out that given the widely felt shortfall of skilled personnel in Europe and the fact that women are likely to make up the vast majority of new entrants to the labour market during the 1990s, there is an urgent need to find ways of making IT-related training opportunities more readily available.   Equality at the point of access to training is not enough. Social status characteristics seem to determine real opportunity rather more strongly than the rational selection of individuals on the basis of merit. IT occupations are potentially less stereotyped as a male preserve, given the break they represent from traditional male characteristics of technology related work, such as physical strength.   However, the requirements of IT jobs are, it seems, becoming masculinized and women are beginning to cluster in the lower jobs in the core IT industries.

Policies to increase access to training have varied between earmarking funds - which raises the problem of 'ghettoising' of the issue - to targeting resources into sectors where women are highly represented - and by so doing perhaps channelling women in to more low level work.   In case studies of the German and UK experiences, Rees extracts a number of critical lessons. First, whilst the larger German firms seem more willing to support women-orientated training, there are inequalities in provision and participation. For instance, a women only scheme run by AEG was successful but did not lead to the full qualification. On the other hand recruitment of women to traditional mixed training courses has been difficult because of entrenched inequalities in access.   These are also found to some extent amongst other groups who have training and retraining access difficulties, such as older workers and ethnic minorities, and can add together to create multiple access problems, for instance in the case of older women workers from Turkey. As Rees notes, women only training can be a way of breaking the vicious circle by which women are excluded from training opportunities, by adjusting the training structure to meet their initial needs such as perhaps accommodating family responsibilities and lower initial qualifications. However, her examples from the UK, although perhaps more extreme than elsewhere, indicate the tenuous and inconsistent nature of these schemes.

The problems of creating appropriate VET Systems in the peripheral regions of Europe are tackled in Chapter 8 by Gareth Rees.   He looks at two countries, Greece and Ireland, which have major areas of Objective 1 status; which are parts of the European Union typified by low value traditional industries such as agriculture and small scale craft manufacturing, with perhaps some tourism. He points out that, despite the recognition of the special problems faced by these areas, central European aid is unlikely to be on a sufficient scale to effect the structural reforms necessary to reform these economies. National governmental action leadership is likely to be the main hope. In Objective 1 regions, however, the starting point for IT strategies is very low, and there is no clear model of best practice in such circumstances. For instance, in Greece manufacturing is a low proportion of GNP and most of the firms are very small, 98% employ less than 50 people, and have low profitability. This means little opportunity for investment in new techniques and technologies. At the same time, the IT infrastructure is very weak, with a minute core-IT sector, a backward telecommunications system and even an unreliable electricity network is unreliable. However, spending on IT has increased in the state and private sectors, and substantial expansion is expected in the IT market in the 1990s. The VET System has responded to the potential new demands by making plans to introduce PCs into school education and there are computer training courses in a number of Universities and technical institutes, with a rise in graduates from 45 in 1982 to 1500 in 1988.

Supply-side actions, in countries such as Greece, are likely to be greater than the growth in demand will merit, given the low base from which it starts. In practice, graduates are likely to look abroad for a more coherent career structure than the nascent IT industry at home can support. Exactly the same situation occurs in Ireland, where there has been a long term commitment to the development of an IT industry and IT training. The IT sector is dominated by US branch plants whose demands for more professional IT expertise are limited. Thus, despite recent growth in indigenous IT production and the shift in transplants towards more high skill work, the demand for IT work has been mainly in direct production. Paradoxically, the integrated Irish VET strategy produced rather more high quality workers than the system could absorb, resulting in substantial emigration, as up to 70% of science graduates have left the country in recent years. The point is not that there is a shortage of vacancies in absolute terms (Irish and Greek firms suffer skills shortages as elsewhere), but that there is an absence of a structure of opportunity in Ireland. Many graduates saw no opportunity for a technically demanding career if they stayed at home.

The final section of the book looks at the less commonly explored issues of work organization and worker participation in technological change. In their chapter on work organization (Chapter 9) Miles and Ducatel reiterate the point made throughout the book that the implications of IT for firm structures are complex and are not simply deskilling, enskilling or polarizing. Cultural factors are at play here, with significant variations in the structure of industrial organization in different countries. For instance, there is a low formalization of job boundaries in Germany with high discretion and cooperative industrial relations styles. By contrast, French and British structures tend to be more heavily demarcated, with higher levels of formalization. In France the demarcations are associated with more elitist technical training as compared to a tradition of strong craft demarcation in Britain, although this has been eroded in recent years. Clearly, however, IT itself affects different workers to varying degrees, for instance office occupations are obviously more immediately affected by IT and some technical workers are also heavy users. Roughly half of office employees are likely to be directly affected by office automation impacts, and 25% of direct manufacturing jobs were affected by IT by the late 1980s. However, diffusion rates are uneven and the intensity of effect varies from occupation to occupation, sector to sector and place to place. Office Automation (OA) has had rather slower development than early forecasts would have suggested, social factors in the workplace seeming to continue to act as a substantial brake on the potential efficiency gains here. The continuing use of secretaries as 'office wives' or to provide 'chauffeured' use of PCs may well cause a more subtle shift in the emphasis of clerical type roles. The shift of data factory work offshore is also a long term spectre that has yet to gain more than rhetorical significance. One clearly important issue, in this area, is the way that IT will restructure the flows of information in the office, so that people no longer need to be co-located both with colleagues and paper based information sources. This must surely change the nature of markets for business services and for labour.

In manufacturing, again, historical and cultural evidence indicates that there can be a variety of outcomes. For instance, the relatively low proportion of supervisory staff in German plants (4.5% versus 9% in France), leads to a flatter hierarchy, thus in a sense the German system can be expected to be initially more flexible than its German or French counterparts. Kern and Schumann's (1992) work in the German automobile industry demonstrates the possibility of new structures of work associated both with the removal of much repetitive work, and the shift of human roles to controlling these systems. On the other hand, as evidence from the UK indicates, flexibility can also be achieved by making the workers themselves less secure, for instance by reducing the security of contract structures (increasing sub contracting, part-time work and temporary work) particularly in non-core areas.

Turning to issues of the quality of working life (Chapter 10) Ducatel and Miles point out that in general IT is associated with lower health risks, because much of the heavy exertion or direct exposure to toxic substances has been automated. However, there is evidence that, although the extremes of physical effort are reduced, work itself is becoming more intensive, the conditions of work may well be more fatiguing, with a 'tighter coupling' in the work cycles. Also, in the process of the replacement of manual by intellectual work there are increased pressures on workers from a number of sources, both direct physical health hazards associated with the use of IT and increased stress associated with work practices conjoined with the introduction of IT in the workplace. The health hazards include the problems of using VDUs, which by now are well documented and include primarily eye problems and lower arm injury associated with intensive use of keyboards. The stresses of modern work styles, to which IT contributes, are also related to the way that the new technologies are employed by managers. Workers may be reduced to the role of machine minder, being expected nevertheless to remain alert in case of a malfunction (which raises stress levels both through boredom and the expectation of a fast response in an emergency). There is also the induced stress where workers are aware that the actions are susceptible to continual monitoring by management. Also with new work organizational structures stressing the importance of employees taking more direct responsibility for their performance, workers can be placed under greater pressure to perform on a yearly, monthly, daily or minute by minute basis.

Despite the negative character which IT can assume in the workplace, there are opportunities for ameliorating working conditions as well as meeting overall managerial objectives. Indeed there is evidence to suggest that a close consideration of the simultaneous development of the quality of working life, human capital (in the form of skills) as well as productivity gains can lead to a smoother transition to a new technological system and to a more sustainable work organization structure, particularly given the importance of human capabilities and flexibility to intermediate between complex integrated systems. This is particularly apparent in the context of worker participation in the introduction of new technologies (Chapter 11), where direct consultation and negotiation can lead to better productivity, higher morale and better industrial relations. However, the evidence on participation indicates that full and wide ranging consultation on the introduction of IT is rather rare. Unions and workers tend to be told about new technologies rather late in the planning stage, often only at the time of introduction. These results hold even in countries, such as Belgium, where there is substantial legal support for the worker's right to participate in technological change. More optimistically, however, there is an expectation amongst both managers and workers' representatives that there will be greater involvement in the future both in terms of degree (ie direct consultation as well as information provision) and the stage at which the change occurs, from planning through to implementation.

To some degree, the effectiveness of trade unions in achieving an influence over the introduction of new IT relates to the degree of centralization and coherence in the industrial relations bargaining structure. For instance, unions organized at the industrial level tend to be much more influential in setting overall terms. Nevertheless, given the flexibility of IT, negotiation at plant level is also important. Discussions at industry level invariably lack the specificity and detail necessary to anticipate the situation in each workplace. Thus, most technology agreements occur at plant level and unions have to meet the challenge of dealing with strategic changes centrally whilst supporting local level negotiations.

The final chapter in the book, contributed by Luc Soete and Chris Freeman (Chapter 12), provides some policy perspectives on the issues taken up by the chapters reviewed above. Soete and Freeman point out that there is a need for major efforts to reduce bottlenecks in order to unleash the efficiency gains proffered by these new technologies. Not only is there the risk of under-utilizing large elements of our human capital, particularly people in the peripheral regions, women, minorities and older workers, but we cannot assume that these technologies will lead to a levelling out of unevenness. One particular need is for a better environment for the diffusion of new technology, especially by encouraging applications of telecommunications. The authors encourage consideration of the possibilities for more coherence between authorities at both the European and national level in their policies on technology, industry and employment. In particular, concern should focus upon the need to match the social with the technological factors in the implementation of IT. These effects include the need to increase the effectiveness of participation in technological change and the preparedness of unions and workers to meet the challenge of new technology. The quality of management of IT introduction also needs more attention, with more effort going into the formulation of best practice in the introduction of new technology. Whilst it is too simplistic to expect uniform policies to produce good results in all regions and industries, there should be at least the opportunity for the sharing of experience from one region to another; such learning effects could be encouraged through staff secondment, workshops and so on.

Soete and Freeman stress the challenge of a heightened rate of redundancy of existing skills. Clearly, the existing profile cannot simply be scrapped and there is also a need for a move towards the widespread acceptance of continual training throughout a working life. Many firms are too weak or unwilling to engage in a high level of retraining and may require more extensive support at a central European level in order for industry to reach an optimal level of competitiveness. These issues are writ large in the challenges facing VET systems at firm-level and in public vocational training and in conventional general education. They emphasize the requirement for transferable skills, especially cognitive skills, the ability to work in teams, communication aptitudes and entrepreneurial skills. It is, unfortunately, not clear that any coherent approaches as to the melding of these approaches is evident in any of the EU countries. There is instead a great variation both in the depth and consistency of training in all countries.

Clearly, efforts to monitor and evaluate the progress of integrated training policies are an important challenge for the future.

SUMMARY

The research in this book is directed towards three key features of restructuring in the European employment system: new patterns of employment associated with the search for responsiveness at the level of the firm; the greater scale of industrial markets associated with the formation of the Single European Market; and the permeation of IT into all industries and occupations. However, despite the self-evident relevance and necessity of such studies, at the time of the research, there existed an inadequate base of pre-existing analysis at a European level. This situation has begun to ease, presumably as more researchers realising the topical relevance of such work have begun to mobilize resources towards the development of a pan-European research frontier in employment research (see as examples Lane, 1989; Ferner and Hyman, 1992; Teague and Grahl, 1992). However, there remain two major gaps in this growing research domain. First, most of the research remains in the form of collections of national studies which are laid alongside, but not fully integrated with results from other countries. There has yet to emerge a widespread internationalism in employment research. Nevertheless, it is to be welcomed that researchers are far more aware of the findings from case studies in other countries, thus perhaps the development of proper international employment research is merely a matter of time. Second, the cross-national research has tended to concentrate on areas of research closely allied to labour market institutions and practices, particularly industrial relations. Whilst this is an obvious starting point, given the immediate opportunities for comparative analysis, it has caused a neglect of other important areas of research such as the consequences of internationalization in the development and application of information technology. It is at this gap that we have aimed this book.

2. The Diffusion of Information Technology in Europe

Ken Ducatel and Ian Miles

The employment changes associated with new information technology (IT) span a huge range of topics. A large amount of research has been carried out on them in many countries and across a number of distinct social scientific disciplines The distribution of effort in this wide range of work, however, is very uneven. Complex problems are posed even in trying to describe and summarize research results, let alone when one is seeking to develop theories or engage in useful forecasting employment trends.

In addition to the wide range of topics covered, and the diversity of their concrete manifestations in specific situations, two additional features make these issues complex. IT is not an homogeneous technology. The term refers to an expanding spectrum of diverse applications of a new 'heartland' technology - a technology at the core of our contemporary industrial system (Miles et al, 1990). Second, the issues cannot simply be 'read off' the technology, as 'impacts of IT'. Rather, they are matters of human agency, with interested agents (social actors - innovators, vendors, distributors, purchasers, end-users, etc.) acting more or less strategically and consciously so as to influence the outcomes of technical and organizational developments. The phrase 'the implications of IT' is used here rather than talking about 'impacts', in order to signify that technical change affects the opportunities available for human action, rather than directly determining action itself.

INFORMATION TECHNOLOGY

The development of microelectronics and, more broadly, semiconductor technology has been central to new information technology. This heartland technology, beginning with the integrated circuit and its subsequent miniaturization, is providing unprecedented information-processing capability to a wide range of activities. Its trajectory of increasing utility in terms of power, price and reliability is at the core of the majority of IT developments

(Miles et al., 1988). The production of chips and related semiconductor based materials is the heartland IT production sector, around this lies a set of related industries which are producing multipurpose IT products rather than IT-using products for specific applications. The telecommunications and computer industries are parts of the IT-producing sector. Computer and telecommunications services are integral parts of the IT sector. They do not merely add value to the hardware, they are the means by which the value of the hardware is realized. As IT is highly software-dependent, these services are intrinsic components of new IT. In contrast, the machine tool or household appliances industries are more focused in terms of markets, and their products may be considered to be IT-using rather than IT products.

IT has a number of key features which mark it out as a revolutionary technology (Figure 2.1). It is programmable and therefore can be adapted to changing circumstances. It has information processing capacity which makes it both a powerful tool of management and creates the potential for machines to talk to one another. The process of miniaturization is making it accessible to even the smallest of enterprises. Increasing user friendliness means that IT is no longer the preserve of a few highly trained technocrats.

Programmability is a crucial characteristic of computer technologies. In many cases, IT systems feature more or less dedicated software running on general purpose hardware. Sometimes hardware appears to be more completely dedicated: some IT-using equipment is employing integrated circuits installed in such ways that the scope for alternative applications is extremely limited. But core IT products like computers and telecommunications equipment are typically general purpose information-processing devices, that can be applied to different tasks, with different software, and in different configurations.

Programmability is responsible for the growing importance of software within the IT producing and using industries, and it reinforces attention on the scope for flexibility in production. It means that the same information technology hardware, even the same semiconductor chips, can be applied to a vast range of problems. If the programmability of IT enhances the flexibility and therefore the general utility of new industrial machinery, the information processing capacity of IT reinforces that trend. The organizational need for information processing power promoted the growth of markets for general purpose software for accounting, payroll and word processing, which despite being standardized are adaptable for use in a wide range of organizations.

Figure 2.1   Key features of new information technology

Programmability   IT systems are essentially programmable.   Any computer can simulate any other computer, though this may occur very poorly and slowly if the architectures are very different. IT devices are 'virtual machines', where the programming determines what type of machine performance is forthcoming. Programmability means the growing importance of the role of 'software' of all kinds, both in terms of contribution to systems performance and utility, and in terms of production costs - though reproduction costs typically decrease very substantially. 'Software' here includes texts and broadcast   programmes as well as systems and applications programs for computers and microprocessor-controlled devices. There is scope for increased systems flexibility, as devices can be programmed to carry out a range of separate tasks, reducing the time taken for retooling.

Hardware   The size of equipment is decreasing,   meaning that new technology can be incorporated unobtrusively into existing devices, or installed in locations where large machines would have   rendered the application unviable. There is increased reliability of equipment, with fewer mechanical components and non-integrated components to go wrong.   The reduced cost of data-processing means that distributed rather than centralized processing facilities become feasible. This may change the 'common sense' methods of handling problems, for instance, the processing power of user desktop computers can outstrip that previously possessed by centralized mainframes. The shifting costs of information-processing as compared to data inputs, and of distributed as compared to centralized processing, makes networks of computers attractive. Data can be rapidly transferred from place to place rather than re-input, data processing tasks can be shared in new ways.

Information-processing activities   The decreasing cost of information processing means very data intensive operations can now be carried out efficiently, cheaply and quickly that would heretofore have been very slow, costly and cumbersome. All forms of information-processing are effectively being cheapened and rendered more effective: data capture, communication, storage, manipulation and presentation are all subject to dramatic quantitative and qualitative improvement. Digitalization of information of all kinds (speech, video, text, graphics, etc) makes it possible to readily transfer data generated via one medium to different media (thus the same material may be embodied in a printed paper text, as 'hypertext' on a CD-ROM, as interactive source material on an online database, and so on). This facilitates the shift to shared information processing using computer networks.

Human-Machine Interaction   The quality and user-friendliness of systems is increased, as 'spare' processing power is applied to error checking, to providing greater immediacy (or interactivity), 'intelligent' or 'user-friendly' interfaces. IT has the capacity to engage in 'conversations' with users, using everyday language or 'common-sense' icons and producing unique output customized to user inputs. As a result of these changes in the way it can be used occupations and work roles relatively unaffected by earlier technological revolutions are being brought into contact with IT, particularly tasks such as management, design and coordination. This changes diffusion dynamics since these users have comparatively greater organizational power.   Also, the more powerful interfaces with the technology allows the use of IT to make IT (e.g. software engineering techniques or the computer aided design of silicon chips). It might be appropriate to think that we are moving on a trajectory from data processing (computers), through information processing (early IT), to knowledge processing (the full extension of IT).

When used in concert, the programmability and information-processing capacity of IT underlie the potential for a new dimension of flexibility of industrial performance. For instance, changes in product specification have until recently required manual intervention. IT permits rapid change in operations to be controlled by software. There are several important implications of this development:

1. it opens up greater scope for integration between design, production and management;
2. it saves on the considerable volumes of down-time consumed during the manual readjustment of equipment;
3. it becomes possible to respond more rapidly to changing demands for products from markets;
4. it becomes possible to reorganize large-scale production processes into a set of smaller-scale processes, resulting in more 'just-in-time' operation with less stock kept waiting around, and permitting continuing flexibility.

Therefore, a key feature of IT is that it produces a more general purpose technology system than any of its predecessors. Adding further weight to this conclusion, miniaturization is the trend towards cheaper, smaller, lighter, faster and more powerful hardware. As IT has become more widely diffused and based on small, cheap hardware the software base has also become more accessible to the lay person. Exactly the same effect is observed with current efforts to improve the human machine interface to create systems which are intuitive and user friendly. Once again, as the technical system becomes available to personnel who are not necessarily highly trained technologists, the technological paradigm becomes more generalized than previous technological systems.

The primary implication of IT in overall terms, therefore, is its massive potential for increased operational flexibility for industrial users. This flexibility derives from its characteristically greater generality of use than previous generations of technology. The issue is whether, when the technological systems are actually implemented within an organizational context, the utility of such general purpose technologies is recognized and realized. Ultimately, the flexibility of IT will be limited by institutional perceptions of how work processes and technological systems go together.

Figure 2.2   Size of markets for software and computer services

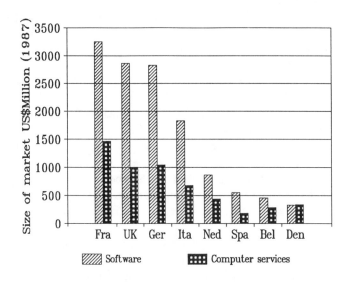

Source: OECD, 1989a

Figure 2.3   Size of IT markets and IT labour force

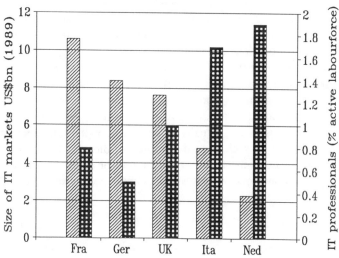

Source: OECD, 1993; IDC survey data, 1990

RATES OF IT DIFFUSION

National Level Evidence

There is no readily available and simple way of describing the situation of different EU countries with respect to IT diffusion. An ideal approach, perhaps, would be to attempt to develop a whole host of IT diffusion indicators, and then to cluster together countries on the basis of these data. However, here we have had to be content with more limited sources of information in order to make some simple international comparisons (Figures 2.2 and 2.3).

Different indicators obviously tell different stories. France, for example, displays vastly more videotext terminals in use than other EU countries (because of Minitel), but on other indicators it appears as a leading, but by no means exceptional, IT user. We shall see later that Germany appears to be most advanced on measures of use of manufacturing IT: but it is widely reported that rigidities in the telecommunications supply system mean that the development of telematics supply (e.g. online databases) and use (e.g. companies' use of private networks) is relatively restricted. Roughly speaking, the level of IT use appears to be a function of national prosperity. The 'peripheral' Southern European countries (less so Italy) and Eire are relatively low users; the UK seems to be a higher user than would be expected in terms of, for instance, GNP/capita.

Sectoral Issues

The implications of IT vary according to the activity it is used to support. Ideally we would develop a classification based upon these core activities. However, the evidence which we are able to draw upon has a number of serious defects from the point of view of providing a systematic overview of sectoral diffusion of IT. Most of the research is several years out of date, and even recent work focuses on older, rather than emergent, IT applications. Thus while we can use these studies to establish structural features of IT use, there is only limited scope for extrapolating from their results to the future. We structure our discussion by looking first at the office applications of IT, which are found across all branches of industry before looking in more specific detail at manufacturing and services.

Figure 2.4 Technological change in office activities

Office Functions	Technologies	
External communications	From	external mail (postal services), telephony, telex.
	To	the above plus electronic mail, new telephone services (PBXs, messaging, etc), telefax, viewdata, teletext.
Internal communications	From	memo slips, telephony.
	To	the above plus electronic mail, new telephone services, electronic bulletin boards.
Data storage and retrieval	From	filing cabinets, libraries, microfiche, tape storage of data on mainframe computers for restricted access to large data files (payrolls, etc.), press cutting services.
	To	the above plus storage of all forms of data (text numbers, graphics and now digitalized video and voice) on new media (hard and floppy disks, CD and videodisc) for distributed or local use by terminals and microcomputers, and accessed by user friendly database management systems, online databases for new items, bibliographies, etc.
Information processing	From	calculators, statistical modelling on mainframes, systematic and intuitive use of human skills and intellectual techniques.
	To	the above plus an array of microcomputer based techniques such as spreadsheets, 'idea processors', interactive graphical systems for data inspection and 'expert systems' of various degrees of sophistication, overhead transparencies and slides.
Information presentation	From	typewriters and electronic typewriters, conventional printing, hand drawn graphics (using transfers and other means of standardization).
	To	word processing (eventually with direct voice input), desktop publishing, computer graphics derived from spreadsheets or graphics/CAD packages, videotapes, videoslides.
Meetings	From	the conventional meetings and conferences.
	To	the above plus telephone conferences, video-based teleconferences, computer conferencing.
Activity management	From	diaries, wall charts, secretaries' memories.
	To	diary programmes on PCs which act as alarms and reminders, programmes to help scheduling and task ordering.

Source: Miles et al, 1988

Office Activities and Technology

Office technologies affect virtually all industries. The generalized role of information management in an organization involves managing, coordinating, and designing both core production functions and peripheral support (Figure 2.4). Office automation is particularly important in large organizations. Offices record activities and store records; they often manage relationships between suppliers to the industry and the industry, likewise for clients; they organize the wages of the workforce and the administration of personnel relations; at least some of the work of drawing up blueprints and designs for new products and new organization of production takes place in offices. These are all information-processing activities, with much scope for application of IT.

A distinction is often drawn between two generations of IT application in offices: (a) office mechanization, and (b) Office Automation (OA). Office mechanization refers to the application of (generally stand-alone) devices in offices, usually with each device replacing some earlier mechanical or electronic device to carry out a specific task. Personal Computers (PCs), dedicated word processors (WPs), electronic typewriters, 'smart' telephones and private branch exchanges (PBXs), and photocopiers are now widely diffused, at least to larger organizations.

Office mechanization has led to significant changes in daily office routines, but the large productivity gains reported in many early trials are less visible. Several factors seem to be at play:

1. organizational change and learning is required to establish efficient ways of using new office technologies;
2. new modes of work organization and new skill structures are required, often these involve changes in management work, which are frequently resisted because these involve changes in the manager's own conditions;
3. new technology increases product quality rather than productivity, for example redrafting for visual effect can be quite time consuming;
4. new technology is sometimes alleged to lead to 'information overload' rather than more efficient use of data (e.g. the proliferation of inter-office memos.

A rather different argument suggests that the important developments are unlikely to occur until the application of IT moves beyond the substitution of new technologies for existing devices, and toward the introduction of new systems used to reorganize the process of office work as a whole. OA may provide the platform for just such a development. To date, however, OA-type systems have been taken up on a much more restricted scale than office mechanization, and almost exclusively by large organizations. OA involves linking together discrete items of office mechanization, typically through Local Area Networks (LANs). In addition to network management equipment (cables, switches, etc.) a key device here is the 'office workstation'. This refers to a PC (itself serving as word processor, tool for analysis of quantitative data, and drawing board, among other things) linked directly to computer-communications systems like electronic mail, and (in advanced versions) using voice and even video messaging systems.

OA systems blend together three types of office IT. Distributed data processing systems provide multi-user access to a mainframe computer -

Table 2.1 Administrative terminals in the Netherlands

Sector	Cost per employee (Fl)	Terminals per 1000 staff
Insurance	15700	355
Banking	17100	288
Business services	8510	152
Chemicals	5820	116
Engineering	3320	86
Manufacturing	3270	79
Trade	2110	55
Transport and communication	1650	51
Food	2050	40
Agriculture	460	15
Construction	500	13

Note: ordered by last column

Source: CBS, 1988

typically used for a small range of standard tasks, but providing little scope for horizontal data communications. Powerful desktop PCs bring high-quality data analysis and presentation to managers with limited keyboard skills. In addition, there is data communications within and between offices and sites.

OA has evident advantages - for instance, the same data need not be re-entered into each device through which it is processed - but has proved difficult to achieve in practice. The move from office mechanization to OA has been impeded by:

1. costs of rewiring buildings and installing new equipment and software;
2. incompatibility of standards (for communication, text management, databases, etc.), which has made it difficult to integrate existing and planned systems;
3. fear of being 'locked-in' to a particular supplier and to particular technical options, when open systems are only of limited availability;
4. slow response of some IT manufacturers to the requirements for networking (e.g. Local Area Networks);
5. organizational difficulties, e.g. conflicts over control of IT facilities, shortages of technical skills, and needs to reorganize work in the light of new technical facilities.

IT finds application in all types of office, and has been the focus of a great deal of case-study research, but rather less systematic survey research. Some data on the diffusion of IT systems to administrative applications across different sectors are provided in a Dutch study (CBS, 1988, cited by Diederen et al, 1990). This reports diffusion rates of terminals for administrative applications as displayed in Table 2.1. The results demonstrate some trends that will be encountered repeatedly: 'information services' dealing with finance and knowledge are outstanding users of IT, followed by high technology industry.

The evidence would seem to indicate that despite the large-scale introduction of new technology, office practices are generally changing only slowly (Webster, 1990). This is especially true for those organizational innovations that redistribute office work over time and space. Offshore office work is commonly restricted to large-scale data entry operations, and 'telework' remains rare. However, the use of mobile communications, while particularly useful for staff who are themselves mobile (e.g. travelling sales workers) are also associated with some change in the location of what was traditionally office work. New communications facilities in transport (in-train and in-plane phones as well as car phones) and hotels (IT business centres), together with new technologies (such as portable cellular telephones and laptop computers equipped with modems), make it possible for more frequent contact between worker and firm, without the necessity to call in on the office in person or via conventional public telephones. In terms of diffusion of technology this is certainly a rapidly growing area. In the UK there were around 600,000 cellular telephones in use in mid-1989, with the number forecast to grow to 1.8 million by 1993 (Williamson, 1989). This was rapid growth, given that the technology was only half a decade old as a commercial offering.

Table 2.2 The installed robots in 18 OECD Countries, 1985

Country	Robot stock	Robots per 10,000 employees	
		manufacturing	ISIC 38
non-EU countries			
Japan	406000	384	83
Sweden	2046	27	55
Norway	3502	114	31
USA	20000	11	25
Austria	170	34	7
New Zealand	262	14	3
Australia	528	not available	not available
Finland	27	5	15
Canada	7003	4	13
Switzerland	290	3	11
EU Countries			
Belgium	975	12	36
Italy	3808	124	32
West Germany	8800	13	25
France	4150	9	22
UK	3208	64	15
Netherlands	350	4	11
Denmark	160	4	10
Spain	693	34	10

Note: Japanese data rendered comparable with other OECD countries

Source: OECD, 1989b

The employment effects of these new technologies unfortunately remains unexplored; however, one can imagine that telecommunications links allow mobile workers, in principle, to:

1. maintain contact with head office to improve scheduling (personal communications enable individuals to be located wherever they are - including whatever office they are in;
2. use private networks and virtual private networks to overcome 'telephone tag' by adding 'call camping' facilities;
3. keep up-to-date with office developments and messages;
4. directly interrogate firm databases while on the job (for example, in helping a client draw up an insurance form or a purchase order, or in order to seek pharmaceutical or other medical data).

As large service firms of all types (and large organizations in other sectors) come to rely more heavily on networking and mobile communications systems, their activities are increasingly determined by the quality of the telecommunications infrastructure. The tariffs charged for conventional and advanced facilities, their availability in different locations, the time taken to install them, etc., are all important determinants of the activity of these firms. Their pace of innovation, their international competitiveness, their locational decisions, and many other features, can be influenced by the direction and pace of infrastructural development.

Manufacturing Systems

Edquist and Jacobssen (1988), focusing on manufacturing technologies and industrial automation, point out that there is still considerable development expected around the current islands of automation (Figure 2.5). Most manufacturing systems are still at an early stage of the product cycle, being neither widely diffused nor 'mature' technologies.

Various analysts, of whom the best-known is probably Kaplinsky (1984), have distinguished several phases in factory automation. In Kaplinsky's account, the earliest phase is one in which specific tasks are automated (intra-activity automation): stand-alone equipment, like numerically controlled machine tools and computer-controlled handling equipment, is used for such purposes. More recently, we see systems integration, where several activities within a sphere of operation are automated: CAD/CAM and Flexible Manufacturing Systems (FMS) are examples, and these applications of intra-sphere automation are generally most advanced in engineering industries. We are only witnessing the beginnings of CIM (Computer-Integrated Manufacturing), in which the whole range of manufacturing functions are integrated under computer control; process industries are in the lead in such inter-sphere automation. Major capital goods suppliers in Western countries have put considerable effort into CIM systems for the 'factory of the future'. There would appear from this account to be long-term pressures towards CIM as a model for all manufacturing - in which case all branches of manufacturing might eventually come to resemble those branches based on continuous flow processes (e.g. much production of industrial chemicals). However, this prospect is certainly a long way off for the great majority of sectors (Senker and Beesley, 1986).

Figure 2.5 Diffusion stages of IT capital goods in manufacturing

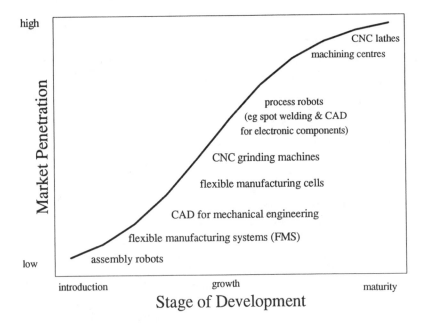

Source: Edquist and Jacobssen, 1988

The OECD's Government Policies and the Diffusion of Microelectronics (1989b) reports a range of statistics on the use of robots and of microelectronics in manufacturing products and processes (Table 2.2)[1]. Based on detailed data for three countries, the authors of the report conclude that '[m]ost robots are installed and used in large establishments, with over 50 per cent of total robots in establishments with more than 1000 employees in France, Japan and the United Kingdom' (p. 24). This type of diffusion pattern is repeatedly encountered in IT applications, as it is with more traditional technologies.

The OECD study also discusses studies of microelectronics use based on sample surveys of manufacturing establishments, for five countries - France, Germany, Japan, The Netherlands, and the UK - from the early 1980s, using methods developed by Northcott at the Policy Studies Institute in London (Table 2.3). These surveys suggest that, in the early 1980s, Japan was leading in microelectronics applications to processes, but level with Germany when it came to products. In the EU, Germany was the leader, followed by the UK and then France.

In terms of sectoral variations, there are unsurprising variations in product innovations, with food, print and chemical products being unlikely to find microelectronic applications, and electrical/electronic products - followed quite closely by engineering and then by vehicles - being major users. Process innovations are more evenly distributed, with differences across countries as to which sectors are leading. Indeed, the French leader (vehicles) lags in Germany and the UK. We would not expect this to be the case any longer (unless it reflects a definitional artefact). It is apparent that the print industry is a leader or near-leader in all EU countries, but the variation in detail suggests that this level of sectoral aggregation conceals important differences in industrial structure across the countries.

Such data do not inform us as to how many workers are directly and indirectly influenced by the use of IT - although there is an attempt to estimate employment 'impacts'. The OECD study does cite skill shortages as a recurrent obstacle to wider and more rapid diffusion of IT in manufacturing industry, and suggests that new technical skills, new skill combinations, and (more ambiguously) higher skill levels in general in the workforce, are common results of such innovation.

More recently, a Danish study (Vilkstrup, 1988) applied similar techniques to the study of microelectronics use in manufacturing processes and CAD in Denmark, France, Germany, Sweden and the UK. Logistic-type diffusion curves are apparent in all cases, with France and the UK lagging behind the other three countries in the case of product applications. CAD methods were found to be diffusing rapidly, but from a low base, and with typically limited levels of application. Again, large establishments were in the lead; sectors applying the technology more extensively included mechanical engineering, electronic engineering, and instruments. Moderate levels of use were found in textiles; some other sectors had limited use on account of the nature of their products (meat and dairy products, food,

Table 2.3 Microelectronics use by industry, 1983
(percentage of manufacturing establishments)

Sector	Country				
	France	Germany	Japan (1982)	Nether-lands	UK
Applications in Products					
Food	0	0	0	no data	0
Chemicals	1	7	0	no data	0
Engineering	23	42	30	10-30	28
Electrical	28	42	42	>30	50
Vehicles	23	9	10	10-30	14
Print	1	6	0	no data	0
Total	6	13	13	5	10
Applications in Processes					
Food	39	46	44	10-30	60
Chemicals	43	52	62	no data	51
Engineering	31	59	71	10-30	45
Electrical	33	54	72	10-30	51
Vehicles	58	39	73	10-30	33
Print	50	77	69	>30	62
Total	35	47	59	30	43

Source: OECD, 1989b

chemicals), and others imply unexploited possibilities (wood & furniture, paper & printing).

The OECD and Danish comparisons draw on survey methods developed by the Policy Studies Institute (PSI) in London. From a ten-year programme of research into manufacturing IT diffusion in the UK (with some international comparisons, as discussed), Northcott and Walling (1988) draw a number of conclusions:

1. there is extremely rapid diffusion of microelectronics in both manufacturing processes and products, in the UK and other Northern European countries where data are available;
2. IT process innovation is diffused over most major manufacturing sectors, notably in food industries, paper, printing and publishing, chemicals and metals, and both electrical and mechanical engineering although remains low in clothing, leather and footwear and textiles;
3. IT product innovation, not surprisingly, is concentrated in electrical engineering, mechanical engineering, and 'vehicles, ships and aircraft';
4 microelectronic use in products and/or processes is most prevalent in larger factories (the data concern plant size, not that of the organization in question);
5. robots are mainly used in large plants, and in plants where other robots are in use, but there are small plants with few robots (many of whom plan to get more robots);
6 robots are mainly used for welding, injection moulding, machine loading, assembly and surface coating, in the automobile industry, plastics, electrical and electronics, metal goods, mechanical engineering and aerospace and shipbuilding.

While these results suggest that firm size is an important determinant of the rate of innovation, it is clear that even small factories can and do make use of the new technologies. As an obstacle to innovation, more respondents in these surveys were prone to mention lack of relevant skills than lack of investment capital - but larger firms may be better placed in the recruitment of specialist workers.

Northcott and Walling (1988) also provide some evidence on the relative prevalence of discrete/stand-alone as against systems/network innovations. The use of the latter, which they term 'integrated central control systems', was relatively uncommon although rapidly increasing. Computer-aided design and automated handling and storage were still fairly rare. Most common was the control of discrete items of equipment or of specific processes. For the immediate future, innovation around discrete stages of the production process is liable to remain dominant.

In summary, the diffusion of IT across manufacturing industry reflects the nature of the core production processes and products of these sectors.

1. Process manufacturing - where there is a continuous flow-type process, mainframe computers have long been applied to process control. The

development of cheap microelectronics, and new types of electronic, optronic and chematronic sensor, means that more precise measurement and control is becoming applicable across a wider range of process manufacturing operations, particularly to smaller scale and more variable production.

2. Manufacturing assembly - increased application of microelectronics in products often makes assembly tasks easier, and more subject to automation, as component numbers are reduced, sizes reduced, and connections standardized. Robotics and planning aids (such as CAD and electronic just-in-time systems) bring new technology to the production processes here, in some accounts making repetitive assembly tasks resemble process manufacturing in terms of the continuous flow of material and products.

3. Variable and complex manufacturing - the reprogrammability of new IT is making it possible to rapidly retool machine tools and other equipment, to convey information from CAD and other sources to the site of direct production, and in other respects to apply IT to tasks that were previously beyond its scope.

The continuing development of IT is likely to mean that firms of all sizes in all manufacturing sectors will substantially increase their reliance on IT systems, both in direct production and in linking production to design, coordination, and related activities. But IT developments will certainly continue to diffuse unevenly across manufacturing, reflecting organizational and market scale, and also the widely different materials handled and final products created. Electronics and clothing industries are illustrative examples of extreme cases. Not surprisingly, quite high degrees of automation are apparent in electronics, where there are also considerable skills available relevant to IT innovation. In clothing, even automation of discrete functions is a fairly novel phenomenon, but some of the largest firms have linked Computer Aided Design (CAD) to cutting operations. CAD equipment is presently used less for basic design of clothing than for assuring a maximum use of material.

Service Sector Use of IT

Most quantitative research into IT use has focused on manufacturing industry. However, services are major users of IT. Analysis of input-output data for the UK suggests that some 70-80% of investment expenditure on the core IT hardware of computers and telecommunications equipment is absorbed by services. Services typically have higher proportions of IT in their total plant and machinery investment than do manufacturing sectors

(Miles and Matthews, 1992). In a 44 sector breakdown of the UK economy in 1984, the highest spenders on IT hardware - computer and telecommunications equipment - were telecommunications, banking (excluding leasing), retail and repair, and business services. Next highest expenditure came from electrical and instrument engineering (twice as high as any other manufacturing sector), followed by wholesale and miscellaneous services. In terms of IT shares of plant and machinery

Table 2.4   Adoption of IT affecting manual workers by size of establishment (percentage of UK workplaces adopting)

Size of work place	Sector							
	Energy	Mineral & Chemical	Engineering	Other manufacturing	Construction	Distribution and hotels	Transport	Banks and Finance
25-49	34	10	27	29	0	13	0	3
50-99	27	13	24	20	5	6	10	0
100-199	24	28	56	41	3	10	21	17
200-499	66	45	68	32	0	5	40	5
500-999	37	71	72	71	0	27	35	5
1000-1999	36	79	79	78	44	15	24	0
2000+	30	100	73	100	-	100	61	16
Avg	37	21	39	31	2	11	11	4

Source: Millward, 1986

investment, telecommunications was outstanding, followed by electrical engineering and instruments, banking, gas supply, wholesale and retail trades, and miscellaneous services.

Similar patterns emerge from other countries' input-output data. In the Federal Republic of Germany, in 1988, three service sectors (insurance & banking, retail, and wholesale trades) spent more on telecommunications

*Table 2.5   Adoption of IT affecting non-manual workers by size of
establishment (percentage of UK workplaces adopting)*

Size of work place	Sector							
	Ener-gy	Min-eral & Chem-ical	Eng-ineer-ing	Other man-ufact-uring	Cons-truc-tion	Distri-bution and hotels	Trans-port	Banks and Fin-ance
25-49	12	19	31	36	36	30	15	53
50-99	35	62	49	42	43	26	12	70
100-199	52	70	81	46	57	32	36	77
200-499	80	69	70	60	32	42	50	88
500-999	98	86	91	76	100	87	64	90
1000-1999	87	89	94	96	34	87	76	100
2000+	100	92	89	100	-	100	100	84
Avg	42	46	52	44	43	30	22	61

Source: Millward, 1986

equipment than the whole of manufacturing, more than half of manufacturing's total spend on DP equipment, and half of its spend on computer services. In Italy in 1988, the same three sectors invested more than manufacturing on DP equipment, and practically as much on computer services and software - and central government was a bigger investor than each of these other service sectors. In the Netherlands in 1987 the total IT current expenditure (including DP personnel) was roughly similar for the three sectors, government, finance, and wholesale and retail, with manufacturing's total only slightly ahead of each.

One result reiterated in the comparative studies of manufacturing IT discussed above, and repeatedly confirmed in other studies, is familiar to analysts of diffusion of industrial technologies of all sorts. IT adoption is clearly influenced by both industrial sector and establishment size. With the exception of multi-site firms with a large number of small workplaces (as are found in retail industries, including retail banking), the larger the workplace the more adoption of information technology has taken place (see also Daniel, 1987).

The application of IT to manual work is low outside of manufacturing. Retail industry workplaces such as banks, building society offices and shops are in the vanguard of the move to adopt IT, particularly computer networks. Thus, sample survey evidence points to over 50% of UK retail establishments (with over 20 employees: the figure would be much lower for many smaller shops) being computer-linked in 1984, and around 90% of banking sites (Table 2.6). The picture since then is liable to show an uneven but generally positive upward trend. Some sectors - e.g. travel agents, insurance brokers - have had a high level of take-up of videotext and similar terminal and network-based services.

A German study of IT use in services (Höflich-Häberlein and Häbler, 1990), drawing on surveys carried out from 1982 to 1987 in samples of all industries, presents estimates of the proportion of white-collar employees working with different types of computer system in offices (Table 2.7). These results show that - in common with the studies in manufacturing described earlier - IT diffusion is proceeding extremely fast. It is also apparent that the change in work experience is more profound than there simply being a computer system on the premises. It is reported that the proportion of white-collar staff using IT rose from 2% to 9% in just three years. This increase is most pronounced with WP systems, albeit starting from a low base - annual growth in the proportion of white-collars using WPs is over 130%.

In services the pattern of diffusion is very much determined by the industrial branch in question. Levels of diffusion in 1985 vary from less than 2% to over 25% of workers using IT systems. Though terminals are the form of IT most commonly used in all sectors, half of the sub-sectors display a shift away from terminals towards PCs and/or WPs, particularly in professional services. But another half show terminal usage to be the most rapidly increasing element of IT use. Presumably these figures reflect the extent to which the technologies are being used for large-scale administrative applications, as opposed to the production of texts or knowledge-based materials.

The detailed results from a British postal survey in 1984 (Yap, 1986) confirms the point that financial and business services were early, and are now heavy, users of computers (Table 2.8). They are particularly intensive in terms of measures such as terminal per employee, reflecting the greater direct use of IT in office environments than in manufacturing. Among computer users, the main applications were credit checking (84% of users), sales analysis (75%), billing (68%) with payroll and stock control at 62%.

Table 2.6 Computer linkage rates by industrial activity: UK services

Industry	Percentage of establishments networked				
	All estabs	Single site	Head office	Admin office	Other
Banking	87	-	84	99	92
Retail	52	27	26	-	57
National government	39	-	71	33	36
Local government	37	0	51	58	17
Insurance	35	-	28	18	40
Business services	28	9	39	-	38
Wholesale	22	7	29	18	24
Cultural industries	20	0	17	56	25
Transport	20	0	35	17	28
Post and comms	18	-	100	16	17
Medical	16	0	-	56	13
Education	11	7	-	8	12
Construction	9	0	4	4	18
Hotels and tourism	8	6	18	43	2

Note: - = no observations in this cell

Source: Millward, 1986

Yap's data also indicate that more experienced users apply their computer systems to a wider range of applications.

Most services have started from a low technology base in adopting IT, and lack of technical expertise may be part of their relative lag in this respect. Rajan and Pearson (1986) report growing demand for IT skills among British managers, whose job is being broadened in many respects. Rajan and Pearson suggest that larger firms will rationalize their

management structures and remove or reduce some layers of management
- but they expect this to be offset in the whole economy by a growth in
managerial staff in smaller firms.

Table 2.7   *PC use in German services*

	Whole-sale	Retail	Trans-port	Banks & Insur-ance	Private Services	Profess-ional Services
Percentage of staff:						
1982	11.2	0.6	0.7	3.0	0.8	1.6
1985	17.2	4.3	3.4	25.4	1.8	10.9
Distribution of IT use: 1982						
terminal	78.1	74.5	90.6	87.0	61.5	88.5
PC	20.9	14.8	9.4	8.6	23.9	9.5
WP	0.9	10.7	0.0	4.5	7.7	2.0
Distribution of IT use: 1985						
terminal	72.3	77.4	84.5	93.3	78.5	59.1
PC	22.1	15.9	9.6	3.1	18.2	23.6
WP	5.6	6.7	5.8	3.6	3.3	17.3

Notes: PC=personal computer, WP= dedicated word processor

Source: calculated from Höflich-Häberlein and Häbler (1990)

COMMENTS ON THE DIFFUSION OF IT

Most of the systematic study of the diffusion of new IT is biased in
significant ways. The majority of studies deal with manufacturing process
technologies, and with nothing equivalent for services or office applications
to the comparative surveys of robotics and microelectronics in these
applications. The focus tends to be on 'stand-alone' equipment: telematics
and network-based applications receive little attention, although there is
some analysis of the integration of different spheres of activity (again,
especially in manufacturing). Nevertheless, the studies do identify some

Table 2.8   Sectoral variations in computer diffusion, use and employment

	Manufacturing	Transport	Wholesale	Retail	Financial	Business services	Misc. services
Computer diffusion (percentage using)							
comupters	78.2	60.3	71.7	54.4	95.6	90.6	64.1
bureau services	23.7	24.2	21.5	20.4	63.6	36.5	28.1
Number of items per 1000 employees							
terminals	83	84	119	54	181	164	82
printers	40	33	53	31	62	76	49
dedicated WPs	9	1	11	9	47	36	4
general purpose WPs	17	5	25	2	77	67	16
phones	495	650	712	518	954	833	707
faxes	1	3	6	4	13	8	2
Percentage of establishments using:							
LANs	8.0	3.1	5.1	2.7	4.4	12.8	6.5
email	9.3	3.1	6.0	5.5	9.1	17.9	4.8
fax	18.2	10.5	12.4	5.4	30.4	18.1	6.5
radio-paging	25.3	23.1	27.4	21.2	29.1	33.0	35.5
teleconference	27.2	16.7	33.8	24.8	34.8	36.2	31.2

Source: calculated from Yap (1986)

features that we would expect to persist in the case of newer generations and applications of IT.   To summarize:

1. nationally, IT diffusion is typically more advanced in the Northern European economies and the 'core' areas of the EU.
2. regionally, IT diffusion is typically most advanced in core centres within countries, in and around their capital cities and growth areas;

3. sectorally, IT applications to sectors' core tasks are typically most advanced in information services, such as finance, business and professional services, and in electronics-related and process manufacturing industries, followed by assembly manufacturing and physical services such as retail and wholesale, and then by sectors such as complex and variable manufacturing, and human services;
4. newer generations of IT, however, are likely to widen the scope for applying IT to core processes and thus change these sectoral patterns;
5. organizationally, IT diffusion is most marked in larger companies and establishments; diffusion among small firms is often related to action on the part of their suppliers or clients.

NOTES

1. Data on robots raise a number of definitional problems, since robots vary considerably in price and capability. Nevertheless, there is considerable variation in the diffusion of robots across countries, with Japan and Sweden being outstanding in robot use.

3. Core IT Skills and Employment

Jacqueline Senker and Peter Senker

Telecommunications, computers and software production are the industries at the heart of information and communications technology (IT). This chapter reviews available literature on the skills implications of the production, installation and use of IT equipment. It also considers developments in the wide range of services now indispensable to IT use, including software production and the provision of telecommunications networks.

IT is pervasive, with a rapid growth in applications across many industrial and commercial sectors. This has resulted in demand for telecommunications and software skills in almost every sector of the economy. In this context, such skills are the 'core' IT skills and there is a widespread need for maintenance workers to acquire these skills so they can keep the new equipment in working order. There are similar trends in relation to maintenance skills across the economy, and they are therefore also discussed in this chapter.

TELECOMMUNICATIONS[1]

Telecommunications employment can be divided into three main areas:

1. the supply of equipment necessary to produce services;
2. the supply of telecommunications services by public network operators and others;
3. consumption of telecommunications services by end-users.

Total EU employment in these three areas stood at 1.8 million in 1987, with 17.5% in equipment industry, 54% in the supply of services and 28% in end-users.

Equipment suppliers and network operators have shown similar trends in demand for labour and skills, although the timing and pace of change varies from area to area. In overall terms, there has been a loss of jobs accompanied by continual changes in skills requirements. There is growing demand for highly qualified people and a sharp decline in demand for unskilled labour (Emeriaud and Paponeau, 1989). Far fewer skilled manual workers are required than previously by both equipment manufacturers and network operators. Where skilled manual roles remain they are often required to have new digital skills. Also, automation is reducing the demand for clerical workers. The decline in demand for lower level skills contrasts with the greater need for highly skilled technicians and software and telematics engineers. Demand is also rising for middle managers with professional skills in marketing and accountancy and more senior managers with the commercial acumen to exploit the expanding markets for telecommunication products and services which are coming about as a result of both technological advances and the liberalization of telecommunications regimes.

In general, the telecommunications industries suffer considerable shortages of appropriately skilled labour in order to meet the considerable restructuring they are undergoing. Traditional education syllabuses in Europe fail to produce people with the necessary combinations of technical, commercial and personal skills. Consequently, the generally long established equipment suppliers and network operators devote heavy resources to internal training and retraining of their own personnel. In many cases, these training schemes are treated as a hunting ground for recruitment by emergent telematic service firms and end-users, who have a rapidly growing need for telecommunications-based skills.

Equipment Manufacturers

Over the period 1980-87 there was continuous growth in the market for telecommunication equipment. This trend is likely to be sustained by the on-going modernization of the European network and by the increase in the number of lines, not only in countries catching up with the digitalization of telecommunications, but in better equipped countries where new services and products are creating additional demand. Although, as would be expected, the largest countries (Germany, France, the UK and Italy) have the highest employment in equipment manufacture, there is some employment in almost every member state. Public procurement has favoured national producers in large countries. Foreign suppliers have been required to set up manufacturing facilities to gain access to local markets in countries lacking a national producer.

Until the 1970s, the telecommunications industry produced a range of electro-mechanical and partially automated switching, transmission and terminal equipment. This was largely a mature market, with the capital equipment installed having a long depreciation cycle. In the decade to

1987, as telecommunications operators began to roll out their digitalization programmes, there was a marked up-turn in the rate of activity as electro-mechanical equipment was replaced by new generations of microelectronic equipment. However, despite a significant growth in turnover there was a 25% fall in employment. At the same time the range of products manufactured has widened to include radiocommunications (satellite communications, mobile telephones) and data communications (answering machines, fax machines). However, many of these latter products are produced by consumer electronics and office systems manufacturers, which are not generally regarded as part of the telecommunications industry. The overall decline in employment may continue in the 1990s. Increased competition from U.S. and Japanese equipment firms (and competition in subscriber equipment markets with consumer electronics firms) could lead to mergers and defensive collaborations amongst EU companies, resulting in pressures to rationalize labour forces.

The restructuring of the telecommunications equipment market results in core skills required of telecommunication equipment workers becoming much more subject to change, much more complex and less unique to the telecommunications industry. Hardware and software techniques used in the telecommunications equipment industry are highly sophisticated and changing rapidly: 18% of employment is in R&D. The number of highly skilled jobs is likely to increase together with those related to marketing and commercial activities. Equipment manufacturers expect to suffer from shortages of software and electronics engineers and marketing managers. They will face strong competition in the labour market from consumer electronics and IT equipment manufacturers, to whom telecommunications expertise has become of strategic importance.

The move from semi-automatic towards totally automated and micro-electronic equipment in telecommunications, has made redundant many traditional manual skills in the industry. For instance, the virtual elimination of traditional metalworking in the industry has resulted in a steep drop in the proportion of skilled manual workers. Unskilled assembly jobs are declining with the automation of production processes (automatic component insertion and surface mounting, automatic testing). Women, who account for a high proportion of assembly jobs, are bearing the brunt of these job losses.

The decline in employment of manual workers has now begun to level off, but new forms of work organization in some companies have increased the need for multi-skilling. However, the amount of training carried out by equipment manufacturing companies varies considerably, and there is no clear relationship between investment in training and the products manufactured or methods of production. Decreases in training for unskilled and skilled manual workers reflect the general fall in the numbers of such workers, with a lack of training to reskill redundant workers. That resources devoted to training are above the general level for manufacturing industry reflects the difficulties that equipment manufacturers throughout Europe find in recruiting highly qualified personnel. University trained engineers receive too narrow a technical education and graduates are not prepared for the management and commercial world of the telecommunications industry. In response, companies have increased in-house induction training for the rising number of graduate recruits.

In some countries, however, there have been efforts to redesign courses for existing workers. For instance, Danish employers of metal workers and their union have jointly identified new vocational training needs and organized courses which have shifted the emphasis from traditional skill development towards systems and corporate understanding. In Germany three new telecommunications-related apprenticeship schemes have been organized for radio and TV technicians; telecommunications equipment electricians and communications electricians. By contrast, Southern European countries face particular problems meeting the industry's needs for very high skills because a high proportion of workers only have primary education. One Portuguese company has met this problem by giving grants and time off to workers who wished to pursue education and training outside in order to lay the foundation for more sophisticated training in new technologies.

Telecommunications Services

Telecommunications services are provided by network operators, their subsidiaries and new telematics firms, representing 50% of total EU telecommunications employment. The large countries, UK, Germany, France and Italy, accounted for over 78% of EU employment in telecommunications services in 1987. Network operators experienced relatively stable employment over the period 1980-87, but there was an eightfold expansion of employment in subsidiaries and new telematics firms, which, by 1987 accounted for over 7% of telecommunications services employment.

Employment in telecommunications services is affected by four principal factors: the market, technological change, the effect of the regulatory environment on operators' strategies, and the status of network operators. Demand for services is growing throughout the European economy, both continued demand for telephone and telex and, where they exist, for the most advanced networks. In most member states growth in the number of main lines is slowing down but businesses and households are acquiring additional lines.

Table 3.1 Network digitalization in EU member states, 1987

	Degree of Digitalization	
Member State	**Local Switching**	**Long Distance Switching**
FRG	3%	22%
France	70%	75%
Netherlands	35%	15%
Luxembourg	8%	10%
Denmark	23%	40%
Belgium	29%	75%
UK	42%	90%
Greece	15%	25%
Italy	25%	36%
Ireland	65%	85%
Spain	5%	45%
Portugal	20%	30%

Source: OECD 1989c

In Denmark, France and Ireland, unlike the majority of member states, digitalization is well advanced, and has destroyed jobs in transmission and switching. It has also created jobs for specialists and in connection with the development of new services. In all countries the number of telephonists' jobs has fallen, but the extent of the fall depends on operators' commercial decisions about the general services they wish to offer.   The number of commercial staff is expected to rise considerably.   The effects of deregulation on employment, particularly its negative influence, have been exaggerated, and cannot be considered in isolation from consideration of network operators' commercial strategies, the services developed, the constraints of their status as public authorities and the extent of computerization.   (In most countries the status of network operators as public authorities means they have to adhere to strict recruitment controls.

This limits their flexibility to adapt recruitment patterns to meet changing demand).

Skills and training in the network operators

The shift from electro-mechanical to electronic switching (or telephone exchanges), the digitalization of transmission and the introduction of optic fibres for transmission systems are causing major changes in the type of skills and numbers of staff required. The changes are not uniform throughout the member states and depend on a number of factors including the extent to which network digitalization has advanced; the country's equipment rate; the availability of skilled staff and/or retraining programmes to equip existing staff with new skills. Table 3.1 shows the extent of digitalization in member states in 1987, both for local and long distance networks. Digitalization has proceeded rapidly since 1987, particularly in Spain, France and Germany (OECD, 1989c).

In all countries there is growth in skilled jobs at the expense of unskilled jobs. Skilled employment is rising in countries which are beginning to modernize their networks. Once modernization has been completed, as in France, skilled employment in technical activities may fall. Most countries require highly skilled engineers, management and commercial staff to develop new services. As in the equipment manufacturing industry, skills for electronic switching are in short supply, and network operators in Italy, Spain and the Netherlands have become involved in programmes for retraining staff who previously worked with electro-mechanical exchanges. New transmission techniques, particularly the introduction of optical fibres, will require large-scale training programmes. Unskilled jobs such as line-laying are expected to be extensively subcontracted.

All network operators devote considerable efforts to induction and ongoing career training for their staff, and this is likely to continue. They use a mixture of both internal and external resources including equipment manufacturers, local colleges and universities. Generally in-house training is used to develop technical skills, for instance converting staff from electro-mechanical to digital skills, developing software engineering skills or, as in Italy, to retrain staff in optical fibres. There are also training programmes for commercial, clerical and management staff.

In Germany, in addition to an elaborate in-house system of vocational and further training for staff at all levels, *Deutsche Bundespost* has a management academy for training highly qualified management staff. Other network operators also have their own schools, including the Belgian and British Telecom in the UK. Portugal has a joint venture with a university for training in high level expertise. The Greek network operator OTE closed its Higher Telecommunications School in 1984. High level personnel are now sent abroad for training in new technologies and management. On their return they become in-house trainers. The French Ministry of Communications carries out training through two National Telecommunications Institutes.

Overall, there is high student demand for telecommunications studies but a lack of training places. New communications courses are being created rapidly at all levels of higher education, but these general courses do not provide the high level training for network managers and designers which industry requires. Appropriate courses provided by French Telecom and the *Ecole Nationale Superiore de Telecommunications* (ENST) are unable to meet the demand. French Telecom recruits most of its management personnel from ENST. In 1987 its 186 graduates were swamped with over 2,500 job offers. Telecommunications equipment is so costly and its technical evolution so rapid that universities are having difficulty in coping with the cost of providing equipment for training. Universities and schools of industrial engineering could provide more training places if they were provided with extra resources to meet the costs of equipment (Bodet, 1989).

Skills and training in the new telematics services
The development of new telematics services (Figure 3.1) is advanced in Germany, France and the UK, but is very new in Spain, Italy and Denmark. Companies providing these services require specialists who thoroughly understand telecommunications techniques, but these skills are not available in the labour market.

Firms providing telematic services have similar skills needs: they require hybrid specialists with thorough knowledge of data processing and telecommunications with knowledge in a specific applications area, e.g. finance or retailing. These multi-skilled experts also require communications skills and the ability to anticipate customers' needs and to provide advice. Firms would also like specialists fluent in several European languages, who have a good understanding of varying national cultures.

Many specialists recruited to new telematics firms come from the sector which the firms wish to penetrate and there is a considerable transfer of staff from users to suppliers of services. Turnover of staff in new services is high. Technologies are continually changing, and in order to get the specialists they require, firms devote a large proportion of their salaries budgets to training. Demand for skilled telematics personnel is likely to continue to increase, but the introduction of common communication standards and user-friendly interfaces may relieve the pressure on demand (Locksley et al, 1990).

Figure 3.1   The main types of value added services

Network administration services	transmit information between different networks, where there are problems of interconnectivity. They also enrich the transmission of information by, for instance, protocol or baud rate conversion. The major firms in this sector have their own networks and personnel with telecommunications and data processing expertise. They need to provide their experts with considerable continuing training to enable them to keep abreast of the latest telecommunications and data processing techniques.
Communications services	including relatively simple electronic messaging services which do not involve sophisticated communications software.
Information services	make databases available to outside users through data processing and communications technology. This sector is dominated by firms specializing in financial information.
Sectoral services	are the most sophisticated, based on complex combinations of the previous three categories adapted to the needs of specific groups of users, e.g. Electronic Data Interchange (EDI) and Electronic Funds Transfer (EFT). Most firms in the previous three sectors are trying to enter this market by forming alliances with other suppliers of value added services, major users or professional bodies.

End Users

Traditional telecommunications jobs in end-users are switchboard operators and equipment maintenance; both are affected by technological change. Switchboard operator employment has stagnated, but there have been profound changes in the nature of these jobs. The volume of telephone traffic has been growing, but new types of terminals have shifted work from operators to users. This trend is most pronounced in large firms which have invested more heavily in new equipment than in medium and small

companies.   When new switchboards are installed, operators are often
expected to undertake additional reception and secretarial responsibilities.
The development of teleshopping has led to growth in employment of
telephone operators able to take orders by telephone.   Technicians'
maintenance responsibilities are declining (see below), but they are assuming
a new role. This is to train users in the new functions available with digital
exchanges and help them to realize the full potential of new communications
resources.

Figure 3.2   Private networks

There are several private leased-line interfirm networks including the Bankers
Automated Clearing System (BACS), the British electronic funds transfer system and
SWIFT (Society for World-wide Interbank Financial Telecommunications) to which
many European banks are now connected.   Other private networks include
AMADEUS, the international airline ticket booking system and GLOBEX, Reuters'
futures trading network. A few major European firms have developed their own
private telecommunications networks in order to transmit voice and data between
computers at remote locations. Apart from these pioneers, most European users have
yet to develop integrated computer and telecommunications networks for intra- and
inter-firm communications.   They are awaiting the implementation of common
regulations and standards and an Integrated Services Digital Network (ISDN).

New employment is being created by the development of private
telecommunications networks   (Figure 3.2).   More private networks are
likely to be set up in the future, but their design and architecture will require
communications systems managers. It is difficult to recruit and train such
specialists, who require both telecommunications and computer skills for
their main tasks: the design and optimization of computer and
telecommunications networks and responsibility for liaising with network
operators and equipment suppliers. No member state provides sufficient
training courses specific to these needs. Demand for these specialists will
grow strongly in large firms.

COMPUTER SOFTWARE PROFESSIONALS[2]

Software employment is growing rapidly in Europe, but lack of quantitative
data and statistics makes it difficult to monitor trends and formulate policy
(NCC, 1987). In some member states official statistics do not take account
of the new and rapidly changing IT occupations.   Moreover, there is no
uniform data on the demand for and supply of computer professionals,
because each member state classifies computer professionals in different

ways. Classifications cluster around six main types of occupation (Figure 3.3). Computer specialist jobs are concentrated in the computer industry itself, in business services, banking and insurance, public administration and retailing. Perhaps as many as three-quarters of these jobs are accounted for by user firms, with twice as many service sector as manufacturing jobs.

Figure 3.3   Computer professional work roles

1 *Systems Design* - responsibility for systems and network management, software or hardware engineering, network engineering or the design of databases

2 *Project and Applications* - design, development, management and analysis

3 *User Support Staff* - a new occupation, not always regarded as a profession in its own right

4 *Managing data processing centres*

5 *Commercial work* - marketing and selling hardware and software, technical assistance for clients and after sales service

6 *IT research* - which is generally considered as a scientific profession.

Overall demand for those with high level qualifications from universities, business schools or polytechnics still outstrips the number of graduates. For example in Germany there are five available positions for each graduate. In Spain, during the period 1985-88, supply only satisfied 40% of demand. Specific skill shortages appear to vary from country to country. France and Denmark are short of applications analysts, whereas Germany, Spain and the UK suffer from shortages of systems analysts. Belgium and the Netherlands have difficulty in finding sales managers.

Training for the computer professions has responded with a rapid increase in the number of degrees awarded in computer studies. Several countries have expanded the provision of short courses to enable graduates from other disciplines to acquire a second computer-related qualification. It is anticipated that growth in demand for computer professionals will continue during the 1990s, but at a slower rate than during the 1980s. In addition, the demand for some groups of computer professionals is showing signs of stabilization and, in countries which are heavily computerized, the market for computer operators is saturated.

Some firms are able to find the skills they require on the job market by offering high salaries, but they may find their 'experts' are head-hunted by other firms offering even higher rewards. Other firms have tried to escape the undue influence of market forces by training in-house to develop the skills of their existing workforce who, although qualified, do not necessarily have computing skills. This route is particularly favoured by user firms in the financial sector (Lochet and Verdier, 1987).

IT service providers and users in the UK are making increasing use of subcontractors. A small core of in-house professionals is usually retained to develop IT policy and applications, but some firms contract out all of their IT activity under a 'facilities management' contract (Pearson et al, 1988). Skills shortages and 'headhunting' have enhanced opportunities for occupational mobility both for highly qualified staff and programmers. Three converging trends are increasing the level of qualifications required for computer professionals. First, program generators and the automation of formal specification procedures have reduced the demand for high calibre programmers and analysts, and training courses focus more on systems analysis and design, to the detriment of programming. Second, increasing diffusion of computers throughout the economy has led to the emergence of new functions, particularly the provision of customer support services. To provide such services, computer specialists are now expected to have qualifications in subjects such as business organization or personnel management in addition to their computing skills. Finally, as IT expertise spreads to every profession, requirements for IT sophistication increase. At the same time the growing complexity of systems and networks requires computer experts who can apply considerable intellectual flexibility to their highly specialized knowledge.

Computer professionals need to update their skills frequently and employers have to invest heavily in continuing training. Employers' needs focus on technical aspects such as operating systems, networks, fourth and fifth generation languages and artificial intelligence. The need for continuing training is creating a market for training, often provided by manufacturers and service companies.

IMPLICATIONS OF IT FOR MAINTENANCE SKILLS

Maintenance is a pervasive activity. In many industries the proportion of maintenance workers has risen rapidly since the 1970s and makes up over 20% of the workforce in some plants (Penn and Scattergood, 1988). In

Benetton's automated warehouse, maintenance accounts for the majority of the workforce (Belussi, 1987). The growth of IT investment by manufacturing firms in the 1980s has not been supported by sufficient maintenance training. Maintenance practices lag behind the advances in technology (Financial Times, 13 June 1990).

By contrast, in the computer and telecommunications industry the diffusion of electronic switching and a trend towards the automation of maintenance is reducing the demand for maintenance staff.

Changing Skill Requirements

The application of IT to products and processes demands that maintenance workers acquire new skills. The precise skills vary by sector, but are usually associated with some combination of electronics, software or telecommunications. Diagnostic equipment has the potential to greatly reduce machine downtime by recognising possible part failure and deskilling some maintenance tasks, but human skills remain vitally important. Similarly, traditional maintenance skills will continue to be important (Penn, 1990). In many instances microelectronics based equipment represents a small proportion of total installed capacity. A good example is provided by the lift industry. Microprocessor controls were introduced into lifts in 1979. By 1989, 90% of new and modernized lifts incorporated microprocessor controls. Despite the rapid diffusion of electronic controls, mechanical controls make up by far the greatest percentage of total installed capacity. These will only be changed to microprocessor controls as their useful life runs out. The use of microprocessor control systems increases demand for installers and service engineers to have knowledge of electronics, but they will also continue to require electrical and mechanical skills for the foreseeable future (Gann, 1991).

Maintenance in Manufacturing Sectors

Shortages of appropriate maintenance skills may lead to under-utilization of increasingly complex capital stock. With high-cost automated systems it is necessary to keep breakdowns to a minimum. A study of a German plant which invested over US $100 million in new plant found that highly skilled maintenance staff could reduce the length of breakdowns. It concluded that 'the more complex and automated the systems were, the higher the skill level of maintenance specialists had to be' (Handke, 1982).

Those involved in the maintenance of computer-controlled machines often have to combine elements of mechanical, electrical, hydraulic, pneumatic and programming skills. In some firms this combination of skills may only be required to diagnose major faults, subsequently repaired by specialists or the equipment supplier. The continuing installation of hybrid plant and the re-assignment of work creates the need for broader training to cope with the increasing range of skills. Multi-skilling is a poorly defined concept, and old craft boundaries introduce complications into training multi-skilled workers. In practice, proper implementation of multi-skilling requires detailed consideration of factors such as the complexity of the job, skills and knowledge available, access to training, impact on the employees affected by the change and the working environment (Keogh, 1989).

Shortages of maintenance workers are a major problem for several sectors, including the automobile industry. Maintenance workers have significantly broadened their skill base and have to work on a variety of mechanical and electronic machinery. But there is no consensus between firms on the skills required by maintenance workers. In some firms maintenance is carried out by specialized workers, in others operatives play a significant role in preventive maintenance and repair (OECD/CERI, 1986).

Traditional sectors such as textiles and clothing face difficulties in recruiting or retraining staff to maintain the new electronic equipment, with the severest difficulties in the least developed regions of the EU. Maintenance workers not only require an understanding of how specific machines work, but a broader knowledge of the scientific and technical aspects of electronics. In many cases suppliers are relied on for maintenance, or to provide maintenance training for textile company employees.

Maintenance in Telecommunications and Computing

There is a trend towards the further automation of maintenance in the computer and telecommunications industry, with an increased use of Expert Systems for fault diagnosis and repair. This trend is reducing the demand for maintenance technicians and is changing the nature and location of maintenance work. Automatic diagnosis has simplified the work of field engineers, enabling identification of the defective unit, which is replaced and returned to the workshop or equipment manufacturer for repair. Previous generations of electro-mechanical equipment used to be repaired in-house. This amounts to a transfer of skills away from the field engineer to the bench based engineers, who are required to have an in-depth knowledge of electronics (Senker et al, 1989).

Telecommunications maintenance
The increasing importance of software in digital exchanges is 'dematerializing' maintenance tasks, and demanding conceptual skills rather

than the manual skills associated with non-digital exchanges. In the UK, for instance, the software-based stored program control in System X should be capable of capturing, interpreting, displaying and transmitting data on all aspects of exchange performance. Self-diagnostic maintenance capabilities are expected to reduce preventive maintenance tasks to a minimum and to change the nature of corrective maintenance. The need for maintenance technicians is anticipated to be reduced to a quarter of the current level (Clark et al, 1988). Complex software related faults are likely to be directed to in-house experts or contracted out to software houses; hardware maintenance will be provided by equipment suppliers. Increasing intervention by equipment suppliers in maintenance, either directly or through diagnostics, is weakening network suppliers' control over the process of maintenance (Valenduc, 1989).

There are similar trends in telecommunications users, where maintenance jobs are decreasing and changing their nature. Greater equipment complexity together with the increased importance of the software component has led to more complex maintenance and operation tasks, for which present staff are under-skilled. Firms are setting up internal and external training programmes to train technicians in new technologies, and adopting changed policies for recruiting technicians.

Computer Maintenance

In the UK most computer maintenance is carried out by the manufacturers' service organizations, but there is a growth in the use of third party maintenance organizations (TPMs) connected with their readiness to service PCs.

When computers break down the faulty unit is replaced, and taken back to central workshops for repair. Powerful diagnostics can be used to locate faults, but the skills required to use and interpret diagnostics increase with the complexity of the equipment. Maintenance of equipment which forms part of a local area network is not simply a matter of exchanging units. An understanding of the whole system is needed to diagnose faults properly. Computer manufacturers' service organizations are now using remote diagnostics for mainframe and large mini systems. This may spread to smaller systems in the future.

Computer manufacturers have traditionally trained their own maintenance engineers and this policy has recently been adopted by TPMs. TPMs' service engineers have to deal with a broad range of equipment, and sometimes have to repair faults at component level. They therefore require a broader engineering knowledge than manufacturers' service engineers. The rapid rate of technological change in the computer industry creates a need for continual updating training (Brady and Senker, 1986).

CONCLUSIONS

The demand for telecommunications, electronic and software skills is generally considered in relation to the telecommunications, computer and software production sectors only. However, the rapid diffusion of IT and its many applications has led to a general demand for these core skills in almost every sector of the economy, with the greatest shortages occurring amongst manufacturing maintenance workers.

In relation to software production, specific skill shortages appear to vary from country to country, demanding differing national training solutions. However, telecommunications has shown similar patterns of changing skills needs, shortages and training throughout the EU. Equipment manufacturers and network operators are active in training and retraining workers, but these are often poached by users. The public sector's contribution to training is limited because of the rapid evolution and high cost of telecommunications equipment. This may suggest the need for public policy to stimulate the provision of courses in the areas of skill shortages. It may be appropriate to support the activities of firms providing training for themselves, since they are also providing much-needed skills for the wider industrial and commercial community. Telecommunications equipment manufacturers are likely to suffer from shortages of software engineers and marketing managers, and will face strong competition in the labour market from data processing equipment manufacturers, to whom telecommunications expertise has become of strategic importance.

The development of new telematics services is at an advanced stage in Germany, France and the UK. They require specialists who thoroughly understand telecommunications techniques, but an adequate supply of these skills is not available in the labour market. There is a need for more very high level courses for network managers and designers. In Spain, Italy and Denmark the development of telematic services is just beginning.

Maintenance, and the effects, direct and indirect, of high machine downtime should not be treated a peripheral issue but central to the introduction of new technologies. Underutilization of increasingly complex capital stock has far reaching effects on the individual firm as well as in the wider economy. Skill shortages in maintenance limit the possibility of realising the full potential of IT.

Automatic diagnostic equipment has replaced certain maintenance tasks and there is increased use of Field Replaceable Units by computer and control system manufacturers. Human skills will be required at most levels of maintenance in the short, medium and probably long term. Maintenance will not necessarily be carried out in-house due to the increasing complexity and variety of manufacturers' equipment installed in a particular plant. There may be a dual maintenance skill structure, those dealing with complex equipment in which they may specialize and broader multi-skilled craftsmen who will undertake fault diagnosis and minor repair.

The trend toward diagnostic skills, multi-skilling and mechatronics is not confined to engineering maintenance. Maintenance requirements across such diverse areas as banking and construction are increasingly moving towards similar broad based skills. While this may allow for a degree of transferable skill, say from construction plant to machine tool maintenance, it also means that the total pool of such skills must be larger if member states are to avoid problems of skill shortages and 'poaching'. This situation can be alleviated by increased investment in training at firm and national level.

NOTES

1. Except where elsewhere referenced, this section draws extensively on Eurostrategies-Planet-Turu (1989).
2. This section draws mainly on CEC (1990a).

4. Information Technology and Skills in Manufacturing and Construction

Peter Senker and Jacqueline Senker

This chapter discusses the growth of information and communications technologies (IT) in manufacturing and its implications for manufacturing employment and skills. The main trends identified are a general decline in manufacturing employment and a convergence in skill requirements across many industrial sectors. Construction is included in this chapter because IT is affecting construction products and processes, and, therefore, has implications for employment and skills in this industry.

Figure 4.1   Extent of microelectronics use in products and processes (percent of workplaces adopting)

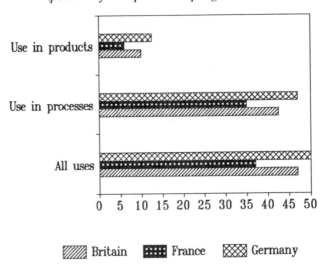

Source: Northcott et al, 1985

*Figure 4.2   Adoption of IT in European factories by size of firm
(percent of workplaces adopting)*

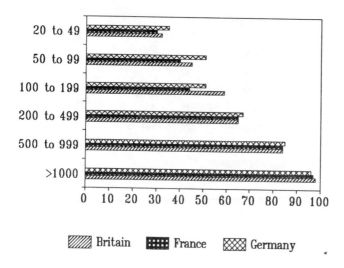

Source: Northcott et al, 1985

GROWTH OF IT IN MANUFACTURING

The adoption of microelectronics by manufacturing increased from less than one half of UK, French and German firms in 1984 (ILO, 1987a) to over two-thirds by 1987 (OECD, 1989d). It is estimated that Europe has more than 250,000 computer numerically controlled machines and over 30,000 robots which represents substantial increases since the early 1980s. Applications of IT to processes are more widespread than to products (See Figure 4.1), with IT use in products being largely confined to mechanical and electrical engineering, vehicle and aircraft production and the electronics industry itself. (Northcott et al, 1985).

The rate of adoption of IT varies between countries, industrial sectors and by firm size. Larger firms have adoption rates over twice those of smaller companies (Figure 4.2). Government policy has aimed to increase the adoption of IT by SMEs in several countries including France, Denmark and Germany.

Figure 4.3   Microelectronics in European industry (percent of firms using)

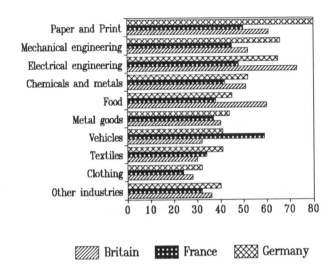

Source: VDI (cited in FAST Programme II Strategic Dossier, no date)

Figure 4.3 shows that adoption of IT is most widespread in engineering, paper and print, food and drink and chemical and metal industries. The following section describe IT applications and their implications for skills and employment in the engineering and other manufacturing sectors.

IT IN ENGINEERING SECTORS

The Development of Advanced Manufacturing Technology

Advanced Manufacturing Technology (AMT) developed mainly in batch production where many benefits were sought including raising quality, accuracy, consistency, increased machine utilization, increased productivity and coping with shortages of skilled labour.

Hard-wired numerically controlled machine tools (NC) controlled by coded paper tapes date back to the late 1940s. Each operation was carried out by a single special purpose machine. The availability of minicomputers in the 1970s led to the development of computer numerically controlled (CNC) machine tools. These built-in computers allow for the storage and editing of a wide variety of programs. CNC machine-tools equipped with automatic tool changing can be used for a variety of functions.

Direct numerical control (DNC) describes a production cell where a master computer controls a set of multifunction machine tools. Flexible manufacturing systems (FMS) are a development of DNC in which a computer also controls the movement of workpieces between workstations by robots, conveyors or automatic guided vehicles (AGVs). Adoption of these technologies is not yet widespread.

Computers are being used increasingly for production planning and materials requirements planning (MRP) and to provide information for decision-making. The main goal to which MRP has been applied is the reduction of inventory and work-in-progress. Interactive computer systems which display data in the form of graphics make it possible for designers to use computers in place of drawing boards. These computer-aided design (CAD) systems can be used for a variety of two- and three-dimensional applications in electrical, electronic and mechanical engineering, textiles, clothing, architecture, construction and other industries. Industrial robots have been widely used for spot welding for some time. They are also used for several other applications such as surface coating and materials handling. At present, the fastest growing application is assembly.

Integration of computer controlled manufacturing systems with computer-aided design (CAD/CAM) and MRP could lead to computer-integrated manufacturing (CIM) or 'the factory of the future'. Experience of integrated systems is, however, extremely limited, experimental and only reflects partial integration. The achievement of manufacturing integration demands preliminary organizational integration. Managerial and work-based organizational changes are thought to have contributed many of the benefits derived from the application of IT.

Implications of IT for Engineering Employment and Skills

Employment

The employment effects of IT are varied. Some sectors have been negatively affected by its use but there have also been job gains from the production of new products and the opening up of new markets. Many studies carried out into the impact of new technology on employment highlight the difficulties in accurately observing and predicting changes at different levels in the economy from the individual occupation, through the level of the firm to the macro-level of the industry or the economy as a whole (Bessant, 1989).

Applying microelectronics to products reduces the number of components, facilitating automated assembly and reducing labour requirements. Increased

60   *Employment and Technical Change in Europe*

reliability of products incorporating microelectronics may reduce demands for service and maintenance workers. IT applied to the production process has reduced the demand for skilled workers and those involved in the transport and loading of materials. The use of industrial robots can replace between two and seven employees, depending where and how they are applied, with most effect on unskilled work (Edquist, 1988). However, applications such as robotics are not solely job displacing. Such applications also creates new jobs, for example in maintenance.

Skills

It is difficult to predict changing skill requirements resulting from IT introduction, because there is a wide degree of choice associated with the technology. There is no single best practice solution in terms of work organization and skill level. It may be practical in one plant to integrate processes and use multi-skilled operatives to perform basic maintenance, programming etc. In another factory, skills may need to be more specialized due to the particular requirements of the product. Between these extremes lie countless other combinations. Work organization is also influenced by managements' motivations for implementing IT on the shopfloor, existing skill levels and trade union power. The skills required to operate a CNC machine, for example, are largely a function of the organizational process of the firm, but the organizational process itself is likely to be radically altered by the application of IT and thus will demand a changing skills profile (ILO, 1987a).

AMT has tended to shift skills from the operator to design, programming and maintenance functions. AMT is also blurring traditional occupational boundaries in such tasks as turning, milling, drilling and shaping of workpieces; they are being incorporated into one computer controlled process. Occupations are gradually moving away from being defined by a particular task towards task integration, occupational flexibility and team working. Operators will continue to need traditional engineering apprenticeships, but these will need to be more broadly based and cover the acquisition of multiple skills (Alderman et al, 1987). For example there is an increasing demand for 'mechatronics' expertise which combines the skills of mechanical and electronic engineering. These trends reflect the requirement for higher, broader and more flexible skills (Bessant, 1989), with growth in demand for 'core' skills of computer science and electronics engineering. Figure 4.4 summarizes organizational practices considered to be required for effective implementation of AMT. Case studies of the introduction of specific AMT equipment and of the wider effects of its introduction in the automobile industry demonstrate that few companies' practices have yet reached this stage in practice.

Figure 4.4   Organizational characteristics of implementation and use of AMT

ORGANIZATIONAL   **COMMENTS**
CHARACTERISTIC

Skill Changes   Different skill requirements ('mental' or problem solving, rather than physical). Usually higher average skill.

Work Organization   Greater interdependence among work and job design activities requiring flexible (multi-skilled) employees responsible for more planning and diagnosis, operating and maintenance.

                                 Work teams to manage interdependent work roles. Decentralization of operational decision-making to work teams. Greater employee commitment needed.

Employment   Need for high retention rate of well trained workers because of: greater investment in training: higher capital investment in training: higher capital investment per employee; and more costly 'down-time'.

Labour Relationship   Strong partnership between management and trade union with greater and earlier information sharing, co-planning and selection and implementation of technology and organizational changes, co-solving of problems.

Source: Human Resource Practices for Implementing Advanced Manufacturing Technology (1986) National Academy Press, Washington, D.C.

Case Studies

Impact of AMT on Engineering Skills
Studies of the introduction of AMT in various European engineering companies demonstrate the difficulty of predicting the impact on engineering skills and qualifications. The introduction of AMT leads to new

skill requirements throughout the workforce, including the loss of some unskilled and semi-skilled jobs. Changes to jobs and in their allocation cannot be explained solely by the characteristics of the technology. The objectives and expectations of management, particularly the extent to which they are prepared train their workers, has an even greater effect.

NC and CNC machine-tools are used to carry out operations which were previously carried out by highly skilled operators, and when these technologies were introduced it was often believed that they would deskill shopfloor jobs, leaving the operator with only unskilled loading, monitoring and unloading jobs. Case studies of the use of CNC have found examples of both deskilled and enriched operator jobs. The evidence suggests that policies of trying to simplify operators' jobs can impair productivity, and this effect could become even more pronounced with more complex technology such as FMS and CIM.

CNC allows operators to program machines, and this practice is more frequently followed in Germany than in Britain where it is more usual for programmers to produce and edit programs in offices away from the shopfloor. Experience has shown that operators with traditional as well as CNC skills, including programming, setting skills, and knowledge of tooling and tool maintenance can produce products faster and more accurately. They can speedily rectify errors in programs, adapt programs for different types of metals or to take account of tool wear.

The combination of traditional and CNC skills is most beneficial when new programs are first used or when operators produce small numbers of components of many different types (Wilson, 1988). Belgian and Danish studies of the introduction of CNC also emphasize that it is not the form of new technology that determines the skill and qualification level of those employed, but wider political and social factors. The Belgian study found that employment and industrial relations policies, rather than the adoption of CNC machine tools, determined changes in work practice, control and qualification (Alaluf and Stroobant, 1987).

In Danish metal working firms adopting CNC, the reorganization of production and product developments constituted a move towards flexibility based on the 'individual employee's, the individual firm's and the individual region's ability to adapt and gain new knowledge' (Kristensen, 1986). Flexibility has been facilitated by traditional Danish education and work practices which have led to a culture able to accept change, with a preference for team working and a willingness for most workers to accept a high degree of responsibility (Hofstede, 1980). Technical and labour relations factors, however, made it easier to introduce new technology in firms which mainly employed skilled workers than in those with a high proportion of unskilled workers. There were also wider employment effects.

Skilled workers increased their skills, but unskilled workers had few opportunities to work with new technology or to upgrade their skills. The existence of a skilled and motivated workforce has made it possible for technical and administrative directors to deal directly with operatives on the shopfloor. In many firms this has resulted in the elimination of intermediate managers, foremen, engineers and even production managers (Kristensen, 1986).

The use of FMS also shows the need for multi-skilling, but adherence to traditional job classifications can discourage FMS operators from working outside their prescribed areas and limit the flexibility of the systems. Effective FMS use requires operators to learn much about the system including programming, inspection, scheduling, operation and machine maintenance, so they can be involved in all the tasks necessary to keep plant running (Jones and Scott, 1987). This requires major changes to operators' skill patterns. In addition to existing skills, operators need to acquire new skills in programming, electronic equipment maintenance, diagnostics and so on. Lack of broad-based skills and training could affect the ability of firms to achieve best practice performance with advanced manufacturing technology systems (Bessant and Haywood, 1988).

Studies of the introduction of FMS systems in both Belgium and France also found that work organization was not technologically determined, but depended on an interplay of economic, technical and social factors (Henderickx and Raeymaekers, 1987). A comparison of three French engineering firms which introduced FMS found a high degree of variation in work organization and skills, but a general rise in the average skill level. The most striking feature of all three firms was the lack of training directed at producing multi-skilling (Rosanvallon, 1986). Another French company which introduced FMS has decentralized departments such as methods, maintenance and programming. Skill levels within the firm have increased, unskilled and semi-skilled jobs have been eliminated and skilled work dramatically changed.[1]

New technology and new manufacturing management practices have important implications for the skill needs of managers and supervisors in the engineering industry. Increasingly, influenced largely by Japanese management practices, British manufacturing firms are putting in place coherent sets of policies embracing Total Quality Management (TQM) and Just in Time (JIT) manufacture. The general aim is to improve service to customers, at the same time reducing work-in-progress and inventories and increasing productivity and profitability. Successful implementation of TQM and JIT demands improved communications and faster response times. This involves moving responsibility and decision-making closer to the point of action on the shopfloor, and removes the need for traditional deep hierarchies of management. At the same time as reducing the number of layers of manufacturing management, firms are increasingly converting to cell production - aiming to increase speed of response and reduce work-in-progress, and transferring more responsibility for quality and output to cell leaders and their teams. For a long time, the role of German *Meisters* has been key to efficient manufacture in Germany. The trends outlined above have led to increasing recognition of the pivotal role of manufacturing supervision in Britain, and of the need for supervisors to receive more and broader training (NEDC, 1991). Such changes may erode the power of specialists such as industrial engineers, personnel managers and training staff, and transform their roles into providing services for manufacturing management and supervision.

Managers often fail to appreciate the need to manage new technology introduction according to a strategy which covers both technical and worker aspects. Communications breakdowns and lack of coordination limit firms' capabilities to get the best performance from their investment. Even in companies with years of experience of CAD or CNC, managers can still lack understanding of the skills needed to obtain the optimum results from the technology. For instance, a British study found that knowledge and experience of CAD has accumulated in relatively junior engineers and managers, but they do not realize the strategic potential of integrating CAD with other company functions. Integration between the functions of various previously separate company departments requires organizational change (Simmonds and Senker, 1989).

This study found that senior managers do not always fully understand the strategic implications of new technology. They are sometimes reluctant to go on training courses for fear that this might reveal their inadequacies. For similar reasons they fail to exploit the accumulated knowledge of their more junior colleagues. CAD could be more effectively utilized if CAD professionals could have more influence on decisions about the need for additional training, or in establishing new links between CAD and other functions.

This suggests the need for new approaches to engineering and management training. Future graduates might be trained as either manufacturing system engineers or business systems engineers. The former would study the range of technical disciplines associated with modern manufacturing, and their links with business, e.g. marketing and finance. The latter would be trained in the implications of new manufacturing technologies as well as in business management (Bessant and Haywood, 1987).

AMT in the Automobile Industry

The impact of microelectronics on the employment and skills levels of automotive workers is difficult to divorce from factors such as competition and the general economic climate. However, the general trend has been a reduction in total employment and the displacement of low level skills.

Robots have diffused very quickly, and are used predominantly for tasks such as spot welding, arc welding, surface coating or cutting. Increasingly, they are also used in assembly operations such as windscreen fitting. Automation of these tasks is responsible for the decline of unskilled, semi-skilled and skilled occupations, but is unlikely to lead to the 'workerless factory'. Increasingly expensive capital equipment needs constant monitoring to enable it to run continuously; any downtime is extremely expensive. High cost capital equipment and the need to maintain quality requires motivated, highly qualified and responsible workers, but as in other industries the way in which new technology affects organization and skill requirements is to a large degree a matter of choice.

In Spain, the introduction of programmable robots and CNC machines has reduced the number of jobs and altered the composition of the workforce. Workers have been upskilled and there is increased employment in quality control and maintenance (CEC, 1987a). There are similar trends in Germany where white collar jobs are increasing slowly, blue collar workers have been cut by 10% but workers in maintenance, quality control and tool making have increased by almost 6% (Kern and Schumann, 1992).

Renault's introduction of new systems into plants was accompanied by a general move towards team working; such systems demand different skills than traditional single man working, for instance the ability to function in a group. Where group work has been introduced it has normally required workers to become, if not multi-skilled, at least multi-functional (OECD/CERI, 1986). The introduction of new technology at Volkswagen led to a company decision to substitute worker competence for the traditional concept of skill. Qualifications now sought from operatives, for example the ability to communicate, plan and cooperate, are similar to those required from professional workers. The OECD/CERI report argues that although such qualifications are not directly related to the introduction of new technology, they are a prerequisite for it. In Germany automobile production has developed a dual structure, combining both high-tech and low-tech areas. At the high tech end most work has become more skilled. Low-tech areas such as grinding and polishing are expected to remain predominantly manual, resulting in high-tech islands with many skilled system control jobs and an environment which is composed of huge areas of manual work (Kern and Schumann, 1992).

New occupations such as 'system controllers' have developed with the integration of quality control, maintenance, machine programming and regulation of workflow. Multi-skilled production workers able to carry out maintenance operations in addition to their direct functions, are much sought after, but several studies have found a lack of workers with medium-level training and education with 'basic knowledge in a number of fields' or workers of 'polyvalence' (Watanabe, 1987). Fiat's engine assembly plant at Termoli in Italy, its most advanced plant, provides an example of the effect of implementing new technology together with profound organizational change. Approximately 150 robots are used in an assembly line process. Assembly is highly automated except for carburettor assembly which is still labour intensive. Engines are transported on pallets which contain all the information on the particular engine. These are read by computers which instruct and control the robot's operation on the engine.

Workers are employed mainly in maintenance, quality control and a newly created occupation of 'conductor'. The conductor's job combines operators' skills with first level maintenance and some programming work. Existing workers were retrained in-house. Training concentrates on electronic and managerial skills and can last from eight to eighteen months. The company has attempted to provide a career ladder from conductor to skilled maintenance worker to technician. Fiat intends that by the year 2000 one third of its workers will be employed as conductors. This implies a transformation of the traditional skills profile of automobile engine production workers with a massive shift from physical to mental skill requirements (Watanabe, 1987).

Robotic assembly tends to be used in the UK as a sophisticated form of special-purpose automation. Firms often assume that operators have few skills and are unable to carry out routine maintenance, clear blockages or amend programs. In contrast to Japanese practice, UK practice tends to be expensive, unreliable and inflexible. Japanese firms use less sophisticated robots but use them more flexibly, and place great emphasis on training workers. Operators play a 'fire-fighting' role as well as performing some assembly work and supplying components, thus keeping the robotic assembly systems running smoothly (Tidd, 1991).

In summary, it has been suggested that new technology and organization in the automobile industry call for a new type of worker, namely one who has not only a greater technical knowledge but a greater adaptability to new situations, an ability to respond quickly to technical problems as well as a capacity for team work, rather than one who possesses physical strength and individual work capacity (Tidd, 1991).

IT IN OTHER MANUFACTURING SECTORS

This section examines the skills and employment implications of the adoption of IT in food processing and packaging, textiles and clothing and printing. There are many technical difficulties associated with automating food processing, which is limiting the diffusion of IT. The textiles and clothing industries contribute significantly to employment in some of the lesser developed countries of the EU and, until recently, had a high labour content. Government intervention has played a significant role in promoting investment and training for new technology. Printing and publishing has been selected because it is one of the sectors most affected by IT, with radical changes to traditional practices throughout the EU.

Food Processing

The diffusion of IT in the food and drink industries is constrained by hygiene requirements which require machines able to withstand steam-cleaning and sterilization; and by variability in the raw materials used. It has been difficult to develop robust sensors to check flavour, colour, texture, etc. and so much reliance still has to be placed on operator tacit knowledge. For example, the automation of brewing fermentation would require robust on-line CO_2 sensors, but these have not yet been developed. In contrast, it is possible to computerize some processes such as sugar refining, because the temperature of the sugar indicates the state of the product precisely.

Integrated systems with programmable controllers are being introduced to many relatively simple processes such as the depithing and canning of fruit; automatic visual inspection is likely to become a common feature of new processing equipment. Future goals include the development of systems which allow management and machines to share the same continuous flow of information.

Computer technology is far more widely diffused in food packaging than in processing. This is due largely to the fact that by the time food reaches the packaging stage the process is simpler and more standardized. There is increased use of microprocessors for machine control functions, incorporating self-test features which eliminate some maintenance work and help to reduce machine downtime. Automated pick and place operations are being introduced, but the most significant trend is towards system integration.

The implications of IT for skills in food processing and packaging are broadly similar to those in other areas of manufacturing, including reduction in unskilled and semi-skilled labour employment. In packaging, some operators' work is becoming less skilled and automatic visual inspection has reduced employment.

In food processing, however, there has been a rise in the importance of skilled staff, while employment has decreased or remained static (NEDC, 1989). Workers have become more flexible and undertake a larger array of low level tasks. Multi-skilling of fitters and technicians has taken place. Electricians have had to learn basic mechanical and electronic skills. Technicians have had to develop extensive electronics expertise and skill levels have generally risen, especially in firms which introduced 'flexibility and or quality improvements alongside new technology'.[2]

Textiles and Clothing

The European textiles and clothing sector has suffered declining employment over the past decades, and most European governments have played an active role in restructuring. Many firms have responded to competition from developing countries by investing in IT. There is a general consensus that continued application of IT to the textile industry will result in further job losses for workers with low level skills, but an increase in demand for qualified labour with expertise in control technology.

Adoption of IT in the less developed European countries is hindered by the low educational attainments of the workers, who, nevertheless, possess high craft skills. Their low wage rates, however, also reduce the incentive for many small and medium size firms to invest in new technology.

IT has been applied to the stages preceding the final spinning and weaving process, for example the opening of cotton bales. It is also used for control and data supply in both spinning and weaving, but spinning is much more automated than weaving. IT has allowed for better stock control and increased use of 'just-in-time' techniques to improve workflow. The use of CAD for design is increasing. There have been fewer IT applications in the clothing sector, where most impact has been on the pre-assembly stage - the computerization of pattern-making and cutting processes; it is most appropriate to mass production of certain fashion lines.

Spain

One report has suggested that the application of IT to the textiles industry has had a significant impact on skill requirements at every level, from shopfloor operatives through maintenance engineers to company managers. All need to be able to operate, programme, adjust, maintain and regulate equipment incorporating electronic technology which was previously unknown in the workshop or factory (CEDEFOP, 1988a).

It is not yet common for Spanish operatives to program or regulate equipment. This is the province of the foreman and in some cases the factory manager. Difficulties in retraining or recruiting staff to maintain the new electronic equipment, leads firms to rely on equipment suppliers for maintenance. The industry lacks any coordinated training policy and its poor image has attracted the least qualified workers. Training has been hampered by the general low level of education in the sector's workforce. Training for new technology has tended to concentrate on key workers, rather than improving all workers' skills as in the former West Germany.

Nevertheless the industry has recently accepted that the skills of all workers needs to be upgraded and five main areas have been identified. These include training and retraining for all workers whose work involves electronics technology, especially maintenance workers and supervisors; and a requirement for technical and programming skills among designers and middle managers. Appropriate training schemes have been implemented by the National Institute of Employment.

Portugal and Greece
The Portuguese and Greek textile and clothing sectors both account for around 20% of GNP, but are in urgent need of restructuring and adoption of IT (CEDEFOP, 1988b, 1989). While this will result in substantial job losses, it has been estimated that new technology adoption will result in far fewer job losses than would result from non-adoption. In Portugal, similar employment trends are anticipated in spinning, weaving and clothing with an increase in demand for senior managers, middle managers, foremen, mechanics and other highly skilled workers; jobs for machine operators will continue to decline, with many occupations disappearing altogether. In Greece, shortages of middle management and technical staff are causing most concern. Some of the key groups where skills are in very short supply are electronics operators and computer programmers, maintenance technicians for the latest machinery and designers with knowledge of CAD.

Government aid has been provided for the purchase of new technology and training. In Portugal, training courses are designed to link traditional skills with the use of computers and electronics. Training has also focused on programming, maintenance and supervisory skills for microprocessor equipment. In Greece, training and retraining opportunities are aimed at technical staff and senior and middle managers.

Many Greek firms have made coordinated efforts to increase production output and quality through the introduction of automation and computer technology. Evidence suggests that even in firms which have committed themselves to new technology, lack of skills among the workers has prevented efficient use and stopped further development.

Belgium

The Government has intervened considerably in the textiles and clothing sectors, subsidizing activities such as R&D and training. In the clothing sector, support was given for the development of a computer-assisted grading and pattern drawing system. A computer integrated materials management system was also developed and a computer-aided production control system introduced.

The Belgian programme has been particularly successful. There has been an increase in employment and share of EU production. It has been suggested that modernization, commercialization, creativity and product innovation, and training played a major role in this success (UNIDO, 1989).

Summary

The Belgian, Spanish, Portuguese and Greek Governments have all intervened to restructure their clothing and textile industries and to provide financial support to modernize equipment. There have been various outcomes from these interventions, depending to some extent on education and training infrastructures in the countries concerned. However, the results of these interventions serve in general to demonstrate that the introduction and diffusion of new labour saving microelectronic based technologies, can be aided by national skills, training and employment plans and policies. The absence of such planning in relation to the British textile and clothing industry is partly responsible for their relatively low investment in capital equipment and training .

A study of British and German clothing firms found three quarters of machinery in UK firms was over five years old. This was in contrast to Germany where three quarters of machinery was less than five years old. Although IT equipment is only cost-effective for some operations in the mass garment market, British companies often used it inappropriately. In Germany 80% of machinists had completed a two year apprenticeship and clothing technicians were used to 'engineer' production patterns to minimize cloth wastage. In Britain, these skills were virtually non-existent. British machinists needed continuous assistance from supervisors and their reliability in terms of quality was poor. German machinists require far less supervision and were able to work directly from technical sketches (Steedman and Wagner, 1989).

Printing and Publishing[3]

Computer technology has revolutionized the production of newspapers, magazines and periodicals throughout Europe. The previous hot metal processes required skilled labour to carry out sequential tasks of typesetting, proof pulling and page make-up. Increasingly, these previously separate tasks have now been combined and merged with the creative work of the author. The pace of change has been most rapid in newspaper offices.

Journalists and workers in the editorial and advertising departments now key their work directly into the computer, where it is stored prior to being output for page make-up. Page make-up can also be carried out on computer, and digitizing optical scanners allow for images to be fed directly into the printing unit. Image processing lags behind computerized text editing, and many papers still use manual insertion because of technical problems. The completed page is output from the photo-typesetter in the form of a bromide, which is used as an input for reproduction by offset lithography, letterpress or direct litho. Newspaper production arrangements have been changed by advances in communications technology. Facsimile transmission enables whole or part pages to be sent electronically to distant printing centres.

Heavy previous investment in offset printing technologies by the French newspaper industry slowed computerization, but it is now diffusing rapidly. Lack of appropriate skills delayed the installation of new computer-aided technology in Greece. Managers and technicians were sent abroad to train in both hardware and software applications, but print technology has tended to lag behind: there is no direct input by journalists: text is rewritten by keyboard operators; and other workers undertake the editing, checking and paging process. In Portugal the national press has been computerized, but most regional newspapers still use traditional technology. Low literacy is a cause of low consumption of newspapers, depriving proprietors of resources for modernization.

In general publishing, the Netherlands is most advanced and tasks such as binding, stapling, packing and shipment of books are widely computerized. In the UK and Italy lack of finance has hindered the diffusion of new technology among small publishers, but falling costs of systems are attracting more firms.

Skills and Employment Implications

The demise of 'hot metal' and direct input by journalists has made skilled work such as typesetting, typography and proof-reading obsolete, with heavy job losses for these skills. In some EU countries, direct input was forbidden under union/employer agreements, but many of these agreements have now been rescinded. Computerized handling of huge paper rolls to the presses and printed newspapers to the delivery vehicles have eliminated unskilled manual jobs in warehousing, binding and dispatch.

A Germany study of the printing industry found that the decline in employment was not as severe as had been expected (Dostal, 1988). The principal impact of new technology had been to shift the demand away from physical and towards cognitive skills. Some unskilled employees have taken over some of the formerly skilled work of inputting such as direct entry of classified advertisement from phone calls. Distinctions between skilled and unskilled work are further blurred when machine assistants take on responsibility as machine managers. The rapid advance of computerization in newspaper offices has led to the introduction of newspaper computer specialists who program, monitor and maintain the computers. Computer specialists comprise retrained printers or new specialist staff.

Alongside the loss of previously skilled jobs, there has been a growth of demand for highly skilled workers who can combine telecommunications with publishing skills, as well as new jobs for computer professionals and training personnel. Technological developments have led to the growth of an 'alternative' print industry, and new jobs have also been created in instant print shops, in-house printing and art and advertising studios. Desk-top publishing is accelerating this process (Pate, 1989).

There is a trend towards training for flexible, multi-skilled workers in most European countries, with training being broadened to include courses in areas such as computer graphics and printing management. In Belgium, for instance, it has been established that graphical workers require broad based training. They need some knowledge of telecommunications technology and computer-aided text editing as well as the skill to combine computer literacy with a deep understanding of graphics. In Italy and the Netherlands the number of occupational classifications in the sector has been reduced. In Italy, machine shop employees are being retrained for work as technical editorial managers, graphic operators or teletype operators. All occupations contain varying degrees of multi-skilling, and printing workers are expected to be flexible, able to carry out all of the technical phases of newspaper production, excluding text input. In the Netherlands, the number of occupational classifications has also been reduced to text producers, editors and managers and in some cases specialist operators. Training aims to create multi-skilled operatives able to undertake several tasks.

IT IN CONSTRUCTION

Construction is not a single industry but a number of industries whose common link is the construction process. The range of activities include building in the residential, commercial and industrial sectors as well as civil engineering projects. In addition the work may be in new build, renovation or maintenance. These activities require a combination of diverse skills, for example architects, engineers and electricians.

Compared to manufacturing, the uptake of IT by the European construction industry has been slow.[4] Indeed, until recently, construction had been regarded as a traditional industry where new technology had little effect. The significance of IT and its skill needs are only just beginning to be realised. IT in construction, especially among larger multinational firms includes computers, automation of the construction process, robotics, electronic based components, software development and design automation. IT is also used increasingly for administrative and professional functions including distribution; production planning and control; data communications; design calculations; personnel/payroll; computer-aided design; finance and accounts; and business planning and statistics (Wix, 1989).

Computerization of construction is proceeding most rapidly in French and German firms, which account for almost 50% of the value of EU construction work. The growing internationalization of construction management is likely to accelerate IT adoption. For example, Bouygues of France, Europe's largest contractor, has bought construction firms in Spain. It uses IT extensively in its French operations and intends to introduce these techniques into Spain. Similar moves into the European Community by firms experienced in the application of IT to construction, from countries such as Sweden and Finland will lead to further diffusion of IT in the construction process, as will the possible penetration of the European market by Japan. Such moves have implications for IT skills across the whole Community.

Effects of IT on the European Construction Industry[5]

IT has implications for the constructed product as well as the construction process, and has led to demand for new types of structures, to change in the nature of structures and the ways they are planned, designed, produced and built/erected.[6] Industry at the 'leading edge' is showing signs of converging with engineering in terms of both processes and skills requirements. Clients, especially in the commercial office sector, are demanding flexible 'smart' buildings which require the installation and operation of a number of 'systems' - such as security, lifts, and energy control, all underpinned by IT. IT is also essential to 'facilities management', in which management and maintenance of sophisticated buildings utilizes computerized controls, records and drawings.

Each stage of the construction process has come under the influence of IT. There has been a rapid diffusion of Computer-aided design (CAD), which has the capacity to 'revolutionize' the design stage. For example, design information, once entered, can be used for structural calculation, drawing production and maintenance planning. IT also has the potential to reduce planning costs, which can amount to as much as 10% of total building costs in complex buildings.

IT applications are also being adopted rapidly by manufacturers of construction plant such as tower cranes and earth-moving equipment, improving both the safety and the precision of operations.

Implications of IT for Skills in the Constructed Product

The use of IT directly related to the construction process is dwarfed by its influence on the constructed product. Buildings have already been affected by developments in office/factory automation (e.g. LANs, CAD, CAM) and telecommunications. The impact is even greater in 'intelligent buildings' which are dependent on microelectronics to control the environment, access, lifts, lighting etc. and maintain security systems. Increasingly, energy management functions such as zonal air conditioning and heating are also computer controlled. The market for intelligent buildings in Europe is large, but the diffusion of intelligent building technologies may be constrained by skills shortages and the lack of system compatibility and standardization.

Skills required for the construction of high-technology buildings are often very different from those needed in traditional construction. In addition to the new skills required to design, install, manufacture and maintain the building, contractors also need to increase their skills: cabling specialists, software engineers, commissioning engineers and facilities managers are in great demand.

Electronic related services in some complex buildings can amount to 50% of construction costs. In the past few years major French, British and German construction contractors have formed strategic alliances with electronics companies, or used them as subcontractors.

Implications of IT for Skills in the Construction Process

Impediments to the diffusion of IT in the construction process include lack of understanding of the construction industry by software designers, lack of construction staff with IT training and knowledge and the low average percentage of turnover spent on IT applications - between 0.1% and 0.25%. Expenditure in areas such as networking and communications are expected to increase by 50% over the next few years, but this is expected to lead to an IT skills crisis (CICA/Peat Marwick McLintock, 1987, 1990). Larger contractors can develop IT skills in-house, and are leading the way in adoption of IT systems, but the vast numbers of small firms within the industry cannot provide the level of training required.

At operative level there will be a growing need for highly skilled specialists in areas where there is a high degree of technical complexity associated with information technology and microprocessor control systems. Alongside the move to greater specialization will be a parallel move toward multi-skilling among those involved in repair and maintenance. Such operatives will need diagnostic skills and the ability to work with systems that incorporate mechanical, electrical and electronic engineering.

There should be caution about the degree to which construction is moving to factory pre-fabrication.[7] However, off-site production is likely to increase, assisted by communications technology which greatly enhances the possibilities for sequencing off-site production, delivery and installation and making the process more economically efficient. Off-site production will be performed increasingly on manufacturing equipment using IT, reducing the numbers of skilled and unskilled workers required on sites. These trends reflect to some extent those found in manufacturing.

The current impact of IT on skills is greater at management and professional level than at that of the operative. CAD is being introduced into companies at a rapid rate; new systems such as 3D walk through design give the architect a far fuller vision of the finished building. Evidence from France suggests that the move from drawing board to CAD will require substantial amounts of retraining.

During the 1990s most medium and large contracts will use IT for project management. This will require the processing of massive amounts of information concerning the many sequential developments on-site, and may demand new high level occupations such as 'site information manager'. These project management systems will network with clients, architects, suppliers and manufacturers, demanding basic knowledge of communications technology by virtually all those involved in the construction process.

The application of microelectronic control systems to plant and equipment known as 'construction robotics' is being developed in Britain for use with minimal labour input. In Japan, equipment already in use requires highly skilled labour, trained to operate programmable machines. Construction mechanization is likely to follow the Japanese approach of employing skilled workers to operate computerized machines.

CONCLUSIONS

This chapter highlights the varying degrees to which IT is being adopted by member states in various manufacturing sectors and in construction, and its implications for employment and skills. A few general trends may be discerned. IT in products, including buildings, has changed the emphasis on skills from production towards the pre-production stage where there is a need for planning, design and software skills. This shift has reduced unskilled work and increased employment in highly skilled occupations.

Investment in IT is expected to result in higher labour productivity and to reduce total labour requirements in traditional craft-based sectors. Boundaries between crafts have been eroded with a rising demand for multi-skilled workers, and the distinction between unskilled and skilled work has become blurred. Generally, craft based skills and unskilled jobs are being replaced by higher level skills based on knowledge and technical skills, with growing demand for computer specialists to program, monitor and maintain microprocessor-based systems.

The introduction of IT has resulted in structural and cultural problems in the readjustment of the existing workforce. Government programmes of support during the restructuring process, for example financial support and retraining for displaced workers, have helped to ease these difficulties in some countries. Evidence from Southern Europe suggests that retraining is only effective where workers have adequate basic education onto which IT-related capabilities can be added through training. Training and retraining of workers is essential for all member states if they are to overcome problems of skill shortages. Some countries train significantly fewer workers than others. France for example trains almost three times as many mechanical and electrical craftsmen as Britain.[8] While these skills do not invariably relate directly to IT, coupled with a knowledge of electronics such skills can form the basis for producing the multi-skilled operative needed for effective installation, running and maintenance of IT-based systems.

The use of IT in products and in production processes has implications for skills at every level of the workforce. Countries failing to train adequately for IT use will find themselves at a competitive disadvantage, because investment in IT cannot increase productivity or competitiveness if the necessary skills are lacking. Pro-active training provision can increase the rate of adoption of IT and its effective use. In order to get the best performance from their IT investments, directors and managers need to become more technically competent and involved with the introduction and supervision of IT systems. Management and supervisory skills will need to be enhanced as integrating technologies such as CAD/CAM move design closer to production. As a result both of the introduction of IT and of associated organizational changes, the number of middle managers is likely to decline, and the functions of those which remain are likely to change.

NOTES

1. *Integrated Manufacturing Systems*, April, 1990.
2. *Food Processing*, June, 1990.
3 This section is heavily based upon CEC (1989a), Gennard (1987) and Pate (1989).
4. The adoption of new technology in the construction industry is inhibited by the fragmented nature of the industry, lack of private or public funded construction-related R&D, regulatory structures unresponsive to rapid technical change and fear of litigation.
5. A report by IPRA for the Department of Employment was used in compiling this section (IPRA, 1991).
6. There is a distinction between the building and erection of a structure. Building suggests a traditional form of construction whereas many of the structures at the leading edge of the industry are increasingly becoming engineered with components produced off site and merely assembled in the field.
7. Prefabrication is used more in some countries than in others. For example, in Sweden, inclement weather, labour costs, close links between design and construction and between construction and manufacturing, and a lower level of social discontent with large building systems has led to a wider use of prefabrication than in the UK.
8. *Financial Times*, 21 June 1988.

5. Skills Implications of Technical Change in the Service Sector

Jacqueline Senker and Peter Senker

Since the middle of the 1980s there has been an enormous increase in the use of IT in many service sectors and great changes in the way it is used. This is linked with the rise of the personal computer (PC), the increasing use of computer networking and a convergence towards common standards.

There is a general trend for the use of IT in service sectors to affect the nature of occupations and change their distribution. Professional and senior clerical jobs are increasing, but demand for junior managers will decrease as IT reduces the need for routine supervision and coordination. Other junior management tasks will be taken over by senior clerical staff supported by on-line technology. Junior clerical jobs are declining, particularly in fragmented data preparation and data entry, and in the future many such tasks will be carried out by part-time staff (Long, 1987; Rajan, 1987; Swann, 1986).

New IT equipment is often introduced into firms without adequate attention to staff training, work organization or the requirement to involve staff in the choice or organization of new technology. Participation in decision-making by those destined to be directly involved in using the technology can yield important benefits. But workers, just as much as management, need to learn about the new technology and its implications in order to be effective in contributing to decisions. Problems are minimized and new equipment most effectively utilized when users are involved in its selection (Huggett,1988; Thompson, 1989).

This chapter describes recent technological developments in IT equipment and its implications for service sector firms, both those bringing old systems up-to-date, and those introducing IT for the first time. The experiences of firms' use of IT in financial services (finance, insurance and banking), retailing and impacts on various office occupations are presented.

Financial and retail sectors are in very different situations with regard to IT. The financial sector was a very early adopter of IT and has accumulated skills over time to enable it to change work organization and seize the business opportunities offered by new generations of IT equipment. Firms using IT have been demanding higher skills from their employees. In contrast, retailing has been a slower adopter of IT and the main effects so far have been decreases in numbers of unskilled jobs together with growing needs for IT expertise in head offices.

TECHNOLOGICAL CHANGE IN SERVICE SECTOR IT

The development of IT dates back to the 1960s, when large companies began to invest in big, expensive mainframe computers to handle large scale operations such as payroll and stock, production and inventory control. They were situated in specialist, centralized data processing departments. Some years later the development of integrated circuits led to the production of smaller, less costly but powerful minicomputers. Computers were connected to 'dumb' terminals ('dumb' because they had no computing power and were communication devices only) for inputting data, and to various output devices, such as printers.

In the 1980s the price of computers fell dramatically with the development of microprocessors which made it possible to produce powerful microcomputers and personal computers (PCs). PCs can run their own software programs or form parts of distributed systems when connected to central computers and used as 'intelligent' terminals. 'Intelligent' terminals can download data from a central computer, and manipulate them.

The second half of the 1980s has seen the beginnings of a wide adoption of PCs throughout organizations, largely due to their low price and high power, and to the development of a wide range of user-friendly software packages for word-processing, database, graphics and spreadsheet applications. PCs are now replacing 'dedicated' word processors and are used as a platform for a wide range of applications, and their flexibility of use allows for standardization between the equipment used by executives and secretaries.

As PCs spread throughout organizations, companies have begun to realize the advantages of connecting them into networks. Computers and associated peripherals linked together for data and text transmission systems within a limited geographic area are known as local area networks (LANs). Wide area networks (WANs) permit links between more remote systems. They are accessed through telephone lines, using a modem to connect the computer to the telephone line. Linkages through LANs and WANs are likely to increase dramatically in the 1990s.

Within this basic framework many specialist applications have been developed for different types of job and for different types of services. In banks and building societies a distributed network may link the head office computer, which holds records of all customers, with bank tellers' computers and with the 'hole-in-the-wall' ATM (automatic telling machine), from which customers withdraw funds.

The diffusion of IT in retailing is now gathering pace, after a slow start in the 1980s. Electronic Point of Sale (EPoS) is a development of the cash register which can capture much more data about a transaction than solely the price. Progress with EPoS has been facilitated by the development of worldwide standards for article numbering, through barcodes, which identify products being traded. Optical scanning of barcodes at point of sale, at goods receiving point and throughout warehousing and distribution is being used increasingly to enter data into users' computers on the movement of goods.

In large shops with multiple sales points EPoS can be operated by 'dumb' terminals (or tills) connected to a mainframe or mini computer in the back office. In small shops an EPoS till based on a PC can both input data and manipulate them. In either case, data recorded in individual stores can be transmitted via WANs to a computer at head office. The low price of PCs and the availability of software tailored to the needs of individual retail sectors is leading to the wide diffusion of EPoS terminals in both large multiples and small independent shops - a point we will return to later in this chapter (see Table 5.3). The data recorded by EPoS can be used not only for straightforward accounting purposes, but also for stock control and for management information systems to aid decision making.

Electronic Funds Transfer at Point of Sale (EFTPoS) involves electronic communication between retail outlets and banks. Plastic cards can be used to make direct debits from a customer's bank account at point-of-sale. Banks envisage EFTPoS as a way of reducing paper payment processing costs, but retailers think the system will involve them in extra expense. EFTPoS has been more widely adopted in some European countries than others (see Table 5.1), but still suffers from the lack of adequate on-line communication systems, or acceptable methods for authenticating customers' instructions (Nichols, 1989).

The use of electronic trading - direct communication between firms' computers via a telephone network for enquiries, purchase orders, delivery notes and invoices - is likely to grow enormously in the 1990s. Direct exchange of electronic data, or EDI, is much more sophisticated than electronic mail. It is the electronic transfer of computer processable data relating to a business or administrative transactions using an agreed standard to structure the data. EDI is used in freight transport, to transfer funds between clearing banks, to exchange information between insurance companies and brokers or tour operators and travel agents (Palmer, 1988), and also for intra-firm transactions. Inter-firm computer communication is facilitated by companies which provide telematic services, i.e. they run third party value-added networks and/or offer value-added services.

IT IN FINANCIAL SERVICES

Worldwide financial markets are changing rapidly as a result of increased competition and the application of new technologies.   In the early days of computing, banks and insurance companies confined mainframe computers to head office in the finance department. Because the computer was so expensive, it had to be used to the maximum. New types of clerical jobs grew up to serve these centralized computers, consisting of batches of narrow sub-tasks, including data preparation and data processing. Large centralized computing facilities can now be used to hold a central database for distributed computing and communications networks. The new on-line systems have facilities for direct entry and amendment of databases from decentralized intelligent terminals, and could enable branch managers to access information on which they could base local decisions. For instance marketing campaigns for new services could be offered to designated sub-sets of customers.

In practice, central control is very often maintained by headquarters staff, eroding the level of responsibility delegated to branch managers. They have lost many of their day-to-day supervisory and training responsibilities and their autonomy over local decisions. Some bank branches without managers are now controlled by senior clerks (Smith, 1987; Storey, 1987). Whilst early computerization reduced clerical skills, decentralized 'on-line' interactive systems could increase them. The outcome rests not on the technology, but on the way it is used (Bertrand and Noyelle, 1988a). There are examples of decentralization where clerks continue to carry out deskilled, routine, fragmented keyboarding tasks (Rolfe, 1986; Smith and Wield, 1987).

The experience of Branch Network Reorganization (BNR) introduced by some UK banks with the aim of reducing operating costs shows that deskilling workers is not necessarily cost-saving. Under BNR, only the central 'hub' branch provided a full range of specialist services and many fragmented data sorting and entry tasks were delegated to clerks relocated to a data processing office, which also served a series of satellite branches. Some clerks from satellite branches were also relocated to the data processing office. Reduced numbers of staff in satellite branches offered only a narrow range of services to personal customers.

In practice, however, BNR failed to yield the intended cost-savings. The time devoted to management and coordination increased and the expected reductions in clerical staff were not achieved. Morale was low among clerks engaged in routine, monotonous tasks at the data processing office. Overtime increased in the satellites and there were difficulties in coping with staff sickness, holidays and so on. Automation of branch accounting led to managers losing customer knowledge (Smith, 1987).

The staff in data processing offices are now being reabsorbed into branches, where they share a diversity of tasks with other clerks. Some bank clerks have been upgraded to become personal bankers, with IT giving them the ability to answer queries on financial services and grant straightforward loans (Swann, 1986). The new personal and keyboard skills required of existing workforces have been developed through training without great difficulty.

Decentralization could return autonomy to branch managers, both in banking and insurance, but some analysts believe that organizational politics will act to maintain control at the centre (Storey, 1987). The extent to which decentralization can be implemented also depends on the skills of the workforce. The reintegration of work tasks and strong competition in the banking sector has led to the need for skilled staff able to identify new markets, products and services (LIBER, 1989). Upskilling is required to enable the workforce to diversify away from routine and repetitive tasks towards a new range of duties including emphasis on customer service (OECD, 1990).

There is a great deal of hyperbole surrounding the potential application of expert systems to the financial services sector, but so far there have only been a few small-scale experimental developments (Stevenson, 1989). Expert systems, for instance, could provide branch managers with information relevant to evaluating lending propositions (Forsey and Finlay, 1989). Evidence is available of one insurance company where an expert system has enabled unskilled clerks to do jobs formerly reserved for scarce, overworked, expert underwriters (Senker, et al, 1989).

Recent studies on the banking and insurance sectors in more advanced countries such as France, West Germany, Italy and the Netherlands show broadly similar patterns. Most countries have moved towards the decentralized mode. Banks that are technological leaders recruit workers with a higher standard of vocational education than those which lag in new technology (OECD, 1990). In Germany, for instance, an increase in employees in the higher wage groups reflects a trend towards higher qualifications. This is expected to intensify in the next few years (Gurtler and Pusse, 1988). Managers also need multiple skills to qualify them to implement decentralization policies: they need to be effective administrators, strategic planners and entrepreneurs. In Italy the need has been identified for banks incorporating advanced telecommunications systems to recruit staff with telecommunications skills. In the past Italian banks hired consultants to implement new and complex automated technology (OECD, 1990).

A wide range of skill formation systems have been identified in the financial sector throughout Europe (OECD, 1990). They ranged from a policy of hiring less qualified workers for entry to apprenticeship programmes, to skill formation systems aimed at recruiting employees with extensive education and placing them in regular jobs at once. Firms are seeking employees with a high level of general education and training in specific skills.   Adjustments of this sort were common to most countries even where socio-economic characteristics differ significantly.

These findings reflect the experience of advanced countries, but Greece may be more representative of peripheral regions of the EU. Greek banks were the first sector in the country to introduce data processing: indeed one-third of established Greek computer systems are located in banks. They linked up with SWIFT (Society for Worldwide Interbank Financial Telecommunications) in 1980, but some perceptions about the progress of automation in Greek banking may be gauged from the fact that capital transactions are often quicker between Greek and foreign banks than between banks within Athens. Fragmentary evidence that the union of bank employees has tried to limit the number of hours which workers spend in front of terminals suggests that Greek banks still operate a centralized form of bank automation. The emphasis on classical training in schools, the small number of IT graduates and the lack of understanding of new technology by consumers, particularly the older age groups, may retard the ability to introduce more decentralized forms of bank automation (Nikolinakos, 1989).

A Spanish study on the effects of introducing new technology into ten credit institutions found that IT had a considerable influence on the organization of work and staff structure. Repetitive tasks and manual handling of documents were reduced, but customer service and other commercial tasks were increased. The associated finding of an increase in the number of employees in central services and a large decrease in the average number of branch employees suggests that this too is an example of first stage centralized banking automation (Castells et al, 1986). It is likely that in due course peripheral countries will also move to a more decentralized form of bank computerization, with the associated need to upskill their workforces currently being experienced in countries with more advanced forms of automation.

EFTPOS - LINKING FINANCE AND RETAILING

EFTPoS (Electronic funds transfer at point of sale) is a method whereby customers pay for retail purchases with a plastic card which debits their bank accounts. In effect, an EFTPoS terminal is an ATM terminal at the point of sale. It could possibly be considered as part of the banking system rather than of retailing, but perhaps more accurately as an important link between retailing and the financial sector. This technology is diffusing rapidly throughout Europe. In 1988 there were more EFTPoS terminals than ATMs in most European countries (Table 5.1).

Table 5.1: ATM and EFTPoS in Europe, 1988

Country	Bel	Den	Fra	Ger	Ita	Spa	UK
January 1988							
No. of ATMs	833	571	11167	4400	3500	7092	12389
No. of ATMs per million population	84	112	204	72	62	186	220
December 1988							
No. of EFTPoS terminals	17050	8736	122000	250	2000	70000	19300
No. of EFTPoS terminals per million population	1722	1713	2230	4	35	1832	342

Source: Hirsch, 1989

The EFTPoS programme in France is the most extensive in Europe as a result of cooperation amongst financial institutions and widespread acceptance of cards (both magnetic strip and smart card) as means of payment. Bank fraud is becoming a major problem since the system currently runs off-line (there is no direct, immediate link between shops and banks). Partly because the use of cheques as a payment method was never widespread, Spain has the second largest installed base in Europe. Banks wishing to increase electronic payments have cooperated to extend the EFTPoS system, so enabling them to bypass the need to develop extensive cheque clearing. EFTPoS is also well established in Belgium and Denmark.

Progress was held up in the UK because the national Interbank scheme has had to compete with a proliferation of other debit card schemes. Individual banks have introduced simple, unsophisticated systems to gain retailer acceptance of their terminals. It is doubtful whether retailers will be prepared to write-off this investment to upgrade to a more expensive national EFTPoS system. German progress is delayed because of lack of agreement between the German Retailers Association and the Interbank Payment Association (Hirsch, 1989). In Greece EFTPoS is in an infant stage and there are very few ATM/cash dispensers (Nikolinakos, 1989).

IT IN RETAILING

A report on the use of IT in French retail trade (OECD, 1990) identified four categories of application:

1. applications related to internal management - EPoS and scanning, which is now used by more than one-third of French EPoS cashpoints;
2. applications involving interactions between the retailer and its suppliers, which follow the implementation of common standards which facilitates the on-line exchange of data for orders, invoices, etc;
3. applications involving technologies which interact with the customer. This includes the use of Minitel for mail order and telemarketing. EDP is also used to store useful customer information;
4. warehouse applications e.g. space management, control of automated vehicle (treated separately below).

Statistics are available on the diffusion of IT in European retailing. Indicators such as the installation of EPoS tills and the extent of barcode scanning are used.

A recent report predicted the potential market for specialized EPoS tills in the leading European countries - UK, France, West Germany and Italy - would amount to more than £11 billion by 1990. Table 5.2 shows the percentage of EPoS terminals accounted for by each of those countries. It also shows the percentage of points at which cash is paid in each country which are accounted for by EPoS terminals. Installation of EPoS in Italy was delayed by the need for EPoS tills to receive government approval under the 1983 law on fiscal receipts (RMDP, 1989). In Greece EPoS is only used in a few shops, for instance the Greek Duty Free Shops (Nikolinakos, 1989). Retraining of checkout assistants to use EPoS equipment takes only a few days at most, and mainly concerns operator

Table 5.2 EPoS systems in UK, France, West Germany and Italy, 1989

Country	% Installed Base	% Total Cash Points	% Growth of Installations 1988-89
UK	46	14.96	42
W. Germany	24	7.83	37
France	17	6.15	22
Italy	13	3.60	13

Source: RMDP, 1989

error or equipment breakdown (Jarvis and Prais, 1989). Table 5.3 shows the numbers of retail scanning outlets in each country.

Barcoding of products by manufacturers has been very labour-saving. Individual price ticketing of products in supermarkets is no longer required. Scanning, EPoS and EFTPoS systems are further reducing the need for labour because the data captured by these check-out systems can be a direct input into a shop's accounting, inventory, marketing and purchasing systems. With the full implementation of EDI, and communication between retailers' computers and those of their suppliers, EPoS data recorded in the inventory system could trigger purchase orders which will automatically generate invoices, shipping orders and delivery notes, without any need for data to be rekeyed. It also has the potential to handle payment for goods. In the UK, Marks & Spencer is already using the information from EPoS terminals in this way for electronic ordering and invoicing (Bradshaw, 1990). These trends will lead to a reduction in clerical staff and purchasing officers. Purchasing staff who remain will have to acquire new analytical skills so they can devote more time to their professional functions instead of 'chasing paper'.

Two further IT developments may further reduce jobs for staff in shops. Electronic shelf-edge labelling will remove the need for shelf labels to be up-dated manually, because electronic shelf-edge label displays will be automatically up-dated from the computer database to which they are linked (Brunton, 1989). A pilot self-scanning experiment being conducted by a Dutch supermarket has been well received by customers. Self scanning has been predicted to have a revolutionary effect on retailing in the 1990s. It reduces the need for check-out assistants, and minimizes the time spent by

Table 5.3 Number of retail scanning outlets in EU member states, 1991

Country	Supermarkets and other self-service grocery stores	Department stores	General merchandise stores and pharmacies	Total of scanning stores
Belgium	1,146	-	505	1,651
Luxembourg	-	-	-	20
Denmark	-	-	-	1,500
France	4,400	180	3,170	7,750
Germany	-	-	-	7,238
Greece	-	1	-	1
Ireland	124	2	1	127
Italy	3,790	160	-	3,950
Netherlands	1,160	60	300	1,520
Portugal	50	7	564	621
Spain (est.)	4,653	-	3,000	7,653
UK	-	-	-	7,869

Source: International Article Numbering Association EAN Annual
Report, 1991

customers in check-out queues (Hughes, 1989).

In different countries differing approaches towards retail training have been adopted. None of them appear to reflect modern trends towards self-service and computerization, and it is not yet clear whether it is important for them to do so. In France in 1982, 24% of salespersons were qualified. Training in full-time vocational schools consisted of specialized product knowledge, selling skills and general educational subjects such as language, mathematics and a foreign language. Unemployment among newly qualified salespeople has been growing and the current trend is towards providing even higher qualifications, even though the trends towards self-service and IT do not justify the high level skills being provided. In contrast only 3% of British retail employees had a qualification. The qualifications available are based on much shorter courses and less rigorous than in the French system.

In Germany the training system is work-based: the school-leaver finds a training place with an employer before arranging vocational training through a system of day-release. Very few German trainees fail to find employment on completing their courses (Jarvis and Prais, 1989). Retailers are using IT technologies increasingly, but these do not play decisive roles in the development of employment, qualification and skill structures, or in vocational education and training. In the past, IT was primarily directed towards purchasing activities, but now it is increasingly being related to sales applications. Sales data are helping local sales managers to make purchasing and price decisions (OECD, 1990). Another report suggests, however, that skills training is the most important factor in increasing productivity (Gurtler and Pusse, 1988).

In the Netherlands, a 1979 survey found that 80% of total employment in retailing consisted of jobs which required low-level skills. By 1985, another survey found that about half of the employees in retailing were skilled at the lower general or lower vocational level with the remaining half requiring higher levels of general or vocational education. Training activities are very modest in retail and most post-formal schooling courses for updating workers' skills are provided by the Organization of Education and Training Retail Sector. Only large supermarkets and department stores provide any in-house training (LIBER, 1989).

In some countries, IT is eroding the level of responsibility of local managers in retail chains. They have lost many day-to-day supervisory responsibilities and their autonomy over local decisions. EPoS data about goods purchased can automatically provide shelf replenishment from the central warehouse. The same data have been used by a British supermarket to determine staff rostering for its stores (Graves, 1989). Work is proceeding on systems to determine the location and amount of shelf space to be given to each product and to provide detailed advice on store layout and merchandising, for instance by Standa in Italy (Rorato, 1989). These systems are examples of Management Information Systems which focus on producing answers to specific problems through the use of objective and quantifiable data, and their use is shifting control from branch managers to Head Offices. Distributed on-line systems could enable branch managers to access information on which they could base local decisions, as seems to be happening to some extent in Germany (OECD, 1990), but this would demand that shop managers receive training to become computer literate.

In warehousing, automation is reducing the demand for unskilled workers. The take up of information technology in warehouses has so far been slow, but it is likely to increase in the future. Software programs can be used to plan warehouse layout, vehicle loading and route planning. Innovations in warehouse hardware include highbay automated storage and retrieval systems (AS/RS) for palletized unit   loads, carousel picking systems, conveyors and parcel sorting systems and guidance networks for automated guided vehicles.   The skill profile demanded of warehousemen has become uniform with the replacement of skilled reach truck drivers by automated retrieval systems.   In Benetton's automated warehouse, for example, the task of the workforce has become limited to maintaining the plant.   Their system requires only 16 people (8 maintenance workers, 1 warehouseman, 6 computer operators and 1 area director).   Without automation it is estimated the operation of the warehouse would require 80-100 workers (Belussi, 1987).

IT IN OFFICE AUTOMATION

IT is affecting the jobs of secretaries and clerks in offices in every industrial sector.   Early predictions of a rapid decrease in demand for secretarial and clerical workers as a result of the use of IT have not been realized.   Some jobs have indeed been lost, particularly junior clerical jobs.   This has been caused by the trend for capturing data at point of origin, self-entry by the customer through ATMs, barcode scanners in shops and the full implementation of EDI, all of which reduce the needs for keyboard data entry.   EDI also eliminates the work involved in correcting errors which inevitably occur when information has to be rekeyed.   Although some types of office work are vanishing, others are growing.   The automation of services has created opportunities to provide a wider range of services, and new jobs.

Secretarial work has followed a pattern of centralization followed by decentralization.   Expensive, dedicated word processing equipment was first introduced as a central facility either to existing typing pools or to new WP pools based on typists who had formerly worked for an individual or small group on a range of tasks.   There are many reports of a lack of job satisfaction for typists working under these conditions and managerial dissatisfaction with the quality of work produced (Long, 1987).

The advent of cheap PCs with sophisticated word-processing software is leading to the break-up of typing pools.   PCs are replacing typewriters and typists are located closer to the people they work for.   Experience has shown that involving secretaries in the selection of equipment to be used for word processing has yielded considerable benefits, including better trained secretaries committed to the new technology and machines able to produce the professional standards of work required.   The standardization of word-processing equipment throughout the organization has facilitated training, and optimized the use of peripherals and shared support staff (Huggett, 1988, Thompson, 1989).

Some managers with PCs use them to write reports, but few are prepared or able to use PCs themselves. Indeed a French study of the introduction of office automation at CNRS not only revealed that researchers had insufficient mathematics training to utilize statistical computer programs, it also showed up deficiencies in their French language skills! Similarly, administrators were revealed to have insufficient accountancy knowledge when they tried to use spreadsheets. While one could have expected that administrators would become the office automation professionals, researchers were somewhat in advance of the administrators in office automation techniques (Bélisle and Rosada, 1988).

Many managers put PCs on their secretaries' desks, delegating to them a wide range of other computer applications, including diary management, spreadsheet, database, accounting, and electronic mail. This phenomenon of senior managers relying on intermediaries to use IT on their behalf has been called 'chauffeured' use (Martin, 1989; McCandless and Duffy, 1989), and can be explained by the lack of management training accompanying the delivery of a PC (Hall-Sheehy, 1988). Managers, however, also fail to give their 'chauffeurs' IT training. Apart from word processing, PCs are mainly used for databases and spreadsheets, but few secretaries understand how to use these applications effectively (Fenton, 1989). Secretaries who can acquire the skills to use these new applications may be able to take on many junior administrative tasks, acting as a personal assistant to their bosses. Too often however, secretaries are not given the necessary training to upgrade their computer skills. This is even true of word processing, where typists find they have to learn a wide range of skills additional to those used by a traditional typist, for instance the requirement to organize the storage and indexing of computer discs and their files, and to take responsibility for their safety and security (Quintas, 1986).

Studies in France and Germany suggest office computerization increases the need for skills. In Germany it was found that after the adoption of new technology, routine, monotonous tasks were confined to unskilled labour (mainly women) who had always done monotonous work. Computerization seemed to reduce the proportion of poorly qualified clerks in the white collar labour force. Workers who had completed occupational training in office work were given a measure of autonomy and opportunities to exercise their skills. Indeed employers are seeking to upgrade the skills of their existing labour force (Lane, 1985).

French companies now have a tendency to recruit only those with high level qualifications, 'capable of taking on the responsibilities arising from the reorganization of work based on new technology'. Their strategy is long-term. They envisage further technical developments in the 1990s and they wish to have staff not only able to use the technology of the 1980s, but to adapt to the technology of the year 2000. British firms, by contrast, tend to recruit office staff with few formal qualifications, and give little thought to appropriate work structures and systems for new office technology (Steedman, 1987). This failure of British management was recognized in a recent report which emphasized the need for computer literacy throughout organizations, not just in computer services departments. 'Hybrid' managers with skills in business management and IT could bring about significant change within organizations. They would have the ability to recognize IT opportunities and understand how to implement them (Palmer and Ottley, 1990).

CONCLUSIONS

'Hybrid' managers with skills in business management and IT could bring about significant change within organizations. Managers need multiple skills to implement the decentralization policies often required for IT implementation: they need to be effective administrators, strategic planners and entrepreneurs.

Office computerization often increases needs for skills. Employers of office staff are seeking to upgrade the skills of their existing labour forces. Secretaries with the necessary training to use IT applications may be able to take on many junior administrative tasks, acting as personal assistants to their bosses. And even word processing operators with new skills, could take on important responsibilities for the storage and indexing of computer files and discs and for their safety and security.

European countries have adopted differing approaches towards retail training. None of them appear to reflect modern trends towards self-service and computerization, and it is not yet clear whether it is important for them to do so.

The way in which jobs change depends not just on the technology, but on how it is implemented. Decisions about the introduction of new technology should not be the sole preserve of management. Participation in decision-making by those who will be directly involved in using the technology can yield important benefits. But workers and management need to learn about IT and its possible implications in order to be capable of contributing effectively to decision-making. Problems are minimized and new equipment is most effectively utilized when users are involved in its selection.

6. IT and Vocational Education and Training in Europe: An Overview

Gareth Rees

As new information and communication technology (IT) have come to be increasingly widely adopted in European economies over recent decades, so the implications for vocational education and training (VET) systems have become a major focus of concern for policy-makers. At the heart of this policy debate has been the capacity of national VET systems to deliver the kinds of technical competencies and behavioural characteristics demanded from different categories of workers in consequence of innovation in the form and implementation of IT. There is no sign of any lessening of this concern through the 1990s, given that the wider diffusion of advanced IT is almost universally identified as a *sine qua non* of the international competitiveness of the more advanced economies, as well as a critical element in the development of the less advantaged European states and regions. This pervasiveness of IT, in turn, implies that the acquisition of the relevant skills is an important factor in determining access to crucial segments of the labour market and thus in shaping the career opportunities of individual workers.

Rather surprisingly, however, there has been relatively little direct academic interest in these issues. The aim of this chapter, therefore, is to contribute to the debate by developing a preliminary framework of analysis, which draws together disparate research literatures. Chapters 7 and 8 in this section of the book build upon this framework by exploring in greater detail more specific issues.

CONCEPTUAL ISSUES

New IT, Work Organization and Skills Development

There is by now an enormous body of research on the purported impacts of new IT on the organization of work (in fact, most frequently, employment) and the skills consequently required of workers. This is not to suggest, however, that there is any straightforward consensus over their nature. Earlier approaches saw the introduction of new IT as an integral part of societal shifts in economic organization and their effects as correspondingly universal. Braverman (1974), for example, emphasized that the 'despoiling effects' of the introduction of new IT are an inherent consequence of management's strategy to control working practices, by removing significant elements of worker autonomy in the labour process. In contrast, other commentators - most notably Bell (1974; 1980) - identified IT as a crucial element in liberating workers from routine tasks and creating opportunities for widespread upskilling and the emergence of a knowledge-based, post-industrial society.

More recent general models have focused more specifically on the role of IT in overcoming the problems besetting Fordist mass-production industries, organized along Tayloristic lines. Here, it is suggested that competitive pressures have demanded far greater product differentiation, smaller batch sizes and greater adaptability to business cycles. These new imperatives imply the radical reorganization of production, entailing the thorough-going utilization of new IT and the consequent development of a highly skilled and flexible labourforce, capable of exercising considerable autonomy over work tasks. However, the introduction of such 'new production concepts' (Kern and Schumann, 1984) or 'flexible specialization' (Piore and Sabel, 1984) is not seen as an inevitable consequence of wider, societal change. Rather, whether or not the new forms of production are put into practice is contingent upon fulfilling the appropriate strategic conditions (such as ensuring a supply of adequately trained or craft-based labour). Accordingly, the actual incidence of new forms of production varies from one society to another or even between different industries (cf. Lane, 1989).

This recognition of diversity is given a much stronger emphasis in studies which are more directly rooted in detailed, empirical investigation of technological change. The effects of introducing new IT are seen as highly complex and dynamic, embodying diverse elements of skill and worker autonomy, which may not all change in the same direction, even for similar types of worker (for example, Elger, 1987; Child and Loveridge, 1990). Patterns of change reflect the specificities not only of national and industry contexts, but also of the localized decision-making as to the form and manner of implementing new IT (for example, Appelbaum and Albin, 1989). In light of this accumulated evidence, therefore, a recent OECD study seems to present a reasonable summary view.

> The relationship between new technology and work organization is characterized by great diversity as well as mutual dependence. New technology promises to revolutionize the way work is organized in many institutions - and has at times already done so. The direction and extent of change, however, is difficult to predict in

particular cases as it depends on a range of factors - among which managerial strategy stands out as the most important. In practice, skill-using modes of implementation prove more common than skill-reducing ones, although there is reason for concern over loss of worker autonomy and initiative. At the aggregate level, where microprocessor-based innovation continues the upgrading of demands made on the skills of the labour force in a wide range of areas, skill enhancement is expected to prove the rule (outside the personal service sector, at least). (OECD, 1988: pp. 87-89)

In short, then, there is considerable indeterminacy, although within broad limits set by an expectation of a general increase in the demands made for appropriate skills. Certainly, the task of relating specific types of technical competence, particular categories of employee and patterns of work reorganization to trends in the implementation of new IT is an extraordinarily complex one. And this complexity clearly poses substantial problems for the development of VET systems which are capable of matching up to future demands for a labourforce capable of utilizing the most advanced IT.

National Models and International Comparisons

These latter concerns over generating the technical competencies relevant to new IT are, in fact, simply a subset of a wider preoccupation with the general capacities of national systems of education and training to deliver a labourforce with the appropriate competencies and qualities or skills. Whilst these concerns have - for obvious reasons - been most strongly expressed in relatively unsuccessful economies, such as the UK, they have been voiced pervasively throughout Europe (and elsewhere).

Here too, there are substantial complexities. Perhaps most significantly for present purposes, even where employers are able to define their skill requirements unambiguously - which is less frequently the case than may be thought (Rees et al, 1989) - they do not entail a particular form and organization of VET. Two enterprises may fulfil their demands for a labourforce with given characteristics by means of a wide variety of labour-market processes, including different types of VET. For instance, one may adopt a strategy of training its own craft-workers in computer-aided manufacturing (CAM) techniques, whilst another may choose to poach employees who are already trained from other firms. Similarly, faced with shortages of software engineers, one firm may intensify its recruitment programmes amongst graduates, whilst another may train up its technicians (cf. Campbell and Warner, 1987).

Exactly these issues are reflected at a macro-economic level too. Hence, although there is a burgeoning discussion of what constitutes the best model of VET (NEDO/MSC, 1984), it is actually extremely difficult to establish *determinate* relationships between the form and organization of a VET system and the performance of the national economy. For example, the strength of the economies of both the former FRG and Japan has frequently been attributed to the effectiveness of their VET systems. Whilst there is undoubtedly considerable force in this, the two national VET systems in question are organized in quite radically different ways. Some commentators have actually contrasted their capacities to respond effectively to the challenges posed by new IT, arguing that the Japanese system of broadly-based general education is more appropriate than the vocationally focused dual system of the former FRG (Senker, 1990).

What this suggests is that whatever causal mechanisms are involved are embedded in wider systems of economic and social organization (as the study of Japan by Dore and Sako, 1989, strongly argues). Hence, in a particularly sophisticated analysis, Maurice and his co-workers at the *Laboratoire d'Economie et Sociologie du Travail* (LEST) at the University of Aix-en-Provence (Maurice et al, 1980; 1986) contend that it is not possible to understand the ways in which skills are construed and the consequent role of VET except in the context of conjunctions of national structures of educational provision and skills development, patterns of work organization, and the style and institutional arrangements of industrial relations. Moreover, it is the systematic differences between national patterns of these conjunctions which are crucial: the 'societal effect'. For example, in France, job allocation and promotion depend primarily upon a combination of general educational attainment and seniority within the firm. This implies, therefore, that the decisions of firms exert a powerful influence over workers' careers. In Germany, in contrast, access to jobs is dependent on the acquisition of certificated vocational qualifications, most crucially the craft apprenticeship, with the consequent lesser significance of general education and the easier movement between work tasks and, indeed, jobs (cf. Rose, 1985).

In general terms, at least, this kind of analysis offers considerable insights, which although developed in a general context, apply equally to the more specific case of the role of VET in the development of IT-related competencies. Indeed, in their later work, the LEST group have applied their theoretical framework to the analysis of new technology, discerning distinctive societal effects in the form of its implementation and consequences (Eyraud et al, 1984; 1988). Their work provides a sustained caution against the widely prevalent notion that there is a single best practice model of VET which provides a universal key to strong economic growth and international competitiveness (cf. Campbell et al, 1989). More generally, it implies that improving the VET system does not in itself lead to better economic performance; education and training cannot generate economic development by themselves.

However, the emphasis of the LEST group on national distinctiveness may be problematic. It is a matter of some importance to assess the extent to which the development of European Union (EU) policies are exerting a substantial homogenizing influence. (In a recent paper, Maurice (1990) has himself acknowledged the significance of what he terms the 'European' actor in future development, whilst retaining his essential emphasis upon societal effects.)   The standardization and certification of vocational qualifications across the EU, for example, may decrease national distinctiveness and encourage greater labour mobility.   However, Prais (1989) has drawn attention to the difficulties involved in reconciling the kinds of demands made by British employers with regard to vocational qualifications and the training which they provide with those of employers in other European countries.

Numerous commentators have also remarked upon the emergence of sharply delineated regional (and more local) configurations, especially in the context of the purported development of flexible specialization (for example, Castells, 1989; Scott, 1988). For some of these, the role played by VET in the context of wider patterns of regional distinctive work organization, industrial relations and so forth, is crucial (especially, Sabel et al, 1989). It is not necessary to go along wholeheartedly with the flexible specialization thesis to acknowledge the salience of these intra-national differences; indeed, a 'Europe of the regions' has become a commonplace of post-1992 forecasters (for a recent discussion focusing particularly upon science and technology, see Hingel, 1990).

Equally, the significance of nationally distinctive conjunctions of the kind emphasized by Maurice and his colleagues, may be undermined by the emergence of transnational structures within Europe (and, indeed, more generally).   Many firms are developing organizational structures which transcend national boundaries, not only through direct foreign investment, but also increasingly through a variety of joint-venture arrangements and take-overs.   These developments pose interesting questions as to their impacts upon what the LEST group contend are clearly differentiated national conjunctions. In the UK, for example, it has been claimed that Japanese inward investment has had important consequences for many dimensions of work organization (including vocational training arrangements), with indigenous firms attempting to emulate what they believe to be Japanese practices (for example, Morgan and Sayer, 1988; Oliver and Wilkinson, 1988).

What these arguments suggest, therefore, is that any analysis of the roles played by VET systems should be highly sensitive to the bases upon which generalizations are made. In the case of, say, direct investment by a multi-national firm, it is clear that such investment may introduce production methods, forms of work organization and programmes of vocational training which are radically distinct from those amongst enterprises indigenous to the national or regional economy in which the investment is made. However, this is no more than a particularly sharp example of the much more pervasive tensions between analysis at the level of the firm or enterprise and at the level of the national or regional environment. There is thus a sense in which all firms develop individual ways in which skills and associated training programmes are embedded into highly specific systems of production and work organization. To put this another way, there is substantial variation from firm to firm within a national or, indeed, regional/local configuration, as well as between the latter.

In analytical terms, therefore, distinctions should be drawn between societal effects, regional effects and firm effects. In purely heuristic terms, however, these distinctions may be separated out by identifying elements of the analysis with greater and lesser degrees of generality. For example, the supply of IT-related skills is shaped by the characteristic outputs of the general education system, whose structure and organization are uniform at least over broad administrative regions, if not the national spaces of whole states. Although again, the situation is considerably complicated by the well established disparities between different areas in terms of educational resources. Similarly, the organization of public-sector vocational training is relatively uniform over whole states or at least administrative regions. However, it is much more difficult to establish generalizations of even these kinds in the analysis of the interface between publicly-provided VET and the training regimes adopted by employers, for here the impact of the firm-based specificities and complexities which have been identified are strongest.

In what follows, an attempt will be made to illustrate these different levels of analysis by reference to contemporary developments in Europe.

LABOURFORCE STRUCTURE AND VET SYSTEMS

Outputs From VET

As this latter discussion suggests, therefore, at the most general level the availability of appropriate labour in particular sectors of the IT-related labour market will be - at least in part - determined by the character of the flows through VET systems. As Wellington (1989) remarks in his study of education and IT-related employment in the UK 'employment in relation to information technology is divided into strata or "segments"... and...

recruitment into these strata is related to levels of education and training...ranging from graduate level and above to school-leavers and YTS trainees...' (Wellington, 1989: p. 254). In other words, the possession or otherwise of different kinds of educational and training qualifications and experience in effect act as key closure mechanisms, rationing access to opportunities at the various levels of the occupational hierarchy.

Figure 6.1   Outline model of the general structure of VET systems

1. Further training
   - for specific occupations
   - for disadvantaged groups
   - for trainers
	2. Continuing
	   education

3. Initial vocational education and training	4. General education

Source: Sorge, 1984

To develop a clearer understanding of the mechanisms involved here, it is useful to outline a model of the general structure of VET systems (Figure 6.1). It is convenient to distinguish conceptually between those elements of a VET system which are primarily concerned with the development of general educational competencies (components 2 and 4 in Figure 6.1) and those whose function is to generate skills with specific applications to employment (components 1 and 3). However, even here the distinctions are far from easy to make empirically; especially as there has been a rather widespread trend toward vocationalization within most national VET systems during recent years (a point taken up later).

Ideally, then, an analysis should begin by presenting the outputs from these components of national VET systems, thus enabling estimation of the supply of different kinds of labour, defined in terms of their educational and training profiles.   Not surprisingly, however, only a very rough approximation of this procedure is possible.

Participation in Education

Cross-national analysis is beset with difficulties even when comparing basic level participation in general education and initial VET (components 3 and 4 in Figure 6.1). Not only is extreme caution required with respect to the basis on which data are calculated; but also they need to be interpreted within the economic and social context of the states in which they are produced.

Table 6.1　*Percentages of 16-18 year olds in education and training (full-time and part-time) in Europe, 1986*

Country	Full-time	Part-time	All	School-leaving age
Belgium	77	4	81	14
Denmark	70	6	77	16
France	66	8	74	16
Germany	47	43	90	15
Italy	47	18	65	14
Netherlands	77	9	86	16
Spain	52	0	52	14
UK	35	34	69	16

Source: UK Department of Education and Science, 1990

Nevertheless, there is every indication of wide variations in participation rates, especially at the post-compulsory secondary and tertiary levels of general education and in initial VET. Something of this is illustrated in Table 6.1. Whilst nine out of ten young people in the former FRG benefited from post-compulsory education and training, only half of the age-group did in Spain, some two-thirds in Italy and the UK.

Moreover, there are sharp differences in the form of national, post-compulsory provision too. Hence, within the EU, at one extreme, the former

FRG's post-compulsory secondary education is strongly biased toward vocational courses, in which part-time education within the dual system plays a large part. Similarly, Belgium, Denmark, France, Italy and the Netherlands each has a substantial - and growing - majority of its young people at this level engaged in vocational and technical courses. In contrast, Greece, Ireland and Portugal have much less developed systems of vocational and technical education. Spain and the UK occupy intermediate positions in these terms, although the former has an expanding vocational/technical sector.

A comparable story may also be told in terms of tertiary education, the sector of post-compulsory education which is likely to be of crucial significance for the higher sectors of the IT-related labour market. Enrolments at this level in those subject areas which - admittedly in very crude terms - have the most direct relationships to IT applications, vary very widely. France, the former FRG, Italy and the UK appear to produce significantly higher levels of enrolments in the natural sciences (including mathematics and computing science); along with the Republic of Ireland, which must be regarded as something of an anomaly in this context (a point taken up in Chapter 8). The participation of students in engineering courses is much more even; although the rather surprising under-representation of engineering in France and in Italy is only partially compensated in the former by enrolments in natural sciences (Eurostat, 1988).

What is perhaps most perplexing of all, however, is that in the EU overall, the percentage of students in higher education following courses in natural sciences and engineering has fallen appreciably since the beginning of the 1970s, in spite of the efforts of many member states to increase the output of highly qualified scientists and engineers. Clearly, should this trend continue, the European capacity to perform at the highest levels of development and implementation of new IT may well be impaired.

The Quality of Educational and Training Outputs

These differentials in the level and form of participation in VET are further compounded by differences in the quality of educational and training provision. For example, in a celebrated series of research studies, the National Institute of Economic and Social Research (NIESR) has argued that the British VET system produces an output which is both structurally very different from that of other advanced countries (and the FRG and France in particular), and whose quality is also lower. Not only are there the well-established shortfalls of qualified school-leavers and workers with intermediate vocational qualifications, but also the levels of competence which are certificated in these ways are inferior too (Table 6.2). Detailed

examination of the content of the education and training which is signified
by various levels of qualification, reveals that the standards required by the
British VET system fall below those of France and the former FRG (except
at the level of research degrees).

Table 6.2   *Numbers qualifying in engineering and technology, 1985
(thousands)*

Qualification	UK	Fra	Ger	Jap[1]	USA[1]
Doctorates	0.7	0.3	1.0	0.3	0.5
Masters degrees	2.0	>6.0	>4.0	5.0	4.0
Bachelor degrees	14.0	15.0	21.0	30.0	19.0
Technicians	29.0	35.0	44.0	18.0-27.0	17.0
Craftworkers	35.0	92.0	120.0	44.0	not available

1. *Figures for Japan and the USA are adjusted for a size of population equivalent to the UK.*

Source: Prais, 1989

The implications of these kinds of qualitative and quantitative differences
for the development and implementation of advanced technologies are
potentially profound. As Steedman (1988) puts it, 'the wider extent of basic
training amongst the workforce makes it easier to provide effective retraining for new technology and for new production organization; it also
provides a reservoir of skills from which employees willing to take on
higher levels of responsibility can be brought forward' (p.67). What all this
suggests, therefore, is that very real limits may be placed upon the capacities
of individual states to respond effectively to the challenges of new IT, not
directly because of their provision (or lack of it) for IT-related VET, but
rather because of the shortcomings of their general education and training
systems.

However, in order to pursue these implications in greater detail, it is necessary to move beyond aggregate analysis. Accordingly, the next section focuses upon a more detailed examination of the relationships between IT-related initiatives and VET systems.

IT DEVELOPMENT AND VET SYSTEMS

Differentiated Demand for IT Skills

It is essential to disaggregate total demand for IT-related labour into different strata or segments. The supply of labour, therefore, may be conceptualized in terms of the availability of appropriately qualified individuals for the different segments of demand. And, as was noted earlier, a key determinant of this differentiated supply is the functioning of the VET system. The personnel delivered by the latter may be distinguished by their educational and training qualifications and experience, which, in turn, may be taken to indicate specific forms of competence. In this way, the flows of individuals through the VET system come to define labour shortages of particular kinds (although the extent to which it is possible to transfer from one route through the system to another is of major significance here). For example, in the UK, it has been a matter of public concern for some time that insufficient numbers of graduates (and above) are being produced to fill the higher-level occupations which are crucial to the successful development and implementation of new IT (for example, Alvey Committee, 1982). In the former FRG, attention focused on the supply of employees with intermediate qualifications adapted to the demands of applying the most advanced IT in key industrial sectors (Gottelmann, 1989).

However, this account omits some important complexities. The relationship between level of qualification and the competencies required in a given job is by no means straightforward. Dore (1976) has described the significant inflation in the demand for formal qualifications which has occurred largely as a result of increasing output of the latter, rather than major changes in the technical competencies which are really needed in the work situation. Campbell and Warner (1987) describe the way in which British firms which were unable to fulfil demand for graduate engineers simply trained up technicians.

In short, employers may seek to use educational and training qualifications and experience as exclusionary criteria, in order to ration access to given employment opportunities. However, other characteristics and, in particular, social attributes, play a key role as well. Certainly, the gendering of occupations is crucial; not only in determining what actually constitute higher-level competencies (skills) (for example, Lane, 1988), but also in shaping access to occupational mobility and the individual career thus implied (Fielder et al, 1990). And in both these respects, the place of education and training is central. (These issues are taken up in Chapter 7.)

Equally, demand for segments of IT-related labour may be defined in terms of the context in which it arises. This demand is concentrated into the core-IT and IT-intensive industries of the advanced economies. Hence, the specific developments in these areas of economic activity may give rise to shortages of IT skills. For example, in a recent study of European telematics firms, Locksley et al (1990) contend that the growth of this major new IT sector is being impaired by shortages of 'technician skills of installation and maintenance of customer equipment'; 'tandem related skills - ie those required to utilize a specific "fault-tolerant" hardware system'; and 'hybrid skills...comprised of selling, technical knowledge of the product being marketed, and technical knowledge of the target market.' (Locksley et al, 1990: 12). Similarly, the dramatic technical changes in the construction industry have given rise to a significant demand for new types of competencies at operative and craft levels, as well as amongst managerial and professional workers, which has been difficult to supply (Gann, 1989).

Accordingly, viewed from this perspective, skill shortages should be understood in terms of the capacity of a VET system to produce personnel who have technical competencies whose content (as well as level) matches the rather particular requirements of employers, especially in the key IT sectors and industries. At the extreme, some skills may be wholly specific to individual firms. And certainly, the broad distinction between those general skills which are transferable between employers and those which are employer-specific is an important one. However, this is not a distinction between more and less valuable skills (as is sometimes suggested by labour economists). Rather, it is to draw attention to types of skill which have different relationships to the organization of production; and which are thus most appropriately supplied by different forms of VET. Contrast, for example, the highly transferable competencies produced in a degree course, with those deriving from a period of on-the-job training: 'sitting by Nellie'.

What this discussion makes clear, therefore, is that the various parts of the VET system may be expected to produce different types of skills, defined in terms both of the level of technical competence produced, as well as its content. Moreover, the capacity of a given system to avoid skill shortages is dependent upon producing an appropriate output defined in terms of both of these dimensions. Hence, for example, in the terms of Figure 6.1 (above), whilst components 2, 3 and 4 bear the principal responsibility for the development of general, transferable competencies, they remain distinguishable in terms of their level and the extent to which they articulate with the specific requirements of employers. Likewise, component 1 is the prime source of employer-specific skills, but again issues of appropriate level remain.

School-based Education

Some of the complexities which are involved here are well illustrated by the changes which have taken place with respect to the development of IT competencies in school-based education. Instruction in the use of new IT has been introduced to the basic school curriculum of a number of states during the past couple of decades; although their lack of development has been a conspicuous cause for concern elsewhere (for an account of the Spanish situation, for example, see Carabana, 1988). Even where they have been introduced, this has been far from a uniform progression, however: for example, the Danish 1975 School Act actually ended experimental work in this field which had been underway since the beginning of the decade; whilst in the former FRG, investment in this type of activity fell during the 1970s (Fasano, 1985).

There is considerable ambiguity as to the objectives of introducing this kind of work to the curriculum and no uniformity in the teaching of new IT. It has been suggested that there are systematic differences between European countries in these respects. For example, France has clearly pursued a strategy of introducing new IT as a vehicle for teaching across the curriculum as a whole; in 1984, the *Informatique Pour Tous* programme initiated the installation of over 100,000 microcomputers in schools and the training of more 10,000 specialist teachers (Gottelman, 1989). In contrast, countries such as the former FRG and the Netherlands have tended to restrict new IT to the vocational education sector (Fasano, 1985).

These examples, in turn, are suggestive of the fundamental tension between a strategy which envisages instruction in new IT as a means of improving general education and one which views it as contributing toward the vocationalization of school-based education. In the UK these strategies co-exist. There have been major, government-funded initiatives aimed at integrating computer-based technologies into the general curriculum, for instance the Micros in School Programme, the Microelectronics Education Programme and the Modem Scheme (Wellington, 1989). Equally, however, the new IT has been integral to attempts to improve the efficacy of the school system in generating the specific skills and behaviour which are deemed necessary to employers, thereby increasing the employability of school-leavers and promoting the growth of the economy more widely. And here the Technical and Vocational Education Initiative has been a prime example (Senker, 1990).

The obvious problem with the vocationalization strategy, however, is matching specialized IT competencies generated within the education system with what employers in reality require. Certainly, past manpower planning attempts to match outputs from the schools to predicted demand for different types of IT competencies have been dramatically unsuccessful (Cerych, 1985). Moreover, demand for *highly specific* IT skills is likely to be restricted to rather limited occupational categories. Employers are placing an increasing emphasis upon the need for *combinations* of general IT skills with other areas of competence (for example, Bertrand and Noyelle, 1988b; Locksley et al, 1990; Senker and Senker, 1990).

Paradoxically, then, the demands of highly innovative new technologies may serve to reinforce the salience of those *general* capacities traditionally fostered by the school system. Far from providing a rationale for the attempt to produce narrowly-based and specific skills, purportedly attuned to the requirements of employers, the development of new IT tends rather to underline the continuing importance of generic, transferable competencies - problem-solving, decision-making and communication; as well as of inculcating self-confidence and motivation in handling the new technologies (Dore, 1987).

In short, therefore, the most effective contribution to the development and implementation of new IT is likely to be made by those school systems which are able successfully to develop these general capacities and attitudes. Moreover, although detailed evaluation research is largely unavailable, enough is known to be certain that, once again, there are significant variations between European states in these respects; in terms not only of the extent to which instruction in IT has been introduced, but also of its form.

Higher Education

Many similar issues arise over developments in the institutions of higher education. Here too, there have been intense pressures to vocationalize the system, especially in those countries where an ideal of generalist education has predominated, for example, the Irish Republic, the UK and, to a more limited extent, France. In the UK, for example, the government has sought to skew the distribution of student places towards the sciences generally and technology in particular. Policies of this kind, however, have only been very partially successful. Of course, this strategy has been implemented during a period of cut-backs in capital account expenditure on higher education in many of the advanced economies, despite rising levels of student enrolments, making it much more difficult to meet the re-equipment needs precipitated by new technology (Ryan, 1984).

More fundamentally, however, it has proved difficult to alter entrenched patterns of student preference. For example, although there has been a substantial increase in the numbers of computer professionals being produced by the Spanish universities in recent years, it remains widely recognized that there is still an enormous over-production of humanities graduates, whom the labour market cannot adequately absorb (Carabana, 1988). Similarly, in the UK, student demand has not increased as rapidly as the supply of higher education places in engineering and allied subjects, reflecting the enduring orientation toward the humanities and social sciences.

This situation is not simply attributable to the immediate preferences of many employers for generalists, but also to deep-seated social and cultural patterns. It has been extensively argued that there has been nothing elsewhere to compare with the distinctively technological culture, expressed most clearly in the concept of *technik*, which has provided the essential context for the popularity of technical subjects within the German curriculum (Hutton and Lawrence, 1981; Sorge and Warner, 1986). However, even this favourable socio-cultural climate provides no guarantee of effective adaptation of the higher educational system to the new IT needs of employers. Gottelmann (1989), for example, has argued that German educational policy-makers have been notably slow in responding to the growth in demand for highly-qualified employees, competent in new IT applications.

What this suggests, therefore, is that there are substantial constraints on simplistic social engineering approaches to creating particular kinds of IT-competent labour. Nevertheless the introduction of new IT across the range of the curriculum in higher education may yield considerable pay-offs, especially given the evidence of growing demands for IT competencies in combination with another substantive area of expertise, as well as more general management capacities (see, for example, Bertrand, 1985, for a discussion of the French situation). It remains to be seen what is the most appropriate means of creating a supply of highly-qualified IT specialists to contribute to the development and implementation of new technologies in the core-IT and IT-intensive industries.

Vocational Training and Intermediate-level Skills

The issue of vocationalization is essentially concerned with the re-drawing of the traditional boundaries between general education and vocational training. However, it is important not to lose sight of the contribution which vocational training itself makes, especially to the generation of the intermediate-level skills which are crucial to the implementation of new technologies of all kinds. Here, the structure of demand for such competencies is again crucial. At the most general level, it has been argued that the application of new technologies is changing the occupational pyramid to a diamond shape in most advanced economies, thereby fostering a burgeoning demand for vocational training for this middle-rank of occupations. Certainly, in France, the development of the technical and vocational *baccalaureats*, as well as the *certificat d'aptitudes professionelles* (CAP) and the *brevet d'etudes professionelles* (BEP), appear to reflect these trends (Dundas-Grant, 1985; Steedman, 1988). Whilst in the former FRG, the whole system of vocational training is best geared to the generation of intermediate-level skills, with its clear progression through the dual system of craft apprenticeship to the supervisory levels of the *meister* qualification (Braun, 1987; Prais and Wagner, 1988). Even in the UK, the ratio of technician to craft apprenticeships in metalwork rose from 29% to 52% between 1967 and 1986 (EITB, 1987).

Within such broad trends of development, however, there are substantial variations between different national economies. Contrast the situation in France or the former FRG with that of Greece, for example. In the Greek economy, the predominance of heterogeneous small firms has militated against a self-generating base of technological development, thereby producing overwhelming dependence upon foreign technology. This, in turn, has led to the gross underdevelopment of vocational training geared towards the exigencies of new technologies (CEDEFOP 1987).

This type of argument has been extended by Gottelman (1989) to embrace the relationship between vocational training and national technology strategies. Accordingly, in France and the UK, it is argued, there has not only been a rapid and extensive introduction of new IT into school-based general education, but also a major priority attached to the integration of these technologies into vocational training at the post-secondary level. These initiatives, in turn, were a logical response to the government policy in both countries to create indigenous IT industries, manufacturing micro-computers, components and software. In contrast, state strategy in the former FRG has, on the one hand, concentrated on the improvement of the supply of professional-level computer scientists and engineers, and, on the other, the careful development of new programmes of IT-related training within the dual system. And this too constituted a rational recognition of the centrality of the highly qualified workforce to the success of German manufacturing, especially in mechanical and electrical engineering, the very sectors which were now required to contribute to the production of the new IT-based manufacturing systems.

This argument clearly has considerable plausibility. However, the fit between national technology strategies and vocational training is by no means exact in these instances. Certainly, extreme caution should be exercised in using these ideas as the basis for a normative model for future policy-making. Gottelman's (1989) analysis implies a degree of rationality and control in educational policy-making which is at odds with most of the general research findings (certainly in the UK). And this scepticism is strengthened by the fact that the rational responses of the three VET systems concerned reflected, to a considerable degree, the *traditional* strengths and weaknesses of those systems.

It should be no surprise, then, that the principal effort in the former FRG has been directed at the integration of instruction in new IT competencies into the established and highly successful system of vocational training, focused on the dual system. Initially, there were difficulties here, with delays resulting both from uncertainties as to what new technical knowledge was required and from the need to develop new behavioural qualities - responsibility, reliability and so forth - which had previously been the domain of general education and the family (Krais, 1979). More latterly, however, the structure and content of training within the dual system has been modernized through the inclusion of new training modules and the discarding of ones which are no longer in everyday use. For example, in engineering, new areas of technical competence (digital devices and control techniques in industrial electrical engineering, for instance) have been introduced and, generally, greater emphasis has been placed upon training in communication, planning and evaluation functions (Buschhaus, no date).

The need to integrate the new IT has necessitated innovations in delivery systems too. For instance, some small- and medium-sized firms have experienced considerable difficulties in covering the entire range of subjects specified in the new curricula. This has led to the creation of multi-company training networks, within which training resources can be pooled (Hoch, 1988). Parallel developments have taken place with respect to clerical and other forms of services-based training as well (Lane, 1987).

This is not to argue that the pattern adopted in the former FRG is either problem-free or a model which other European states should seek to emulate. There are major concerns over the extent of vocationalization in the treatment of new IT competencies, as well as over the preoccupation with intermediate-level skills. Moreover, the dual system generally is experiencing problems over, for example, funding arrangements, the transition from training into the adult labour market and so on (Braun, 1987). Rather, it is to emphasize the continuities between the approach to training in the new IT and the historically constituted German VET system. Again, whatever the innovations embodied in the technologies themselves, this has not generated parallel transformations in the training infrastructure.

Developments in France too have largely been contained within the existing system of vocational training. At the intermediate level, instruction in the new IT has been absorbed into the established, predominantly school-based structure of VET, focused on the CAP and, more recently, the expanding BEP. On the other hand, the *Institutes Universitaires de Technologie* have been developed since the 1960s and now compete with the technical *lycees* to produce higher-grade technicians; and these institutions are particularly concerned with training in computing and electronics (Bertrand, 1985; Dundas-Grant, 1985).

Even more interesting, perhaps, is the case of the UK. The British VET system has aroused considerable concern, especially over the generation of intermediate-level skills, largely as a result of the short-termism and lack of investment in training by employers (for example, Finegold and Soskice, 1988). Clearly, then, the established system of vocational training has been in a very weak position to meet the challenges posed by the new IT. Accordingly, the state has responded through the 1980s with a plethora of initiatives, ostensibly aimed at remedying these shortcomings. Following the so-called New Training Initiative of 1981, the Youth Training Scheme (subsequently the YT Programme) was introduced, which guaranteed all school-leavers initially a year and, from 1987, two years of training and work experience. Moreover, IT literacy was identified as one of the core skills to be imparted by YT (Wellington, 1989).

What is instructive here is that the levels of technical competence imparted by these means are extremely low and relate only in the most approximate way to the supposed needs of employers. The revamping of the vocational training system appears ultimately to replicate the traditional polarization which has been endemic to Britain; with a sharp divide between the kinds of access to training in technical skills available to the majority of (in this case, younger) workers and those available to an educationally selected elite. In fact, as Wellington (1989) points out, it may be that the syphoning off of young people into the only marginally IT-related YT is having the effect of reducing the flows into more advanced forms of vocational training, given the extreme difficulties within the British system of transferring from one stream to another. Once again, therefore, despite the surface appearance of fundamental change, it is the continuities which are more substantial.

It is not, of course, a particularly original point that administrative structures are not only difficult to change, but also exert significant influences over the delivery of services such as training. Certainly, the British experience in these respects is mirrored by that of other European states. Gottelman (1989) has contrasted the highly centralized system of vocational training in France (although even here there has been significant regionalization latterly) with that in the former FRG, with its division of responsibilities and powers between the federal government, the *Land* and other regional/local bodies. In the latter, it was not possible to adopt such a *dirigiste* mode of operation as in France, precisely because of the decentralized nature of the administrative system. Whether one of these organizational models is superior to the other, however, remains a moot point.

The tension between centralized and devolved structures is reflected elsewhere. Analytically, the issue is the extent to which a vocational training system, mostly provided by public authorities, can respond effectively to regional and local conditions. As has been seen, it has been claimed that the development of such regional/local responsiveness has been a key factor in the relative success of some European regions (see, for example, Sabel et al, 1989, on Baden-Wurttemberg). Other evidence is less clear-cut. Italy, for instance, operates both a central state system of schools and colleges delivering vocational training and one based upon regional training centres. In principle, the strength of the latter is its sensitivity to local conditions. However, major difficulties arise in the development and implementation of new IT from the enormous economic disparities between the regions. Certainly, there is no evidence that the provision of vocational training itself contributes significantly to the reduction of these disparities; in fact, increasing levels of technologically-advanced vocational qualifications in these circumstances is as likely to intensify such disparities through labour migration (CEDEFOP, 1985). Much of the responsibility for training in IT-based competencies in Italy has therefore fallen upon major IT firms, such as Olivetti.

More generally too, there is considerable evidence that one effect of the development and implementation of new technologies has been to increase generally the extent and scope of vocational training provided by employers (for example, Campbell, et al, 1989). For many firms, the considerable costs involved are outweighed by the benefits of a labourforce whose technical competencies and behavioural characteristics match up to the requirements of their production systems; and, of course, the implication here is that the public sector is not able adequately to fulfil these requirements, whether in terms of the quantity or the quality of IT-related employees.

However, this trend, in turn, has a number of significant consequences. Firstly, there is a shift towards firm-specific skills at the expense of generic, transferable ones, because of the problem of poaching. Secondly, there is a tendency for larger firms to benefit at the expense of smaller ones, as a result of their greater capacity to fund and organize training effectively; and clearly, transnational companies comprise a major element here. Thirdly, and as a partial consequence, the differences between sectors in their provision of training is deepened. Fourthly, all of these are likely to contribute toward the intensification of disparities between regional and local economies.

CONCLUDING COMMENTS

Two central themes can be distilled from the foregoing analysis. Firstly, the VET infrastructure is distributed very unevenly between European states and, perhaps more significantly, the regional and local economies which comprise them. This is paralleled by the uneven development and implementation of the new IT itself. There are, therefore, major contrasts both between and within European states in the resources which are currently available to meet the new demands which will be made of VET systems. Equally, the factors which determine these disparities are highly complex. It is clear, for example, that patterns of work organization, industrial relations and market structures provide an essential context for decisions by employers over levels of investment in training and the forms which it should take. Similarly, public provision is subject to convoluted mediation within the political process. Moreover, the attitudes towards VET of both employers and employees are shaped by often deep-seated cultural orientations.

One implication of this complexity is that it is difficult to manage the disparities in VET infrastructure through public policy measures. This, in turn, has especially important implications for those individuals whose access to employment opportunities is significantly shaped by this infrastructure (this issue is taken up in Chapter 7). Secondly, it is arguable that there are increasing tensions between the relative stability of national VET systems and the apparent volatility of the requirements of firms for IT-related competencies. It is already abundantly clear that quite radical changes in the needs of at least some employers with respect to IT-based technical competencies are in train. Moreover, all the indications are that such trends will continue into the future, although their precise form remains a matter of debate. Of course, these technologically shaped changes will interact with other labour-market shifts (resulting, for example, from demographic trends) to produce distinctive hybrid effects on future labour demand.

However, the evidence suggests that VET systems have responded only partially to these new challenges. Despite a substantial rhetoric of fundamental change, in reality it has proved extremely difficult to break out of the constraints imposed by established administrative structures, funding patterns, recruitment channels, student/trainee preferences and a host of other factors. Moreover, whilst the configuration of these constraints has been shown to vary substantially between national VET systems and undoubtedly some systems are adapting more successfully than others, it is not at all clear that any one such system has produced patterns of adaptation sufficiently successfully to provide a normative model. The question thus begged, particularly in less advantaged states or regions which may see in the new IT a route to economic growth and development, is what form of IT-related VET system to implement. We explore this in more detail in Chapter 8.

7. Information Technology Skills and Access to Training Opportunities: Germany and the UK

Teresa Rees

The European Union (EU) faces a number of challenges in the next decade, such as an ageing workforce, increased competition with Japan and the US, and a growing shortage of high level information technology (IT) skills. All these factors imply that more attention should be paid in future to training and human resource management, and in particular to the under-utilization of women in the workforce. An emerging awareness of the adverse economic consequences of inequalities in education, training and employment coincides with a more pressing climate of opinion favouring social justice between people with different characteristics, for example, gender, age and ethnic origin. But how equal is access to training opportunities in IT in the EU? Are training systems acting as a catalyst for change, are they reinforcing the status quo, or indeed, are they aiding and abetting further polarization between social groups in the labour market?

As previous chapters have shown, technological changes are creating a need for a more skilled workforce. IT itself provides one imperative: the development, manufacture, service and repair of the technology, and the training and support of users in a wide variety of sectors all require growing numbers of people with technological know-how of various degrees of sophistication. Moreover, the all-pervasiveness of IT means that few workers remain untouched. Even those in caring professions, such as nursing, or 'front-of-house' occupations, such as hotel receptionists, find that increasingly, despite the people-based orientation of their work, they need to be technologically literate.

Specific skill shortages in IT are already being experienced in tight labour markets. The lack of people with 'hybrid skills' combining business sense and technical competencies for example, is recognized as a threat to the competitiveness of the EU. Moreover, the combination of skills required is changing: increasingly IT skills are required alongside 'social skills', known in Germany as the 'new pedagogics'. These were listed by Mercedes Benz[1]

113

as a capacity for abstract thinking, team-working, self-reliance, enhanced communication skills, a greater degree of responsibility, and so on. The emphasis in training for IT at Mercedes Benz now includes training in social behaviour, group work and communication, in order to ensure that workers are able to discuss and solve problems amongst themselves (see Rees, 1990).

The use of IT is closely related to patterns of work organization (see Chapter 9) and the need to cope with the perennial problems which face industry, such as wanting to be more efficient, improve products and levels of productivity, streamline work processes, and increasingly, enhance standards of quality control and customer care. IT throws question marks over the appropriateness of traditional forms of work organization, in particular rigid structures of labour market segmentation. There are new pressures to increase the adaptability of an ageing workforce, currently socialized into thinking of training as an initial one-off experience rather than a life-long process.

The effective introduction and development of IT implies job redesign, continuing training, and changes in patterns of work organization. IT can enrich jobs or deskill and enlarge them (Gallie, 1991), according to how people are trained to use them, how jobs are designed and how work is organized. Continuing training in IT can potentially facilitate career development and progression, and the breakdown of the manual/non-manual divide.

Social characteristics, in particular gender and race, are key organizing principles in the allocation of workers in a segmented labour market. To what extent could vocational training systems in the EU facilitate the movement of disadvantaged workers such as women, ethnic minorities and the disabled from low skilled jobs up into more highly regarded and highly rewarded work? A key issue here is access to training. Training systems can be an agent of change and open up opportunities to women and people from diverse backgrounds disadvantaged in the labour market by increasing their cultural capital and making them more marketable. Alternatively, they can in effect reinforce the status quo or even polarize people further by allocating opportunities for advancement to those who already have the correct combination of ascribed characteristics. Vocational and educational training systems tend to be as segregated as the labour force itself, further exacerbating patterns of segregation. The question then is to what extent will these new imperatives leading to enhanced training, open up access and create a labour force less structured by ascriptive characteristics?

This chapter explores access to training for IT in the European Union, and in particular access for women, through a focus on three arenas. In the first section, access to EU funded training measures are examined. There is currently a deepening concern at EU level that a *laissez faire* approach to training for women reflects the inequalities that characterize the member states, leading to widening gaps in skill levels.

Two country case studies follow, focusing on Germany and the UK. The German case study explores change through work reorganization and the development of continuing training for upskilling in some state of the art high-tech companies. Here the economic imperative is leading to policies which should benefit unskilled and semi-skilled workers who have previously not enjoyed opportunities for progression.

The German dual training system, which is generally well regarded, offers young people a highly prescribed programme of credentialized hands-on work-based learning experience alternated with classroom based theoretical instruction. But access to the system is uneven, and it is facing challenges in adapting flexibly to the speed of development of IT. Meanwhile, access to continuing training is playing an increasingly important role in determining occupational life chances. The reorganization of work, the need to enhance the skill level of all workers and increased expenditure on continuing training bodes well for widening access for some workers previously denied opportunities for progression, but again, access is dependent upon a range of determining factors such as sector, size of enterprise, and location.

By contrast, the UK case study focuses on women-only workshops outside mainstream training, designed to bring trainees up to the level of skills and experience necessary in order to compete for intermediate level IT jobs, or to be accepted for further training in the mainstream. The workshops target disadvantaged women returning to the workplace after a period at home looking after children. In the UK, the training culture is not as developed as in Germany, gender segregation in the labour market is particularly marked and vocational education and training systems are as segmented as the workplace. The case study demonstrates the effectiveness of positive action training specifically designed to meet women's training needs and highlights the inappropriateness of much mainstream training for transforming women's skills and filling skill shortages in IT.

Widening access for all is recognized as of growing significance at the European level. However, for three related reasons, reflected in the case studies in this chapter, the issue of access for women in training for IT is of particular concern. Women are seen as playing an increasingly important role in the labour force; gender segregation is particularly marked in the IT, and there is a problematic relationship between women and technology.

WOMEN AND THE NEW TECHNOLOGIES

Increasing Dependence on Women in the Workforce.

Women will represent the majority of new labour market entrants between now and the end of the century, given the decline in school-leavers. They constitute the majority of the EU's unemployed, part-time workers, unskilled and semi-skilled, and economically inactive latent workforce.   As technological developments even out in different parts of the global economy, it has been argued, it is the use made of human resources and the speed of adaptation to new products and services and markets which determine competitive edge.   This puts the emphasis on developing 'intangible capital', that is, the skill levels of the workforce, and enhancing its adaptability and capacity for innovation (European Round Table of Industrialists, 1989; Schmehr and Millner, 1992). Women's training is therefore a priority. There is a particular need to address the training needs of women returning to work after a period of child-rearing, whose skills may be out of date because of technological change, and whose confidence may have eroded, affecting their ability to learn.   The under-utilization of women's potential generally is increasingly being recognized as an economic as well as a social issue.

Gender Segregation in Employment[2]

The EU workforce is highly segregated, both horizontally (whereby women and men tend to work in different industries and occupations) and vertically (whereby women are clustered at the bottom of occupational hierarchies). Segregation has been described as the single most significant determinant of the differences between women and men's access to training, promotion, and equal pay (Walby, 1990). Over three quarters of working women in the EU are in the service sector (compared with just over half the working men), many of them are in low paid part-time jobs in catering, cleaning and retailing. In Southern European countries, the agricultural sector remains an important, if declining source of employment for women.

   The EU's 'dissimilarity index' seeks to measure segregation by comparing women's participation in each sector with the percentage of women in employment in each member state. The results show that despite an overall increase in female economic activity rates in the last five years, and despite the growth in qualification levels among women in the EU, segregation patterns remain clear cut in every member state (CEC, 1992b)

   Training can make an impact on women's occupational lifechances, particularly in those areas of work where entry requirements are clear.

Women tend to fare better in gaining entry to professions for which there are laid down entry qualifications, such as medicine, law and teaching, than those where internal labour markets operate with cloudier criteria, for example business and management (Crompton and Sanderson, 1990). Here informal criteria such as networks and 'fitting in' can effectively exclude women generally, together with male members of ethnic minorities.

The new jobs evolving as a result of IT are less tainted with the history of sex-stereotyping, and demand less use of brawn and more of brain. Moreover, IT jobs have a clean (superclean sometimes) image compared with some of the old male dominated industries such as steel and coal. All this might be expected to contribute to less gender segregation in IT. However, women tend to be concentrated in very low level work, as Connor and Pearson (1986) report in a study of the UK:

> The IT profession is characterized by a low representation of women, although large numbers of women are employed in IT at lower levels on data input and electronics assembly operations. Women typically represented only 1-2% of a company's electronic engineers, although they could be as much as 10% in the larger electronics and telecoms groups. In software jobs, the proportion of women was generally higher, averaging 15-20% (Connor and Pearson, 1986: p. 75).

In occupations whose main component involves the design, development, and service of use of IT, women are predominantly found in relatively low level work, and have no access to career tracks that would lead to their filling high level skill shortages (see Rees, 1992). Women predominate in the lower rungs of IT work, such as secretarial and word processing work, stock control, clerical and office VDU users, data preparation, data entry. They are also increasingly found in user support where their abilities to communicate and appease are considered significant attributes (Fielder and Rees, 1991). Men, meanwhile, are dominant in the top jobs: systems analysts, engineers, software engineers, designers, programmers, management, administration and planning operators. There are few routes of progression: distinctly different recruitment mechanisms are used for the two categories of jobs.

Finally, there are national differences in patterns of gender segregation. The numbers of women entering computing employment, for example, is increasing in some member states but decreasing in others. Computing is seen as a more woman-friendly profession in France but less so in Denmark and the UK (Rubery and Fagan, 1992).

The 'Masculinization of Technologies'

It has been argued that women's access to training and employment in high level IT (where skill shortages are growing) is compounded by the growing 'masculinization of technologies' (Cockburn, 1985; Rees, 1992; Wajcman, 1991). High level IT has become male territory, hence women feel relatively technically incompetent and are deterred from trying to learn what they perceive to be 'male skills' (Cockburn, 1985; 1986). As a consequence women have specific barriers to face such as low levels of confidence, lack of appropriate initial qualifications to gain entry to IT courses, and exclusionary mechanisms practised by men.

There is a powerful association between men, machinery and the concept of technical competence. Children learn early on that computing is male territory. Male computer hacks are accused of indulging male fantasies of sport, adventure and violence through the design of games of speed, war, and 'alien zapping' (Wajcman, 1991). Computers in schools throughout the EU are usually linked with mathematics departments, which are often devoid of women teachers (Pelgrum and Plomp, 1991), when they could logically arguably as easily be located in language departments, emphasizing the communication element. School based computer clubs quickly become male dominated space. In the UK, parents are far more likely to buy computers for home use for their sons than for their daughters (Newton, 1991).

IT is perceived as the territory of the young-white-middle class male (encapsulated in the stereotype of the computer 'hacker'), and this operates as a barrier to the training and recruitment of women and some men. The pool of people from which people can be recruited to fill skill shortages is circumscribed, and it ensures that the masculine ethos of IT, as reflected in computer games, and the use to which it is put, are self-perpetuating.

Limitations are imposed upon technically competent women in a number of workplaces. As Cockburn (1986:p. 185) says 'For a woman to aspire to technical competence is, in a very real sense, to transgress the rules of gender'. In her study in the UK of women and men working in three fields where new technology had been introduced (warehousing, manufacturing and hospital X-ray), and in the engineering firms which developed these technologies, Cockburn (1985) revealed that gender divisions remain clear cut. Even where women learned new technologies, men continued to be the 'technologists' and women the low paid 'operators'. She argues that:

> Whatever opportunities the new technologies appear to offer the operator, they do not in themselves enable her to cross a certain invisible barrier that exists between operating the controls that put a machine to work and taking the casing off it in order to intervene in its mechanism. This is the difference between an operator and a technician or engineer. For an operator there is always someone who is assumed to

know better than she about the technology of the machine on which she is working. That someone is almost invariably a man (Cockburn,1986: p. 181)

Wajcman (1991) argues cogently that technology is a cultural product which is integral to the constitution of male gender identity. The female gender identity is the negation of that of the male, and so the stereotyped cultural ideal of a woman, in the ideology of sexual difference, must be technically incompetent. She underlines the significance of this technological 'ownership' as a source of power in gender relations.

In seeking access to training for IT, then, women and men do not start from the same base position. The masculinization of technology means that girls are far less likely to leave school with appropriate qualifications to move on to higher education and training courses which would equip them for work at technological frontiers. Women are far less likely than men to be given employer sponsored training which would enhance their promotion prospects (Deroure, 1990). A policy of equal access in training for IT which relies on participants putting themselves forward, therefore, will inevitably generate more men than women, just as training for 'feminized' jobs such as secretarial work attracts more female trainees than male. Equality of access does not generate equality of outcome, as the next section on the European Union demonstrates.

WOMEN AND ACCESS TO TRAINING FOR IT IN THE EUROPEAN UNION

The issue of access to training is taking on a new political significance at the EU level. The European Commission has published a proposal for a Council of Ministers' Recommendation on access to continuing vocational training (CEC, 1992a), while the Social Partners of employers' and trade unions' representatives (UNICE and ETUC) have issued a Joint Opinion on access to continuing training (Task Force, 1991). Access to training for IT is increasingly recognized as vital. However, it is access for women which has attracted the most attention: indeed the Social Partners have now agreed a Joint Opinion focusing specifically on women and training, and the European Commission is seeking to ensure that its resources, both through the Social Fund and the innovative programmes developed by the Commission's Task Force Human Resources Education, Training and Youth (the Task Force) are designed to address women's training needs more effectively.

Table 7.1   *Students in IT related degree and postgraduate degree
                    courses in the EU (percentage female)*

	Natural Sciences	Mathematics and Computer Sciences	Engineering
Belgium (combined)	39.6		11.9
Denmark	30.4	22.9	12.0
France	32.5	17.0	16.1
FRG	30..9	23.6	6.5
Greece	37.0	36.0	19.7
Italy	53.4	43.3	54.7
Netherlands	23.0	14.4	8.4
Portugal	63.8	54.0	22.0
Spain	45.5	37.5	10.7
UK (combined)	32.1		8.7
Europe 12	36.6	30.0	9.0

Note: No figures available for Ireland and Luxembourg. These headings refer to ISCED Fields 42, 46 and 54. Figures include full and part-time students.

Source: Calculated from Tables 4 and 5, Eurostat, 1988

Gender Segregation in Training in the EU

Women comprise less than half the EU undergraduate population overall and considerably less than half the post-graduate population in the EU. As girls are less likely than boys to leave school with appropriate qualifications to study IT related subjects, women are less likely to have had training in high level IT skills. The training they do receive tends to lead overwhelmingly to jobs traditionally done by women.

In courses particularly associated with IT, women remain in a minority, ranging from just over a third of all students in the EU in Natural Sciences, under a third in Mathematics and Computing, to only 9.0% in Engineering (Table 7.1). Women constitute less than a third of employer sponsored trainees on in-firm training and are less likely to be in management posts, or other senior posts where in-firm training is often concentrated. There are variations in the different member states. In Southern European countries undergoing massive restructuring and modernization, gender segregation in education and training at least appears to be less entrenched than in some of the more stable Northern countries.

Women in EU Funded Training Programmes

The Treaty of Rome in 1957 enshrined the principle of equal treatment for men and women, and in general terms it could be argued that the Commission has acted as a catalyst to the promotion of equal opportunities within the member states. In 1987 the Commission adopted a Recommendation on Vocational Training for Women which called upon Member States to ensure that women have equal access to all types and levels of vocational training, particularly in professions likely to expand in the future and those in which women have been historically under-represented (CEC, 1987b).

But what effect have the various EU funded training programmes had on women? Has that effect been transformative? In other words, are women's employment prospects qualitatively improved, both in terms of being able to obtain a job in IT, and by securing a job with prospects of further training and promotion, as a result of their participation? Or does their access to and participation in training opportunities merely steer them into low level, low skilled, low paid 'women's' work, with poor terms and conditions of employment?

The Directorate-General for Employment, Industrial Relations and Social Affairs (DGV) of the European Commission has wrestled over the years with the issue of women's training as an identifiable heading: the Organisation for Economic Co-operation and Development has similarly oscillated from the view that earmarked sums are potentially ghettoizing and patronzing through to focusing on the fact that women tend to lose out in mainstream provision despite 'equality of access'. Earmarking has moved from targeting poorly qualified unemployed women and returners (from 1977-1983) to funding training and employment measures in sectors where women are under-represented (1984-89). Women received 41% of European

Table 7.2   *Women's training and the European Social Fund, 1987*

	Number of Female Trainees	Females as percentage of total trainees
Belgium	15,637	45.3
Denmark	10,124	49.2
Germany	38,167	47.1
Greece	107,394	40.8
Spain	211,590	31.8
France	95,490	42.1
Ireland	69,874	43.3
Italy	197,872	37.3
Luxembourg	1,339	31.6
Netherlands	8,055	33.6
Portugal	112,207	39.0
UK	354,456	43.7
EU	1,222,205	39.3

Source: extracted from Table 5.7 CEC, 1989c

Social Fund (ESF) resources in 1990 (CEC, 1991), an increase from previous years (Table 7.2). In individual countries the figure ranges from a third to almost half. However, it is difficult to judge to what extent these resources are effective in transforming women's skills rather than channelling them into low level 'women's work'. The Commission is setting up a more systematic procedure for assessing women's participation in ESF activities. The Commission does support a New Opportunities for Women (NOW) programme aimed at the integration of women into the workforce through training as part of its Third Action Programme on Equality between Men and Women.

Table 7.3 Task force education and training programmes, 1986-1993

Short title	Full title	Duration	Current budget (MECU)
COMETT	Programme on cooperation between universities and industry, regarding training in the field of technology	1986-94	282.5
ERAS-MUS	European Community action scheme for the mobility of university students	1987 on	300.0
EURO-TECH-NET	Action programme to promote innovation in the field of vocational training resulting from technological change in the European Community	1990-94	7.5 (90-92)
FORCE	Action programme for the development of continuing vocational training in the European Community	1991-94	32.0 (91-92)
LINGUA	Action programme to promote foreign language competence in the European Community	1990-94	200
PETRA	Action programme for the vocational training of young people and their preparation for adult and working life	1988-94	218.9
TEMPUS	Trans-European mobility scheme for university studies	1990-94	318.0
YOUTH FOR EUROPE	Action programme for the promotion of youth exchanges in the European Community	1988-94	45.5
IRIS	European network of vocational projects for women	1988-93	0.8

Source: CEC, 1993

Task Force programmes are directed at a range of target groups and for the most part involve transnational partnerships and exchanges of young people, trainees, trainers, higher education students and staff, employers and employees (Table 7.3). Figures on gender distribution among participants on Task Force funded programmes have not been kept systematically by the projects: on some there is excellent information, on others it is patchy. Following a question asked by Madame Fontaine in the European Parliament on the participation of young people, ethnic minorities and women in the Programmes, the issue of gender monitoring (but not ethnic monitoring) is being addressed more systematically in the new round of programmes due to be launched in the mid-1990s. Research commissioned by the Task Force revealed that women's participation rates, not unexpectedly, broadly reflect their existing pattern of representation in the various target groups (Rees, 1993). PETRA, for example, which is aimed at young people in initial vocational training, where there are likely to be broadly similar numbers of young men and women, shows a strong trend towards equality of the genders. COMETT by contrast, which is concerned with continuing training in advanced technologies, is drawing from a pool of potential participants which is overwhelmingly male: this is reflected in the figures of actual participants. Projects are, as Bucci writes (1992: p. 25) 'obviously affected by the balance between the sexes of those who are its potential beneficiaries'. They reflect existing patterns, and hence reinforce existing gender divisions in level and type of skill.

In COMETT however, one of the 125 University-Enterprise Training Partnerships (UETPs), Women in Technology (WITEC), focuses specifically on the needs of women in technology and has played an active role in alerting other UETPs to issues relating to women and technology. There are some noteworthy and innovative COMETT projects featuring women, but the figures on female participation vary in relation to the rough proportions of women in science, engineering and technology. Interestingly enough, in line with women's much greater participation in engineering in Eastern European countries, Christiansen (1992) points out that Bulgaria has imposed a 50 per cent ceiling on women in engineering participating in TEMPUS in response to a fear that they will 'take over'.

The Task Force's new initiative, FORCE, is designed to ensure more even access to continuing training for people with different socio-economic and demographic characteristics, but it is too early to judge its effectiveness in terms of access to women. The Task Force has also funded several initiatives in women's training, in particular IRIS, the European Network of Training Schemes for Women, which facilitates women's training projects to visit each other and develop transnational training.

The Task Force is seeking to improve women's access to training, but has limited resources, and therefore impact, compared with the structural funds of the EU. Both DGV and the Task Force are considering methods of ensuring higher female participation within existing programmes by making them more compatible with women's needs and the reality of their daily lives. A draft joint communication on women and training has been prepared for the Council of Ministers underlying the importance of women's role in the economy. If future programmes were systematically designed to ensure better participation of women, then the Commission would be in a strong position, through its management of substantial resources for training, to act as a catalyst to member states' own policies and practices in the future.

GERMANY: IN-FIRM CONTINUING TRAINING

The dual training system of former Federal Republic of Germany has been described as the envy of the world, certainly in terms of training for intermediate qualifications. Training regulations governing the competencies which must be achieved before an individual can become a qualified worker are strictly controlled. The two sides of industry cooperate with the state in identifying the required skills for any occupation. Some 70% of school-leavers enter the training system, a far higher figure than in other member states, and a further 20% stay on in full-time higher education. More resources are spent on training than elsewhere in the EU, some 3% of the national pay-roll (Federal Minister of Education and Science 1992). There are attempts to ensure that as far as possible, the same standards operate across regions, firms, industries and state recognized occupations. Training is part of the work culture of those people in occupations for which a system of tiered qualifications exists, linked to occupational status and pay.

Companies in Germany have adopted IT to a far greater extent than elsewhere. A Commission survey discovered that 90% of firms in mechanical engineering, textiles, retail trade and services used information and communication systems, 68% had centralized computer systems, and personal computers were used by 61% (CEC, 1988). Given the importance of training in extracting the full potential of what IT has to offer, it is presumably no accident that Germany has some of the most successful companies in the world, not simply in using new technologies, but in their development and manufacture as well. This is a major reason for selecting Germany as a case-study.

However, the very strengths of the dual training system can also be seen as weaknesses in the context of the training needs created by emergent IT. The system provides systematic delivery of carefully considered curricula for occupations in a range of industries, and the opportunity for both college-based teaching for theoretical aspects of the work and firm-based practical learning. The impact of IT on patterns of work organization is having the effect of breaking down barriers between recognized occupations: workers are now required to be more flexible. The nature of some jobs is changing dramatically: the new skills required are not simply technical, but include the new pedagogics (team working, ability to take responsibility, diagnostic and communication skills etc). These qualities are not traditionally taught in the dual training system, and trainers are not used to bringing them out in their trainees. There is increasingly a blurring of the functions of classroom based training and in-firm learning where established staff are now expected to take on a training role.

The dual training system has also been accused of being inflexible: there is a long gestation period for introducing changes into the training regulations which govern occupations. IT is developing with great rapidity, there is a danger that the training can lag behind by many years.

Finally, demographic changes imply that there will be a shift from initial training to continuing training, as older workers are retrained, women returners are recruited, and the unemployed and ethnic minorities are increasingly looked to as a new source of labour. Unlike initial training, the state does not regulate continuing education and training. As a consequence, access to it varies considerably, and the quality can vary too. Moreover, whereas young people are well socialized into accepting the importance of the initial training for their career prospects, there are cultural factors which restrict the enthusiasm of existing unskilled and semi-skilled employees for continuing training.

There are some tensions between what is clearly a highly developed initial training system and the demands of IT in Germany. There are likely to be increasing disparities between experiences at the level of the firm, the region and the individual. Patterns of polarization are already developing. In that sense, one of the strengths of the dual training system, in offering at least a limited standardization of access, is potentially threatened. The discussion here focuses on the effect of these changes on patterns of individuals' access to training.

An individual's access to quality training will depend upon the region in which they live and in which industrial sector they work. There are different standards in the dual training system between the northern and southern *Länder* because of differences in the quality of the training schools and in the standards of the enterprises, despite the attempts to standardize monitored by the Chambers of Industry and Commerce and the Chambers of Crafts and Trades. Larger companies in the commercial sector and the high technology industries are having few problems in arranging the training to suit their needs. However, smaller companies, in the craft sector in particular, are experiencing some difficulties although size is not the only variable (Rees, 1990).

For major companies, spending on continuing training has increased dramatically in recent years and is projected to continue to rise substantially.

Bosch, for example, spent approximately 90,000 DM on continuing training in 1988. In AEG spending increased by 15% in 1988 and a similar percentage again in 1989. Siemens too are now spending nearly twice as much on continuing training as they do on initial training.

There are some jobs whose incumbents never expected to have to undergo further training, or, indeed, to have the prospects of more rewarding work and better pay opened up to them. One respondent from AEG reported:

> People who had been employed to manufacture cables had been working in one of our firms without training. The new recruits are skilled workers who know the new technologies. The unskilled workers can now have opportunities for training as we now need more skilled workers. The machines now require people who have more knowledge about them, those who work with them need more skills. We used to have six different machines involved in the process of making cables, whereas now all that work is done by just one, highly complex machine (translated from an interview with Head of Technical and Professional Training, AEG, Berlin).

However, the response to such opportunities has been mixed. AEG reported that some unskilled Turkish women workers, for example, are not enthusiastic about any changes: cultural factors associated with the family and gendered roles within it intervene in responses to new opportunities and roles. Nevertheless, half the AEG workforce have taken a course within the last year.

Trade unions are keen supporters of continuing training as an alternative to redundancy for workers whose skills have become outmoded. 'Employment plans' were introduced in many German firms facing mass redundancies in the 1980s combining company funds with public resources for regional development to offer people who would otherwise become unemployed places in training or job creation schemes (Bosch, 1990). Collective bargaining has been used effectively during rationalization agreements to encourage employers to invest in the training of their older workers. There are subsidies available from the *Länder* in the case of industries which are being completely restructured and where wholesale redundancies would otherwise have a major impact on unemployment in the region. But, more generally, firms are expected to fund their own programmes of continuing training, with perhaps some contribution from the individual employee.

Access for Women

Gender segregation in the labour force in Germany is as entrenched as in many other European countries, despite a number of measures designed to dilute it. A major difficulty facing young girls wanting an apprenticeship in one of the major companies specializing in training in the new technologies, is that they are less likely than boys to have taken the appropriate qualifications at school. Fewer girls take computing and mathematics, for example, and the number of girls who do diminishes dramatically as they grow older (Schiersmann, 1988). Siemens confirmed a shortage of young women with the basic technical qualifications; despite an increase in the number of girls coming on to apprenticeships, it was felt it would be some generations before substantially more women are taken on.

Women may well benefit from the growth in continuing training, given that they are disproportionately in the unskilled and semi-skilled jobs. Some companies run women-only training to try to break down what are seen as particular barriers facing women wanting to learn new technologies. AEG, for example, run a course for women in electronics: they are not awarded the full qualification, but they can enhance their pay and get better jobs within the company. Computer courses run by women for women tend, as in the UK, to be highly successful in training women in IT. One evaluation emphasized their 'stress free' atmosphere, and the fact that tuition is offered at times of the day suitable for the women. In the afternoons, the equipment is made freely available to the women for practice (see Sessar-Karp, 1988).

Older Workers

It is often said and frequently believed that older people have more difficulty in learning IT than younger workers, who are increasingly likely to be brought up with video recorders, microwaves and home computers. It is difficult to find empirical evidence for this, but it is likely that the belief informs certain training strategies. Moreover, older people's own attitudes towards such training opportunities may well be affected by such perceptions. Clearly, the push for more continuing training can only be to the advantage of older workers, but not all will welcome it, many will feel threatened. As older women are expected to comprise the bulk of new labour market entrants, their age disadvantage of not having grown up with new technologies, will be compounded by that of their gender.

Siemens discovered, like some other companies, that apprentices learn the new technology so quickly that they are in danger of rapidly eroding the skill differentials between them and the older workers. This can cause problems of resentment given the traditional status difference between qualified workers and apprentices, so it has been necessary to introduce special policies. Ways are found to retain the status and pay differential; for example, by rewarding their seniority. Old systems of production are retained to be used by some of the older workers alongside the new ones.

Continuing training is used to up-date the skills of other older workers. In effect, social policies are needed as a complement to training policies. However, older workers are also encouraged to take early retirement, at say 56 or 57, rather than 60 or 63.

More generally, some older workers will clearly benefit from having career trajectories opened up for them, as a result of IT and new working arrangements. There are reports of skilled workers going to university. Qualified workers in the banking industry, for example, are increasingly taking a degree in accountancy as mature-age students. They then have excellent prospects for their remaining careers.

Ethnic Minorities

The old FRG has a migrant population of about 4 million. The sons and daughters of migrant workers have experienced particular difficulties in securing access to the dual training system: they figure disproportionately among the small minority of school-leavers who neither stay on at school with a view to pursuing higher education, nor enter the dual training system. There are, of course, differences between the different ethnic groups. Participation in the dual training system was much higher in the mid 1980s among the Spanish and (the then) Yugoslavians, at around 22%, compared with the Portuguese and Turkish populations (nearer 11%). Turkish girls are the least likely of all to secure an apprenticeship. Those with the greatest difficulties appear to suffer language problems (particularly written skills) and/or to have arrived in Germany relatively recently (Schweikert, 1982).

It is unlikely that the changes outlined above will have much impact on their opportunities for training, except insofar as there will be a general increase in the demand for labour. There have been a series of special projects for the children of migrant workers (Schweikert, 1982). But ethnic minorities may have lost their place in the queue for attention in training matters, given the urgency of harmonizing the training of the New *Länder* and the need to up-date the skills of New *Länder* workers in line with the technical demands of Western industry.

The Unemployed

Opportunities for the unemployed are simultaneously improving because of specific labour shortages, and diminishing because of the political imperative of training people from the New *Länder*, and the recession. There has been an increase in the number of private sector companies providing training in IT for the unemployed, prompted by the availability of finance for such courses through the *Länder* and through ESF monies. The first six weeks of such courses focus on motivation: the trainees have to start at 7 am. They can train in manual qualifications and can then specialize in IT such as computer numerical control (CNC) for metal cutting, industrial mechanics or hydraulics.

The New Länder

Unification between the FRG and the DDR prompted a major task in merging the training systems.   It is clear that in the New *Länder*, qualifications and trades are much more specialized than those even, for example, in the metal trades that have just been replaced. Much attention is being focused on rapidly training residents of the New *Länder* in accordance with the training standards and practices in the old FRG. A particular problem is the fact that the New *Länder* have a very small commercial and service sector where demand for trained people is likely to increase dramatically.

Conclusion

In the main, changes in the training system in Germany are being introduced to reflect the reality of the changes in the working world brought about through the introduction of IT. The rigidity of the dual training system is creating difficulties, in particular in ensuring a standard currency in the value of that training in different parts of the country. Continuing training is opening up more opportunities, but some are better able to take advantage of this than others. There is a danger of the gap between the skill level of the employed, and the unemployed and non economically active, widening even further.   Members of ethnic minorities, in the context of an increasingly racist Europe, face additional problems of access, especially if they are located in those regions where small and medium sized enterprises are having difficulty in collaborating to provide adequate initial training. Older people face erosion of the value of their skills and seniority. The merger of the two Germanies in itself poses a major challenge in harmonization and improving training in IT.

Overall, IT has opened up opportunities for enhanced training in what were routine jobs, and career trajectories where none existed before. It is clear however, that access to these opportunities will not be evenly distributed through the population.   Social characteristics and spatial specificities will influence the allocation of training opportunities.

UK: WOMEN-ONLY TRAINING WORKSHOPS

Gender segregation in the UK is particularly marked. Forty per cent of the female workforce work part-time: the fact that the level of child-care provision for the under fives is among the lowest in Europe is undoubtedly a contributory factor. Opportunities for part-time work in professional and intermediate grades remain few and far between however, and tend to be negotiated on an individual basis. Career breaks are associated with downward occupational mobility, particularly when women return to work part-time (Lindley, 1992). It is clear that women in the UK are grossly under-used as a human resource.

The UK has been described as having a poorly educated and trained workforce compared with its competitors (Finegold and Soskice, 1988). If levels of expenditure are any guide, UK employers cannot be said to set a great store by training: considerably less is spent than by their counterparts in Germany. Most employers do not have a long term strategic commitment to training despite providing training for their employees (Clarke, 1991). Moreover, recent reports suggest that most UK companies are 'still using IT to cut costs rather than underpin their business strategy...Only 39% of a sample of more than 70 companies indicated that they were fully aware of the benefits of IT' (Cane, 1990). Only one in five companies were reported by Cane as relating their business strategy to their information systems.

Training and Enterprise Councils (TECs) were set up in England and Wales, and Local Enterprise Companies (LECs) in Scotland as part of Government policy to ensure private sector involvement in the identification of local training needs and the delivery of training (see Meager, 1991). Executive boards are made up predominantly of chief executives of major local employers, the vast majority of whom are men. TECs and LECs in effect privatize and localize training service delivery, leading to sharper spatial inequalities in the amount and quality of training provided, and as a result, greater polarization in patterns of access. The policy of gearing training to the needs of local industry is likely to have a particular impact on women wanting to return to the labour force, whose needs are ill understood, and met in a haphazard way. Early reports suggest a disappointing performance overall, and considerable variation between TECs (Equal Opportunities Commission, 1993). Resources are made available from central government for the training of the registered unemployed, but this tends to be low level and in any case many married women are ineligible to register[3].

Women predominated in the development of programming and software in the early post-war days of computers (Wajcman, 1991), however, the proportion of women in IT in all but low level data preparation work has since diminished (Perry and Greber, 1990). Wellington (1989) notes that now, 95% of data preparation staff are women, but only 18% of programmers and 2% of data processing managers.

It was only in the 1970s that a well defined education and training route to high level IT jobs emerged in the UK. The decline in women's involvement in programming and software is reflected in IT training and education. In the mid 1980s, women formed a fifth of high level computing workers (Newton and Haslam, 1988);by that time the proportion of girls taking degrees in computer science and computer studies, the main access route into programming and systems analysis, had diminished to 10%. University admissions figures reveal a fall in female students in IT related subjects from 26% in 1979 to 14% in 1986 (Blaazer, 1988). In 1989, women formed only 12.7% of new graduates with first degrees in computing in the UK. Lovegrove and Hall (1987) recount the specific example of Southampton University where women made up a third of computer students in 1978/9 but by 1985/6, there were no women at all enrolled in this subject area.

In the mainstream of training, then, IT have become clearly colonized as male territory except in low level skills. However, there have been some highly innovative positive action training projects in the voluntary sector, often started by groups of women themselves, which meet Cockburn's (1985) criterion of effectiveness by being women-only. The availability of funds from the ESF enabled such groups to persuade local authorities (in the main) to provide matching funds, although funding has remained piecemeal and precarious. Such training in other member states is more likely to be integrated into the mainstream. While for the most part such positive action projects have been in low level IT skills such as keyboard skills, word processing, spreadsheets and basic programming, (and have therefore been successful in attracting disadvantaged women), they have paid particular attention to career guidance and progression, confidence building and assertiveness training, and destereotyping the masculine ethos of IT, thereby going beyond ITeC and further education colleges which prepare young women in 'office skills'.

Women-Only Training Workshops in IT

Women-only training workshops evolved in the mid 1980s as a direct outcome of the women's movement. Although set up on the whole by feminists, they were aimed at training disadvantaged women who were quite unlikely to see themselves as part of the women's movement. The motivation for setting them up came from a recognition of the importance of training to occupational life chances, an understanding of the needs of women wanting to return to the labour force after a period at home with children, and an observation of the inadequacies of existing training provision to meet those needs. Women-only training emerged as a strategy to provide a comfortable environment for women to learn skills not usually associated with their gender. Indeed, some of the early workshops were in construction skills, but latterly IT became the main focus. The tutors tended to be female too, again to provide a woman-friendly learning environment and to offer role models of women competent in IT. Trainees' child-care and other domestic commitments have been included in the planning of the courses: some have on-site creches, most are organized in school term times and during school hours.

South Glamorgan Women's Workshop

One of best known examples and longest running examples of a women-only initiative in this field is the South Glamorgan Women's Workshop (SGWW), a member of the IRIS network, which was set up in 1983 by a group of women in Cardiff operating as a collective co-operative. Funded by ESF and local authority monies, its aim was to train poorly qualified, disadvantaged women over 25 who wanted to return to work, in particular single parents, and black and ethnic minority women. Women from low income families and with disabilities are given priority (see Essex et al, 1986; MacNamara, 1990).

Training is offered in skills judged to be in demand in the local labour market, micro-electronics and computing. Some 50 women have been trained each year, on a part-time basis, between the hours of 9.30 am and 3.00 pm, which both accommodates childcare commitments and allows women to travel in daylight hours. In addition to the specific skills training, there is attention paid to social skills, confidence building, destereotyping, work placements and counselling. Work placements with local employers improve skills and confidence and have led to trainees being offered employment, while enabling employers to recognize that such women are capable of the work. The Workshop is located centrally near bus and train stations, as women on the whole have relatively poor access to private transport, even when there is a car in the household.

The vast majority of trainees go on to further training or employment. Often employment has to be part-time because of the lack of child-care facilities in the area, but the Workshop has provided some places in its on-site nursery to ex-trainees who have found employment places they could not otherwise take up. One group has started a co-operative, advising firms on software choices.

There are now two part-time courses, in Business Computing and Electronics, and a series of short courses in evenings and weekends on various business computer packages: over 350 women attend courses each year. Recent activities supplementing the Workshop's main training courses include a computer club for girls and an access course for Asian women, some of whom then graduate on to the main course at the Workshop. Mature aged Asian women often find mixed gender courses unacceptable, particularly where women will be in a small minority.

The SGWW is now offering EU funded advanced training in Computer Networking and Telecommunications, its reputation as woman-friendly helping to overcome the reluctance of some women to put themselves forward for such training. Skill shortages in the area ensure the women are likely to be recruited into high level IT employment.

Conclusion

The SGWW is an example of 'best practice' positive action training which gives disadvantaged women confidence and skills, and demystifies technology. It has potentially wide application elsewhere. Like other such heavily oversubscribed workshops in Northern Ireland, Liverpool and London, further training is a major destination of trainees (Murphy and Mullan, 1989; Women's Technology Scheme, 1989). By the time they leave the women-only environment, they have developed sufficient confidence to tackle a traditional course where they are likely to be the only woman: they would not have done so before. Such workshops provide a new route back into traditional vocational education and training systems which currently divert women away from training for high level IT.

However, the provision of opportunities for women returners wishing to train in IT in women-only workshops are few and far between. Such workshops continue to operate on a shoe-string at the margins of mainstream training. TECs have not on the whole taken advantage of their existence to improve opportunities for women, nor have they emulated their example. The increased complexity of European Commission funding limits access to experienced European players, this combined with the withdrawal of the Urban Programme as a source of matching funding further constrains the growth potential of such initiatives, despite their success.

CONCLUSION

The effective utilization of IT is crucial to the EU's future competitiveness. Yet these core technologies are currently colonized by young, white males, so that access to jobs in and training for IT is restricted to a small segment of the population. Broadening access to training is crucial to widen the catchment of employment in the development, manufacture, service and utilization of IT. It is particularly important to demythologize the association between masculinity and technology, so that women can benefit from training in IT.

The European Commission is seeking to ensure that resources put into training benefit men and women more equitably in the future, but so far funds have merely reinforced existing divisions.

In German high-tech companies, the increasing emphasis on continuing training, work reorganization and career progression across the old manual/non-manual divide implied by IT may well open up opportunities to both men and women.

In the UK, changes appear to be increasing rather then diminishing gender segregation in the high level IT skills. Successful examples of positive action training for women in IT remain outside the mainstream, and funding is increasingly scarce. Traditional vocational and educational systems may open up a little to mature aged women in the light of demographic changes, but there is little evidence that women are taking up training in computing - quite the contrary.

Patterns of gender segregation, the masculinization of technology and the male-centredness of mainstream training provision are so entrenched that even the combined weight of the economic imperative and social justice demands are unlikely to lead to better access to training in IT for women or for other disadvantaged groups. Strategic policy development is needed at all levels: the European Union, the member state, the region, the firm and the training provider.

NOTES

1. This chapter draws upon documentary material and interviews conducted by the author with training and personnel directors of major companies using advanced technologies in Germany. The study was conducted with Gareth Rees and the original report of the study is Rees (1990).
2. Over half the women of working age in the EU are economically active, although the rates vary by country and by region. Some 28% work part-time, compared with 3.8% of men. The registered unemployment rate for women is 11.9% compared with 7.0% for men (1990 figures: CEC, 1990b). Much of the paid work which women undertake in the EU, for example by Italian homeworkers or Greek family workers, is under-recorded. Steps are being taken by the EU to try to make women's contribution to the agricultural sector and to family businesses more visible.
3. The UK is an exception to the general pattern because of restrictions on certain women, particularly those who are married or who are only available to work part-time, qualifying to receive unemployment benefit.

8. IT Skills and Economic Development Strategy at the European Periphery: An Analysis of Greece and the Irish Republic

Gareth Rees

The overall social and economic configuration of Europe, within which new information and communication technologies (IT) are being implemented, is currently being transformed. The European Union (EU) is proceeding towards the full implementation of the Single European Market, intended to secure the free movement of goods, services, capital and labour, by means of the removal of physical, technical and fiscal barriers between member states (Palmer, 1989). The effects of these changes are compounded by the upheavals in the countries of Central and Eastern Europe, as their former state-socialist regimes are replaced, in different ways and to different degrees, by some form of market-based system (for example, Ray, 1991). Moreover, these developments share more than a common theoretical emphasis upon the efficacy of markets. Although the enlargement of the EU is currently in abeyance, there seems every prospect that in the medium to long term a number of Central European countries will become increasingly involved in the dynamic of the EU Single Market (along, of course, with the European Free Trade Area countries) (Palmer, 1991).

To the extent that this greater market integration does come to characterize the trajectory of change, it will have to come to terms with the enduring processes of uneven regional development within Europe. Within the EU, one of the most persistent problems has been the 'divergences' in economic performance and material welfare between different parts of the Community. At one level, this may be represented in terms of the relationships between member states: hence, the nature and extent of regional disparities were transformed on the accession of Greece, Portugal and Spain. However, the situation is clearly more complicated than this, as there is substantial regional variation within member states too. For example, the 'North-South Divide' became a commonplace of academic and

*Table 8.1   Regional disparities for member states and Level 2
Regions of the EU, 1989 (EU average = 100)*

Country	National average	Percentage of regions below EU average	Number of regions in country	Lowest regional rating
Federal Republic of Germany	131	5	37	92
France	116	18	28	84
Denmark	115	0	3	not available
Belgium and Luxembourg	101	50	10	78
United Kingdom	100	59	44	64
Italy	96	40	25	37
Greece	60	100	12	54
Portugal	58	no regional analysis available		
Spain	53	100	22	59
Ireland	48	no regional analysis available		

Source: CEC, 1989b

political commentary in the UK during the 1980s. Whilst even in the former
Federal Republic of Germany, undoubtedly the most prosperous state of the
EU, debate has focused upon the *form* of urban and regional inequalities,
rather than the fact of their existence (for example, Esser and Hirsch, 1989).

   A crude indication of the empirical contours of this highly complex
pattern of uneven regional development is provided in Table 8.1, based upon

official calculations of levels of economic development and prosperity. In terms of EU regional policy (as revised in 1989), the problem regions identified in Table 8.1 fall into two categories. 'Objective 1' regions are concentrated into the southern and western periphery of the Community, in Greece, large parts of the Italian Mezzogiorno, Portugal, Spain and Ireland (including Northern Ireland). Their production tends to be concentrated into agriculture, low value-added manufacturing and, in some instances, tourism. They are characterized by low *per capita* income and productivity, generally high unemployment, structural underemployment and an expanding labour force (despite high levels of emigration). 'Objective 2' regions, on the other hand, tend to be found in the north of the EU and are defined in terms of industrial decline. They are highly developed and industrialized regions which have lost out through industrial restructuring. Whilst *per capita* income is not especially low in these areas, they have high levels of unemployment. Their problems are perceived as arising from the difficulties of making the transition from declining industries to new ones, especially given poor environmental conditions, conflictual labour relations and an inadequate training infrastructure (for example, Lythe, 1991).

Historically, the EU has attempted to promote 'economic and social cohesion' (the opposite of regional disparities) by directing benefits to both types of region from the European Regional Development Fund (ERDF), as well as the more generalized assistance available through the European Social Fund (ESF) and substantial loans from the European Investment Bank (EIB). In 'Objective 1' regions, the intention has been to counteract the effects of their peripherality, especially through the promotion of investment in communications infrastructure, including new IT. In 'Objective 2' regions, the primary emphasis has been upon human capital, fostering 'entrepreneurship' and higher level 'skills', as well as encouraging the transition of these regional economies to more modern - usually 'high-tech' - forms (Cutler et al, 1989).

In both cases, therefore, the improvement of competences directly related to the development and implementation of new IT has been a necessary element of regional development strategy. This has been attempted not only through ERDF and ESF programmes themselves, but also through specific education and training initiatives such as COMETT, aimed at the development of higher-level IT competences, EUROTECHNET which is concerned with innovation in basic and continuing vocational training, as well as, more recently, FORCE, focused on continuing vocational education and training (VET) (CEC, 1993).

There are, however, important questions to be asked about the overall impact of these EU programmes on established patterns of regional inequality. Total expenditure on *all* education and training programmes amounted to only 0.6% of the EU budget in 1992. Similarly, despite expansion during the latter part of the 1980s, the ERDF constitutes only some 7% of the EU total (which is itself only 1% of EU GNP). This suggests that the redistributive impacts of such activity are likely to be limited. Indeed, some commentators have suggested that, given the preponderance of disadvantage in the 'Objective 1' regions (see Table 8.1), commitment to facilitating the transition of the 'Objective 2' regions is likely to be finite (Begg, 1989). Moreover, it remains to be seen whether the full implementation of the Single Market achieves the kinds of overall benefits officially envisaged in the 'Cecchini Report' (Cecchini, 1988), thereby facilitating 'harmonization' between different parts of the EU; or conversely, whether inter-regional disparities will actually be intensified (a point taken up later).

What this suggests, therefore, is that EU actions are best viewed as complements - albeit very important ones - to the programmes undertaken by the member states themselves. Nearly all national governments have, of course, been committed historically to regional development policies, aimed at ameliorating economic and social disparities between different parts of their national territories. More recently, many of these have paralleled EU strategy in attaching considerable significance to the diffusion of IT, whether in terms of basic infrastructure or applications in key industrial sectors.

What is less clear, however, is that the implications of such initiatives for VET provision have been adequately recognized. In part, this reflects the very scale of the problems of uneven development which are to be addressed. In countries where there are very high concentrations of, in particular, 'Objective 1' regions, the starting point for *any* IT-related development is extremely low and this is reflected in the extent to which the VET system is required to change in order to meet the emergent demands for IT-related competences. Equally, however, the generation of appropriate initiatives with respect to the VET infrastructure is severely hampered by the absence of any adequate normative model which would specify 'best practice' arrangements for the relationships between VET and the growth of new IT (a point which was raised initially in Chapter 6).

In what follows, these issues are explored in greater detail by means of national case-studies of Greece and the Irish Republic. These have been selected as two EU member states which both have high concentrations of 'Objective 1' regions, but which exhibit contrasting profiles with regard to the development of new IT, as well as related VET initiatives. They thus provide an excellent context within which to analyse some of the problematic relationships between new initiatives in VET provision and regional strategy aimed at combating uneven development.

IT DEVELOPMENT AND VET PROVISION IN GREECE

Industrial Development and IT in Greece

Greece exhibits the problems of high concentrations of 'Objective 1' regions in an especially acute form, with generally poor indicators of economic performance (see Table 8.1). More specifically, manufacturing constitutes a very low proportion of total economic activity; indeed, at 17% of GDP it is the lowest in the EU. Even this is carried out within an industrial structure which is highly fragmented: some 98% of establishments have less than 50 employees; whilst the larger ones are mostly foreign-owned. Moreover, average declared return on equity in industrial manufacturing enterprises has also been very low (only 4% at the end of the 1980s, for example) and was even negative between 1980 and 1985. Perhaps not surprisingly, then, Greece has the lowest ratio of research and development (R and D) expenditure to GDP of all the EU member states, at only 0.3%. The infrastructure is also very underdeveloped. The telecommunications network, for example, is extremely old and inefficient; there is no X-25 packet-switching network. Similarly, the electricity system is unreliable and subject to frequent breakdown, especially in rural areas. Even air connections for business purposes are very costly and inconvenient.

The Greek industrial environment in its current form, therefore, is inimical to the development of an IT industry and to the widespread diffusion of IT products throughout Greek society and economy. Although the share of GDP of services at 60% is suggestive of a 'post-industrial society', the reality is entirely different. The Greek economy is characterized by a 'merchant' culture, orientated toward the short term and a quick cash return. Certainly, it would appear that IT-intensive management and accounting methods, which are common in much of the rest of Europe - budgeting and control, marketing and financial planning - are not widely practised in Greece. Moreover, the state sector represents a large area of 'featherbedding' and under-employment, which places a massive fiscal burden on the economy, as well as presenting severe obstacles to efficiency in public administration (Stefanou-Lambropoulou, 1987).

As may be expected, therefore, the indigenous production of IT is currently at a very low level. There are only three hardware manufacturers. One, Intracom, operates in the non-traded telecommunications equipment sector and employs approximately 600 people. The second, Ergo Data, is an open-market operator and manufactures IBM-PC compatibles for the local market. A third company is involved in minicomputer production. Of approximately 150 software companies in existence, perhaps only 20 could be considered to be very active and successful; and there is a high proportion of 'moonlighting' companies.

Equally, by European standards, there is a very low level of diffusion of IT applications through Greek society. However, there are a number of mainframe and mid-range sites in the public sector, in the major banks and other service industries. In addition, there is an apparently plentiful supply of vendors of computer equipment, ranging from high street operators to specialized suppliers. Nevertheless, in general, diffusion is poor both in quantity and quality.

Employment and Training in the Greek IT sector

Table 8.2   IT workers employed in the Greek civil service

	Numbers	% Male	% Female
System Engineers	20	100.0	0
Analysts Programmers	837	73.0	27.0
Computer Operators	190	62.0	38.0
Data Entry	1,431	0.5	99.5
Total	2,478	30.5	69.5

Source: Stefanou-Lambropoulou, 1987

Given the absence of reliable data, it is difficult to build up a more general picture of IT-based employment in the private sector, although it is certainly relatively low. Even in the public sector, estimates vary widely. For example, according to figures supplied by officers of the Federation of Workers in the Public Sector, there are between 1,600 and 1,800 electronic data-processing (EDP) workers in the public sector in Greece (out of a total labour-force of approximately 360,000). However, an independent study estimates that the numbers are as high as 2,500. The break-down of these employees (shown in Table 8.2) highlights the preponderance of lower-level occupations, most of which are filled by women (Stefanou-Lambropoulou, 1987).

Some 80% of these employees work in the EDP Department of the Ministry of National Economy. Many are employed through political patronage and clientelism, rather than on the basis of professional credentials. This has obvious implications for the level of training of EDP employees upon commencement of work; in addition, this is related to the very striking gender disparities within the various occupational categories. For instance, people employed in data entry are not expected to have prior training and those who are employed are overwhelmingly women. The majority of programmers and analysts are reported to have very little in the way of formal qualifications, although those who do tend to have degrees in mathematics or physics. Accordingly, most people receive their training on the job. Much of this is provided 'in house', with the occasional seminar organized by equipment suppliers. From time to time, there are training trips abroad for the lucky few.

All in all, then, EDP in the public sector is not an attractive proposition for the aspiring IT professional in Greece. Working conditions appear to be very poor. There is no career structure for EDP employees and so very little opportunity for advancement beyond the junior grades. Indeed, employees with qualifications often have to take second and third jobs. As a result, there is currently little or no recruitment of qualified IT personnel into the public service. Most graduates seek work in the private sector or emigrate.

Future Developments in IT

It is important to emphasize, however, that this situation is by no means static. EU intervention, especially through its Integrated Mediterranean Programme, has been crucial in stimulating a number of new developments. Hence, both state and private investment in IT research and development have been increasing substantially, albeit from a very low base. By the end of the 1980s, for example, the Ministry for Industry, Energy and Technology calculates that some 23% of private R and D expenditure was on IT-related work.

Moreover, it has been officially estimated (in studies carried out for the Integrated Mediterranean Programme) that there will be a very substantial expansion of the Greek IT market through the 1990s, settling down to an annual increase of some 17%. These estimates partly reflected the expected consequences of one-off initiatives, such as the Fiscal Cash Registers (FCRs) Programme, making FCRs compulsory in all Greek shops and clearly operating to the substantial benefit of indigenous IT manufacturers. More generally, however, software and computer services (rather than hardware)

are expected to be central to IT growth, reflecting a number of important trends. The market-share of software which is produced in-house (and therefore is not traded) is expected to decline; there will be new projects in the field of public administration which are expected to spur the development of customized software, training and support through the mid-1990s; and new value-added network applications are expected, although not until after the mid-1990s.

Clearly, however, this stops a long way short of an official government policy for the development of an IT-based industrial or service sector. Indeed, there is no state organization responsible for industrial development in Greece. Equally, it remains to be seen what impacts these future developments will have on the demand for labour with IT-based competences in the Greek economy. In the most general terms, of course, this demand seems set to rise. In the following sections, attention is turned to the capacity of the Greek VET system to fulfil such a rising level of demand.

IT and the Greek VET System

There are clear indications that the Greek VET system has been attempting to meet some of the new demands which are being made of it. Within the schools sector, for example, as a result of a successful pilot programme, there is now a plan to introduce personal computers across the whole of second-level education, from third grade in high schools (age 15-16 years). To this end, the pilot programme has already been extended to a further 300 schools. However, the longer-term impacts of these initiatives are likely to depend upon a wide variety of factors, including the availability of trained teachers, the method of integrating computer studies into the wider curriculum and so forth.

Similarly, there has been a steady expansion of IT-related provision in tertiary education institutions. The first full Department of Computer Science opened at the University of Padras in 1981, offering degree-level courses in hardware and telecommunications engineering. This was followed in 1984 by a department in the University of Crete at Iraklion, offering degrees in software engineering; and then at Athens University in 1990, also in software engineering. Prior to the establishment of these full departments, computer studies were undertaken as part of degree courses in physics and mathematics; indeed, the Technological University of Athens has been offering degree courses in hardware and telecommunications engineering for some time. Currently, the Greek government has proposed that the Technical Education Institutes should be made Technological

Universities, with the prospect of further development in advanced-level work in IT.

Nikolinakos (1990) estimates that the annual output of computer studies graduates rose from 45 in 1982 to 919 in 1985 and 1,532 in 1988, clearly a very substantial increase. Of those graduating in 1988, 54% were in hardware engineering, 10% in business informatics and 36% in systems design and programming. It is, of course, difficult to relate this output to future labour demand, as not only is the character of future employment opportunities not yet established, but also the interaction of individual career trajectories and emigration may play a significant role (a point taken up later).

There is also evidence of significant new initiatives aimed at improving technological training at the intermediate level. The Hellenic Productivity Centre, which is regarded as one of the premier training institutions in Greece, has been increasing its IT-related provision, although places remain somewhat limited. More significantly, the Hellenic Manpower Organization (OAED) provides a number of IT training courses. For example, high-school graduates, aged between 15 and 23 years, are eligible for programmes of instruction in industrial automation (programmable logic controllers); whilst CAD courses are available for designers with at least two years experience. Similarly, training in data processing is offered to office employees with at least two years' experience; and computer-assisted accounting to accountants and accounting department employees with at least two years' experience, aged between 18 and 50. Computer programming is available for college graduates, with a knowledge of English. Whilst no systematic effort appears to have been made to evaluate the impacts of these courses, OAED is clearly taking the challenge of new IT seriously. It remains to be seen, however, how far these initiatives achieve their goals in the longer term.

VET and the Demand for IT-based Competences

It is widely argued that there is already an under-supply of skilled and trained IT personnel for end-user organizations (for example, Nikolinakos, 1990). Moreover, given even a modest growth in the Greek IT sector, there will be an increase in demand for qualified IT personnel of all kinds. However, insofar as it is possible to judge, it does not seem that even this expanded demand will be such as to outstrip the absolute capacity of VET institutions to supply it. And, as has been noted earlier, there are indications of changing IT-related outputs at all levels of the VET system.

Nevertheless, it is clear that a number of problems do remain. There is strong evidence of some very poor attitudes towards training in both the public and private sectors. This is so amongst both managers and workers, but is particularly evident among management. Characteristic attitudes combine the view that training is not really necessary with an unwillingness to undertake the requisite investment. Certainly, many employers prefer to recruit staff who have already been trained, rather than committing the necessary resources to the training and up-skilling of existing staff. Hence, the shortage problem may be not so much a matter of insufficient capacity at the institutional level, but of insufficient numbers of people coming forward, or being allowed to come forward, for training. What this suggests, therefore, is that there is a need for a fundamental restructuring of Greek industrial culture and organization, if the full potential of IT-induced economic growth is to be realized.

Equally, for those who do attain IT-based competences and qualifications, the crucial issue is whether their career prospects can be maximized given the opportunities available within the Greek employment structure. There is already a significant drain of graduates with IT training from Greece (as there is from other parts of the European periphery too). Again, it would appear that it is not that there are no jobs available, but that the quality of jobs on offer is not appealing or challenging enough, given the generally depressed and underdeveloped state of the IT sector in Greece. Whilst the wider diffusion of IT through Greek society will raise the levels of demand for skilled IT personnel, the quality of the jobs generated and, in particular, the opportunities of individual career mobility are no less significant. Clearly, the Greek government faces a long haul in successfully promoting these objectives. And in this regard, the Greek case illustrates the problems confronted throughout the periphery of the EU.

TRAINING FOR WORK IN NEW TECHNOLOGY INDUSTRIES IN THE REPUBLIC OF IRELAND

Development Policy for the IT Sector

Whilst the Republic of Ireland also exhibits the problems of a high concentration of 'Objective 1' regions, IT-based development has followed a very different trajectory from that of Greece. Irish governments have for some time been committed to developing a strong IT sector, not only in electronics and microelectronics, but also in software and other information technologies. Industrial policy for the electronics sector generally has three major objectives: the attraction to Ireland of new overseas investment; the adding of strategic business functions (for example, marketing, product development and materials purchasing) to the manufacturing activities of

146   *Employment and Technical Change in Europe*

overseas firms with subsidiaries already located in Ireland; and the development of a viable Irish-owned electronics sector. It uses a variety of instruments to these ends, from fiscal measures and grants to industry, to training assistance and research support. There has also been a series of special initiatives, aimed at creating the infrastructural supports for the development of new IT. For example, the National Microelectronics Research Centre was established to assist the development of a semiconductor and microelectronics industry; and the National Microelectronics Application Centre Ltd. (MAC) was established in 1981 as a commercial state-sponsored company to improve the competitive position of Irish companies through the application of microelectronics technology. More recently, policies have been developed for the software industry by the Department of Industry and Commerce, in conjunction with the Industrial Development Authority (IDA). In short, therefore, by the end of the 1980s, the Irish state had taken substantial steps towards meeting the challenges and demands of the new international environment in new IT.

Patterns of Change in IT Production

Table 8.3   Growth of IT electronics production in Ireland, 1984-1990   (1985=100)

1984	1985	1986	1987	1988	1990
97.9	100.0	121.5	167.0	210.2	237.2

Source: Economic Review and Outlook Stationery Office, Dublin, 1990

Certainly, there has been significant growth in key IT sectors. Table 8.3 shows the growth of electronics production during the later 1980s. However, a strong feature of the electronics industry in Ireland is that it is dominated by foreign-owned (especially American) companies. Foreign firms produced no less than 99.4% of total gross output in 1986. Equally, as Table 8.4 shows, the employment structure is similarly dominated.

More recently, however, the indigenous Irish sector has grown substantially. Almost a hundred Irish companies produce an annual output of IR£104 million (1989 figure); in 1982 the figure was IR£30 million. Nevertheless, the indigenous industry remains very small by international standards and future growth is likely to be limited.

Table 8.4 *Electronics industry in Ireland: workforce size and occupational distribution, 1985*

Product Sector	Irish Owned		Foreign Owned		Total	
	Plants	Jobs	Plants	Jobs	Plants	Jobs
Components	17	419	34	4422	51	4841
Consumer products	13	315	12	1335	25	1650
Computer subassemblies and peripherals	10	363	27	5074	37	5437
Industrial control and instrumentation	23	255	31	1787	54	2042
Telecommunic-ations equipment	9	270	10	1853	19	2123
Totals	72	1622	114	14471	186	16093

Source: EOLAS, 1989

One consequence of this predominance of foreign-owned firms is reflected in the employment structure, which is dominated by direct production workers (see Table 8.5). Key research and development work is carried out elsewhere; most of the materials and components are imported; and most of the substantial profits are taken out of the country. For instance, in 1986, only 8% of materials for the production of office and data processing machinery were sourced from within Ireland.

There are signs, however, that both of these features are beginning to change, with almost all American electronics companies opening up some research and development functions in their Irish operation. Certainly, the IDA is actively trying to match Irish suppliers to branch plant requirements. It is these kinds of changes in the structure of production and in the technological base, rather than any gross increase in demand *per se*, which will have the greatest implications for labour demand through the 1990s. As was already clear from the 1980s data (see the final column of Table 8.5), all sectors of the electronics industry will require increased numbers of qualified workers, while fewer machine operators will be needed. It remains to be seen how well VET provision can be channelled to meet such needs.

Table 8.5   Occupational structure of the Irish electronics industry, 1985

Occupational Group	Male	Female	Total	%	1981-85 change (1981=100)
Managers	841	31	872	7	126.2
Engineers	691	44	735	6	-
Scientists	183	22	205	2	223.7
Other Professionals	307	86	393	3	-
Technicians	1,095	78	1,173	9	137.8
Supervisors	535	141	676	5	120.9
Administrators	321	323	644	5	145.7
Clerical Workers	214	727	941	8	117.6
Craft Workers	269	2	271	2	79.7
Production Workers	1,935	4,298	6,233	50	92.1
Others	192	145	337	3	92.1
Totals	6,573	6,537	12,480	100	121.2

Note: Sample (1985) n = 144 plants

Source: EOLAS, 1989

Not dissimilar considerations apply to the Irish software industry. According to figures supplied by the IDA, total employment in the industry was some 5,000 at the end of the 1980s. Although this is tiny by international comparison, growth rates were very strong during the 1980s (some 30% growth between 1986 and 1988, for example) (Durkan, 1990). In part, this reflects the presence of some 50 branch plant operations of overseas giants, with Lotus, Ashton-Tate, Claris (Apple), and Microsoft, among others, having based their European manufacturing headquarters in

Ireland within the last few years. Although originally intended, in the main, as packaging operations for a product made elsewhere, almost all of the bigger foreign-owned companies have more recently taken on skilled staff for production within Ireland. Equally, the indigenous software industry has mushroomed out of almost nothing, with an average of 21 new company start-ups every year since 1983. Although these indigenous companies tend to be quite small, almost all of their employees are involved in high-level skilled design, production or marketing occupations. Moreover, it has been forecast by the Information and Computing Services Association (ICSA) that employment will grow by 20% per annum through until the mid 1990s. Again, it remains to be seen whether such increased demand for qualified labour can be met adequately by the Irish VET system.

VET and the Production of Qualified Labour

The implications of the development of IT production for labour demand and the VET system have been a key element of the Irish state's strategy for some time. As early as 1978, the government appointed a Manpower Consultative Committee to carry out studies and advise on manpower policy; and in 1981, the first attempt to estimate the likely impact of microelectronics on the Irish economy was published by the National Board for Science and Technology (NBST). As a result, the IDA's strategy for fostering advanced manufacturing and services industries, especially through substantial inward investment, was paralleled by a policy aimed at a greatly increased output of graduate engineers, technologists and computer professionals. Most unusually, therefore, the VET system was recognized as a central part of wider economic development strategy.

It is somewhat ironic, therefore, that, certainly during the earlier 1980s, there was only a limited expansion of demand for employees at the higher, 'skill' intensive levels of the occupational hierarchy. Indeed, as was seen earlier, even by the mid 1980s, the electronics industry in Ireland, for example, remained dominated by direct production workers. Hence, one of the key outcomes of the Irish state's policy of increasing the output of graduate scientists and technologists was to contribute towards the conditions for substantial emigration amongst highly qualified Irish professionals to other parts of the EU (and elsewhere); thereby continuing an established dimension of the Irish social structure, albeit in a new guise (Murray and Wickham, 1982; 1983; 1985).

Partly in response to these unforeseen results of the VET strategy, official concern over the employment implications of the development of the IT industry in Ireland has continued through the later 1980s. In particular, in 1989, EOLAS (the Irish Science and Technology Agency) published the results of series of studies of labour requirements in the electronics sectors (EOLAS, 1989). Significantly, these confirmed the high propensity to emigrate amongst highly qualified technological professionals. Asked by the EOLAS review team if they were contemplating moving abroad to work, 46% of the engineers and 34% of the technicians reported that they were. More generally, up to 70% of science graduates from some Irish colleges were said to have left the country during recent years.

Crucially, what appeared to lie at the root of this pattern was not the absolute quantity of job opportunities within the IT sector, but rather the lack of clear *technical* career structures in Irish-based operations. The EOLAS surveys revealed that the desire for technically-demanding work was regarded as the most important factor in the choice of a new job by young engineers (41.4%). Many of them saw their future prospects as better in the long term if they stayed abreast of technical developments and it might not be possible to meet this ambition in their present companies or even in Ireland. Hence, the incentive to leave is strong, especially as a number of the major European electronics giants 'poach' Irish graduates by headhunting them for their research operations in, for example, Germany or the Netherlands.

Equally instructive in this context were managers' views as to the suitability of Irish graduates to work in their plants and factories. For them, the key problem was not with the technical content of engineering education, but with the almost total lack of a non-technical content. Many of the managers said that they would like to employ engineers with a knowledge of project management techniques, systems analysis, operations research, materials buying and management, financial procedures and sales. Engineers with good 'people management' skills were also in demand, as were engineers with knowledge of a foreign language. Engineers of the future will need to be 'more rounded' in their knowledge and have an appreciation for production issues, in particular quality control. Some respondents argued a need for what they called 'components engineers' to work in areas of sourcing and monitoring suppliers. In other words, the engineer of the future will have to be more orientated to the reality of the production and business environment in which he or she works and will be expected to give informed leadership across disciplinary boundaries.

Their responses therefore highlight the tensions between the industry's requirements and the aspirations of the young engineers. The EOLAS report characterizes the situation as follows:

> On one side are the employers, offering limited career paths and usually expecting engineers to move beyond purely technical tasks to seek promotion into management instead. On the other are the aspirations of the engineering graduates themselves, who seem more interested in research work than jobs in production plants and have a strong

sense of their own worth on the international labour market. 'Academic R&D' is a term often heard among engineering graduates when they describe the type of work that they regard as the most desirable (EOLAS, 1989: p. 94).

However, this has to be regarded as a curious attitude given the noted reluctance of electronics graduates to undertake postgraduate research in Ireland, particularly at PhD level. Indeed, if anything, it is the *scarcity* of qualified PhDs in the electronics sector which is giving rise to an industrial development problem[1]. Nevertheless, the attitude of Irish engineering graduates which places high value on 'academic R and D', whilst ascribing low status to manufacturing projects, may well reflect a rather elitist and narrow form of education within the Irish tertiary system. As the EOLAS study suggests, there is good scope for attaining excellence in basic manufacturing techniques at all levels of the industry in Ireland. A change in orientation at this level would probably do much to increase the productivity and competitiveness of the Irish electronics sector.

Nevertheless, it should be emphasized that there is no clear evidence of *shortages* of young engineering graduates in the electronics sector currently. The only area of 'skill' shortage identified by the managers in the EOLAS research was that of senior project managers, with between five and ten years' experience. It appeared to be particularly difficult to attract experienced engineers back to Ireland, perhaps again reflecting perceptions of career prospects.

It remains to be seen, however, whether the emergent pattern of restructuring of the Irish electronics industry (which was outlined earlier) will generate in the future demands for graduate engineers which cannot be met. Certainly, the estimates by the Information and Computing Services Association indicate that the growth of the software industry and of major end-users such as financial services will lead to very substantial shortfalls of computer graduates by the mid 1990s.

In short, therefore, the evidence which has been presented suggests a more complex picture here than is frequently imagined. The electronics sector has not as yet experienced substantial graduate-level 'skill' shortages, in spite of the fact of considerable emigration amongst younger engineering graduates. Where this pattern of labour mobility does have an impact, however, is in the under-supply of more experienced personnel to fill more senior positions. Moreover, it is clear that Irish graduates will continue to seek opportunities abroad, so long as the technical career opportunities remain limited in the domestically-based industry and wider 'quality of life' disadvantages remain. It has to be seen, however, whether the Irish electronics industry will continue to be able to sustain this loss of potential recruits as it develops through into the next century.

The evidence also suggests that for the software industry and for major end-users, there is already an emergent crisis of undersupply of IT specialists at the graduate level. As earlier experience with respect to electronics indicates, however, any development in VET provision to counteract this undersupply will only proceed effectively to the extent that it takes due account of the total structure of labour-market opportunities available.

CONCLUDING COMMENTS

Despite the pervasiveness of IT-based strategies for combating the regional disparities which arise from uneven development, what the two case studies highlight are the complexities of their successful application. In particular, the recent experience of both Greece and the Irish Republic illustrates the dilemmas of adequately planning the kinds of innovation in VET provision which are a necessary part of this kind of development strategy. Hence, where the objectives of state policy with regard to the VET system are modest, it is inevitable that competitiveness is not transformed and the disadvantages associated with peripherality persist. Conversely, grand policy objectives are set and a large investment is necessitated, although without any certainty of a substantial pay-off.

As the Greek case demonstrates, given the severe underdevelopment of IT production and application in the economy, the rates of IT growth which are currently envisaged are unlikely to outstrip the capacity of the VET system in Greece to supply sufficient qualified labour. But neither are they sufficient to alleviate significantly the social and economic disadvantages which Greece experiences relative to other parts of the EU. However, the alternative would be to try the heroic option of upgrading 'skills' in the hope that inward investment and/or indigenous growth would at some later date produce appropriate jobs for the trainees. This would clearly involve a large, speculative investment, with no assurance of long-term success. It would almost certainly be beyond the resources of the Greek state too.

This latter danger, moreover, is clearly exemplified in the Irish experience. Here, substantial investment in increasing the supply of highly qualified professionals appears to have had only limited impacts - so far - on the character of growth in the Irish IT industries, which continues to reflect overwhelmingly the priorities of multinational corporations. Whilst individual Irish citizens may certainly have benefited from the state's investment in VET, many of them have done so by emigrating to countries whose economies offer employment opportunities which match more closely their career aspirations. What have emerged within the Irish economy, therefore, are shortages (albeit limited ones) of IT professionals, at the same time as continuing net emigration amongst these groups. Ironically, therefore, pre-existing disparities between different parts of Europe may actually have been reinforced by these patterns of highly 'skilled' labour migration, in ways which parallel the experience of dependent industrialization in the Third World (Irizarry, 1980).

National governments of states at the periphery of Europe are, therefore, in a rather weak position to combat the disadvantages which flow from their peripherality. Moreover, the changes taking place in the configuration of the EU as a result of the progressive implementation of the Single Market seem unlikely to compensate for this weakness. On the contrary, the intensification of competition which lies at the heart of the Single Market strategy will clearly threaten most gravely the less efficient producers, who are likely to be disproportionately concentrated into the disadvantaged regions. In the absence of effective counter-measures, therefore, the completion of the Single Market will have the effect of further deepening patterns of uneven regional development, thereby actually exacerbating peripheral disadvantage.

NOTES

1.   This has recently been officially recognized by the introduction of the Post-Graduate Awards Programmes, which offer inducements to (informatics) graduates to stay in Ireland and pursue post-graduate research careers.

9. Technology, Occupations and Work Organization

Ian Miles and Ken Ducatel

In this chapter we examine the implications of the technological diffusion patterns described in Chapter 2 for work organization. In particular, we are interested in how changing work organization structures associated with technical change affect different occupational groups. We first present some evidence on the general level of change in work structure associated with technical change. Then, we focus on the job types concerned in the office, on the production plant and in service sector organizations.

TECHNICAL CHANGE AND WORK STATUS

Broadly speaking there are three views on the general effect of IT on work; that it will downgrade or upgrade skills, or that it will encourage a polarization of skills in the workforce. The view that the application of IT results in a general deskilling of jobs stems from the path breaking work of Friedmann (1955) and later Braverman (1974). Technology is seen as part of a long-term management project to exercise complete control over the labour process, primarily through the Taylorization of production work. Taylorization proceeds through careful monitoring and description of the constituent parts of a work process. These analyses provide production engineers with the means to devise the 'one best way' to carry out a production process together with information on the time that each task within the work process should take. Moreover, it has always been assumed by 'Scientific Managers', adherents to the Tayloristic approach, that workers are inherently idle and potentially disruptive. Work analysis is also used by managers to gain as much control over each worker's actions as is possible, thus reducing the autonomy of the employee. One way to do this is to fragment work tasks as far as possible, which reduces the need for managers to rely upon the goodwill and collaboration of the employee, as an individual's performance is routinely monitored within the fragmented work process.   IT offers the Tayloristic manager the opportunity to exercise greater control over workers through techniques such as telesurveillance, and through the use of rigid technological formats which reduce the autonomy of the employee.

A major criticism of the deskilling thesis is that it portrays management aims in too simplistic a way: control of the labour process is only one of the goals being pursued, and Taylorism is only one strategy of work organization (Jones, 1982).   Moreover,   the Braverman perspective in particular has a tendency to ascribe   an unlikely omnipotence to technological change for explaining work organization, and omniscience to managers and engineers in shaping technology to fulfil specific aims. Technology is treated as if its design and implementation were completely expressive of the values of its designers and purchasers.   In practice, information is often limited, existing constraints have to be accommodated, and different actors impose different value sets; the result is often a messy compromise (see Wood, 1982).

The second view, that technology is associated with a general upgrading of jobs, was typical of early discussions of automation and post-industrial society (e.g. Blauner, 1964; Woodward, 1958, 1965; Bell, 1974). It has, more recently, been reiterated by many commentators on the IT revolution, who have been able to draw on official statistics concerning occupational structures (Attlewell, 1992).   The increase in skills is related to increased needs for qualitative workforce flexibility to cope with more rapid product and process change, rather than being a direct product of the technology itself. Multiskilling and the creation of new combinations of technical and social/managerial skill is often seen as critical here.

The third viewpoint argues that it is frequently the case that IT-based change typically involves a differentiation between the best and worst jobs, with a variety of 'middle-range' jobs disappearing. Middle management are seen as being particularly vulnerable to displacement under the polarization thesis. A persistent theme in this literature concerns the problems created for career paths, as the middle rungs of career ladders disappear. The role of technology in polarization varies. Sometimes it is suggested that IT is specifically suited to automating many middle-level information-handling jobs, leaving basic physical work and customer interfaces at one end, and senior management knowledge-based work at the other extreme. Other commentators put more stress on managerial strategies aimed at making firms more responsive by reallocating responsibilities and reducing intermediation of information flows (see for example Adler, 1992; Zuboff, 1988).

In practice, there is likely to be a movement towards more flexibility in work organization structure, stimulated by industrial needs for workers to be

Figure 9.1   IT and working conditions in Finland, early 1980s

blue-collar workers

labour demand falling, content of work more demanding & versatile, better opportunities for promotion & training, growing job satisfaction, though increased stress & social conflicts.

lower white-collar workers

labour demand growing, content of work more fragmented & repetitive, less independent, but better opportunities for training; decreased job satisfaction, growing mental stress & social conflicts.

upper white-collar worker

labour demand growing, better opportunities for promotion & training, no difference in work content or satisfaction, though criticism becomes more marked.

Source: based on Kortteinen et al, 1987

able to adapt to changing circumstances. The flexibility of function of IT (as discussed in Chapter 2) is an important positive attribute, which, if it is to be capitalized upon, requires a flexible workforce.   This approach is compatible with both the upgrading and the polarization theses. Organizational flexibility can be acquired both ways. In the future, the primary components of skill will, we suspect, be adaptability to change rather than the notion of manual dexterity acquired through years of experience, which is employed by the deskilling theorists (see Gallie, 1988 for a useful discussion of this point). This is particularly important given our earlier point that we should expect there to be increased movement towards 'flexible' modes of work organization as the full significance of informatized work filters into more and more branches of industry.

TECHNICAL CHANGE AND WORK ORGANIZATION: NATIONAL LEVEL EVIDENCE

Available empirical material shows us that developments of each sort are observable, with the most common tendencies appearing to be upgrading and polarization of work. The only large-scale survey studies which we have located are of Nordic provenance. A Finnish study (Kortteinen et al, 1987) is particularly worthy of mention, not least because of its use of Labour Force Survey methodology in order to study the implications of IT for working conditions. This demonstrates the potential for studying diffusion, implementation, and implications of IT from a labour force starting-point, in addition to the workplace approaches which have been the core of most of the empirical research. Rather striking results on the introduction of IT in the early 1980s seem to support a version of the polarization hypothesis. The authors summarize their results in terms of three classes of occupation (Figure 9.1).

It is clearly inappropriate to generalize from one non-EU country to the whole of Europe. It cannot be assumed that these Finnish results are good guides as to future trends: they deal with IT-related change relating to earlier generations of equipment. The outcome of IT applications will be at least partly a matter of management strategy as conditioned by labour market and industrial relations circumstances. Nevertheless, less ambitious studies carried out within the EU often paint a similar picture of polarization. Many studies have demonstrated different patterns of implementation of IT, having major implications for working conditions, being associated with different national characteristics (see Hofstede, 1980; Lincoln and Kalleberg, 1990).

An early example is Littler's (1982) comparative account of three major EU economies' predominant work organization features at the beginning of the wave of new IT diffusion (Figure 9.2). Littler draws on the debates and empirical studies about how the labour process is controlled, which emerged after the publication of Braverman's work. Braverman had described a global process of deskilling modelled on Taylorism: but this is only one strategy available to management. One of the chief alternative approaches, 'responsible autonomy' (Friedmann, 1977) places more control and responsibility in the hands of (some of) the workers themselves, who are given rewards in order to maintain quality, work flow and flexibility of production. In Littler's appraisal, French firms typically pursue more of a Tayloristic strategy, German tends more towards responsible autonomy, with the UK between the two.

Figure 9.2   Work organization strategies in three countries, to the early 1980s

Germany

Division of Labour: Large proportions of highly skilled workers, with formally certified qualifications. Low formalization of job boundaries, both horizontal and vertical; workers expected to have flexible skills. High level of discretion for core workers.

Structure of Control: Predominantly ideological: loyalty won through rewards, cooperative industrial relations style, and through training in respect for supervisory and management expertise.

Employment Relationship: High employment security for core workers. Use of 'guest workers' for unskilled mass production jobs.

Workplace Implications: Thriving sector of small and medium sized artisan firms. Development of highly competitive industries based on high-skill labour. Relatively low levels of economic dualism.

Britain

Division of Labour: Large mass-production sector with largely deskilled workforce, with pockets of high skill in craft activities. Job boundaries: both horizontal and vertical highly formalized, in large part due to exclusion practices adopted by unions. High division of labour in mass production, rigid separation of planning and implementation. Low levels of discretion for workforce (except in craft production).

Structure of Control :   Weak task control, weakness partly due to union resistance, partly to low technical levels of management.

Employment Relationship: Low levels of interaction between workers and management. Workers treated as completely substitutable.

Workplace Implications: Relatively inflexible production. Political influence mainly from larger firms.

France

Division of Labour: Workforce largely deskilled. Job boundaries: only vertical boundaries highly formalized. Jobs classified rather than worker skills. Low level of discretion.

Structure of Control: Strong task control, with remnants of early ideological control systems (especially in paternalistic small firm sector).

Employment Relationship: High employment security for core labour force.

Workplace Implications: Little development of multiskilling, and tendency toward Tayloristic organization.

Source: based on Littler, 1982, Table 12.2, and text; and subsequent commentary from Lane, 1989

We might expect that Denmark and the Netherlands are more like Germany, and Southern European countries more like France, in their work organization in factory settings. Such summary reviews, however, should be treated only as a general guide (and a partial guide, based only manufacturing industry). There is of course considerable diversity between countries, based upon national cultural factors, workforce skills, union organization, availability of labour, etc. Also these views represent the starting-points of a widespread period of change and modernization of work organization.

TECHNICAL CHANGE AND OCCUPATIONAL GROUPS

Our analysis of the implications of IT on work organization presented in Chapter 2 can be deepened by an examination of sectoral and industrial diffusion of the technology. It is necessary to consider occupational types in discussing the implications of IT within sectors, and within the economy as a whole, since the use of technologies in an industry is uneven. For instance, managers may often use different hardware and, especially, software than secretaries even though they may be sitting side-by-side in the same office.

In order to consider the differential impact of IT amongst different occupational groups it is interesting to consider two datasets which give different insights into occupational divisions across Europe. The presentation of each of these datasets is followed by a commentary on what the implications of the findings are for occupational structures in different national environments in the EU.

Technical Change and Occupational Groups: The UK Case

To gain a detailed appreciation of the occupational effects of IT diffusion we have produced data for just one member state. Table 9.1 presents data for the UK based on the 1986 Labour Force Survey, using a more useful classification of occupations and industries than we were able to derive from the ILO statistics. The use of these categories will need to be undertaken with due caution. Indeed, when we are discussing the application of IT, one of the most common arguments (with which we have considerable sympathy) is that a blurring of occupational categories is underway. Thus, demarcation lines may be changing; skill requirements may shift out of one category and into another.

Table 9.1   *Occupational and industrial constitution of British Labour Force[1]*

Industry	Occupation (% of sample)						base
Primary	1.1	1.8	1.2	8.0	0.8	0.2	9165
Process	0.4	0.2	0.4	1.1	2.7	0.1	1565
Assembly and variable	2.6	1.3	2.7	11.8	1.7	5.6	14516
Material	1.2	4.6	9.8	3.2	9.0	3.3	19734
Social	5.4	1.3	3.8	1.3	7.6	4.9	17051
Information-al	3.1	0.9	4.7	0.8	0.7	0.6	7495
Column total	13.8	10.1	22.7	26.4	20.2	6.8	100

Source: British Labour Force Survey, 1986

IT and Occupations: Nordic Evidence

Table 9.2 summarizes major results from the Nordic labour force studies concerning occupational incidence of IT use. It will be noted that the data from the different countries spans much of the 1980s - and where comparisons are possible, a rapid IT diffusion is apparent. We do not know how far results from these countries will generalize to the EU countries. However, although the results have considerable plausibility, and their consistency suggests that similar patterns will be found more generally, unfortunately the results to hand are not fully comparable, and there is some blurring of industrial and occupational categories. In all cases the high IT-using occupations are office occupations - administrative and clerical, especially in sectors such as finance. Technical, engineering, and certain professional workers are also typically high users, while agricultural workers are at the bottom. Sales and transport staff are typically moderate users. We would expect broadly similar results in EU countries in general (but some care will need to be taken, on account of, for example, the 'high-tech' nature of Norwegian petroleum industry).

Table 9.2a   Occupational distribution of computer use (percentage of occupational type using)

Finland

Occupation	1984
Administrative and clerical	42
bank clerks	*83*
Sales	24
Technical, natural science, humanistic	20
technical	*32*
teaching, health care	*12*
Industry and mining	9
chemicals, pulp/paper	*48*
printing	*15*
Transport & communication	6
communications	*11*
post	*6*
road transport	*2*
Other services	5
Agriculture and forestry	3

Norway

Occupation	1986
Clerical	60
Miners, quarry workers, etc	46
Administrative, executive & managerial	43
Professional, technical & related	26
Sales	23
Transport & communication	13
Craft and process work, labourers	10
Service, sport & recreation workers	4
Farmers, loggers, fishers	2

Sweden (1984/1989)

Occupation	1984	1989
Clerical	54	76
Administrative	50	64
Technical work	46	61
Other commercial work	37	55
Sales	18	40
Transport	18	24
Engineering & metalwork	16	24
Teaching	11	21
Other production work	10	16
Medical work	10	12
Services	7	10
Agriculture, forestry, mining	6	8

Table 9.2b   Computer users by industrial sector (percentage using)

Norway

Sector	1986
Finance, insurance, real estate, business services	68
Public administration and defence	36
Transport, storage & communication	25
Construction	24
Extractive, manufacturing and utilities	24
Wholesale and retail trades, restaurants and hotels	11
Social and related community services	11
Sanitary, recreation & cultural, personal services, etc	7
Agricultural, hunting, fishing, forestry	2

Sweden(1984/1989)

Sector	1984	1989
Finance, banking etc	52	66
finance	80	87
insurance	80	87
Utilities	43	55
Wholesale, retail hospitality	31	43
wholesale	38	57
retail	31	40
Transport	29	38
Mining, manufacturing	26	38
engineering	30	44
Education and research	12	26
Public administration	14	21
Construction	9	14
Social and medical services	8	12
Agriculture, forestry, fishing	7	9

Sources: various statistical studies and correspondence with researchers in each country

IT and Occupations: Commentary

In terms of gaining a more solid notion of the scale to which IT is liable to be encountered at work, we need to consider the occupation-by-industry structure of the economy. Our depiction of the occupation-industry map of IT applications (Figure 9.3) needs to be interpreted in terms of quantitative information on the proportion of the workforce falling into different locations on the map'.

We can use the summary of EU occupation-by-industry data to quantify IT implications in a very basic way. If, as a rough estimate, we take the proportion of workers likely to be affected by office automation as all the professional, managerial and clerical workers in the labour force, the relevant proportion of the British labour force (from Table 9.1) is 46.7%.

Figure 9.3   Occupational groups and industrial types

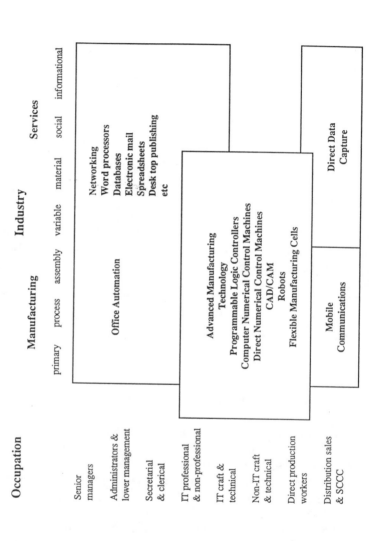

Occupation

	Manufacturing	**Industry**	**Services**
primary process assembly variable material social informational			

Senior
managers

Administrators &
lower management

Secretarial
& clerical

IT professional
& non-professional

IT craft &
technical

Non-IT craft
& technical

Direct production
workers

Distribution sales
& SCCC

Office Automation

Networking
Word processors
Databases
Electronic mail
Spreadsheets
Desk top publishing
etc

Advanced Manufacturing
Technology
Programmable Logic Controllers
Computer Numerical Control Machines
Direct Numerical Control Machines
CAD/CAM
Robots
Flexible Manufacturing Cells

Mobile
Communications

Direct Data
Capture

Rather rougher estimates from ILO statistics indicate that for other EU countries this proportion is typically in the 40% plus range in Northern European countries (and Italy), and between 20% and 30% in Southern European countries with Ireland falling between the two groups (ILO, 1987b, 1988). The comparative data we have here for manufacturing jobs combines these with other 'production' jobs. But given that our more detailed UK analysis yields an estimate of workers affected by manufacturing applications at around 25%, and the UK data are fairly typical of Northern European countries, we may expect a rather similar figure to be attained here, with Southern Europe again achieving a lower score (due to the preponderance of agricultural and other primary sector workers). These estimates should not be taken as saying that all workers in these groups will be immediately affected. Diffusion rates are uneven and sometimes slow, and it is often not cost-efficient to apply IT in particular locations (whether to displace jobs or, as often, to augment them). But with continuing cost reductions in IT, even more pervasive diffusion is probable. These statistics place a sort of upper bound on the workforce that may be confronting these new systems in their everyday activities.

On an industry-by-industry basis, clearly, the manufacturing application 'effects' are greater in industries with a higher proportion of both production workers and professional staff. The existence of professional workers constitutes evidence of some degree of competence to undertake technological innovation, within the industry as a whole. In process as well as assembly and batch-orientated industries between 60 and 70% of the workforce are liable to be affected by manufacturing applications of information technology.

In contrast, OA should be more preponderant in industries with high proportions of non-manual workers. The information services are the most obvious area of application: in the UK nearly 75% of workers in this sector are either professional or clerical. In material services, workers are not as heavily clustered into one or two categories, but the majority of the workforce are either in sales or managerial positions. Sales workers are a special case in the automation of working conditions, as electronic point of sales (EPoS) techniques are gaining wide acceptance in retail industry in many countries, often with scant regard to job design. The social services are predominantly either professional or security-cleaning-catering-caring (SCCC) occupations (53.5% in the UK). A large proportion of these professional workers are teachers (school and higher education), medical workers and government officers. The SCCC workers, on the other hand, are mostly fairly lowly skilled, female, part-time workers (Ducatel, 1989). Thus, within the social services there is a split between the highly qualified and the under qualified in this industrial grouping.

OFFICE WORK

The Distribution of Demand for Office Workers

Statistical accounts such as those given above need to be qualified by considerations of differential diffusion rates and the ongoing shaping and reshaping of applications if they are to be utilized in forecasts, such as those set out here. The employment implications of new office technology have so far been much less dramatic than was suggested by forecasters in the 1970s, reacting to the first wave of reports about the productivity gains of WP. Nevertheless, at the level of individual organizations, some reduction in clerical employment is often visible, and in some cases this has been considerable - see, for instance, the Finnish study cited above.

Growing demand for office services in this period may have offset efforts to use OA to reduce staffing levels. Will such demand continue to increase? We would expect so in Southern Europe, as the industrial and service branches of these economies expand. In Northern Europe the picture is more cloudy. On the one hand, concentration and economic restructuring (including increased routinization and accountability for many welfare and professional services), together with greater administrative needs associated with increased product and market differentiation, may increase demand for such services over the 1990s. On the other hand, increasing automation of production, and the application of data capture techniques and EDI to distribution and exchange, may reduce the need for information workers to mediate production and distribution processes in many industries. In any case, there is little reason to expect a surge in demand for office functions on a scale equivalent to the potential improvements in productivity associated with office technology.

Another factor widely documented as restricting the wholesale restructuring of office jobs (at least those of secretaries) is the desire of individual managers to retain their ''office wives' - all-purpose status symbols, coffee-makers, typists and confidants. Offices that cater to individuals in this way are likely to display quite different patterns of IT use than are typing pool-based offices. Typists and clerical workers may be displaced, while secretaries may find IT used to increase the range of services they provide managers. Furthermore, organized resistance to job loss in offices may well grow. These jobs have become more important to family living standards with the growth of dual-career households. And, despite management requirements for flexibility, information jobs have been increasingly demanded by women who require work that has more of the attributes of a traditional secure career than those of a temporary interlude between school and childbearing.

The shift of office functions to suburban and even offshore locations appears to be an effort to pre-empt such developments (Posthuma, 1988). Many of the more mobile elements of office work that have been relocated in this way have been forms of basic data entry (e.g. keyboarding in data from claims, invoices and ticket stubs). The development of data capture technology of various kinds - in EPOS systems, ATMs, portable equipment for sales staff, etc. - is liable to reduce the demand for this sort of work over the long term, and sooner in some sectors (e.g. finance, retail).

This point should be stressed. Changes in office work are not just related to the use of office technology to process information flows within the office and with its environment: changes in technology used in the environment may dramatically reshape the requirements and opportunities for processing these data.

Data that previously required entry in office environments may be acquired by data entry on the spot in retail and manufacturing work. But this need not mean a simple substitution of (manual or automated) data entry at one site for manual entry at another: with growing volumes of data available in digital electronic form, there are liable to be changes in organizational practices to capitalize on the newly available data. One obvious manifestation is the emergence of client databases in the financial sector, which are used for marketing and for product differentiation strategies. More office work may be created by these responses.

Even if data factories may become less common - and we suspect that this will only evolve over a long period - other forms of office work are becoming more capable of geographical dispersal. For instance, telephone interfaces with clients are now routinely routed to distant offices by large organizations, who find telecommunications costs more bearable than the difficulties of acquiring cheap and socially skilled labour in urban centres. On the industrial relations front, an important issue will be the extent to which collective representation can be obtained for such spatially scattered workforces: the low unionization of office work and the geographical remoteness of these workers may well pose difficult challenges. The 'office of the future' will emerge more slowly than the development and diffusion of IT itself would suggest. Levels of demand for office services in aggregate across Europe will depend upon such political factors as investment in social services.

The Occupational Specificity of IT

What happens to working conditions in practice depends upon how technology is used in organizational restructuring. Technological choices are associated with job design. Whether the WPs that are acquired are readily capable of performing other functions, whether staff are trained to make use of these - such decisions will affect the range of tasks that WP operators can be assigned to, for example. The evidence suggests considerable diversity in outcomes in different organizations and among different groups of worker.

Thus Crompton and Jones' (1984) detailed analysis of clerical work in three British companies, where they studied the level of control and supervision in clerical jobs (reaching conclusions on the basis of cross-sectional comparisons rather than before-and-after studies) found computerization tending to be associated with deskilling for women. This reflected them being effectively excluded from internal labour markets; men were more able to gain promotion. Webster (1990), in contrast, found little evidence of deskilling in offices in the early 1980s, and stressed the variation in outcomes related to the existing organizational structure into which new office IT was introduced. In a key study, Rajan (1985) reports very different patterns of work organization emerging in two bank back offices that had introduced similar IT systems. In one case, the new arrangements involved a further segmentation of work between part-time unskilled clerical staff (all women) and workers who were on a career path which entitled them to new technology training; but in the other case they involved a general upgrading of staff. This study underlines the role of choice in job design around new technologies.

These results are mainly derived from case-study work. The large-scale survey Finnish study (Kortteinen et al, 1987) suggested some divergence in working conditions between different groups of office workers. This type of development has been noted in a number of case studies. But, as we have seen, other studies demonstrate that this is not an automatic product of technological change.

Thus the implementation of current generations of new technology, in new or traditional organizational structures, is having at best a mixed impact on office workers. It is clear that management strategy plays an important role, and that new technological opportunities offer scope for experiment with different modes of office organization. The research literature is far from conclusive as to the determinants and consequences of choice. Perhaps the most consistent themes in the literature are (a) that women tend to be more vulnerable to impaired working conditions than men and (b) that polarization is more likely in large offices (organized especially with typing-pool arrangements) than in smaller ones.

We have focused on secretarial and clerical work so far. What about management and professional workers themselves? If successive generations of IT are to diffuse throughout the economy, a variety of technical IT-related office occupations will necessarily grow, although the exact specification of these occupations is liable to change quite markedly, as more established aspects of IT become routinized and new areas appear as bottlenecks.

There has been considerable attention paid to the improvement of productivity for professional and technical workers through the application of advanced OA. Some commentators argue that the greatest increases in efficiency can be obtained by such 'knowledge workers' rather than by clerical and secretarial 'information workers'; and thus that the major implications of IT for working conditions actually refer to middle and lower management. Long (1987) presents a sophisticated version of this argument, based on US and European research. It should be noted that the Finnish study which found major negative trends in working conditions reported by lower-grade white-collar workers was mainly referring here to clerical and secretarial staff. In any case, as Long argues at length, earlier generations of IT have different managerial implications from the newer systems. Various studies have demonstrated that while these staff account for a disproportionate amount of office expenses, much of their time - perhaps well over half - is devoted to relatively unproductive activities (which often could be undertaken by clerical staff, or automated). Long concludes that in large organizations:

> For supervisors, there will be a reduction in the numbers needed within a given organisation, and in some cases the first line of supervision might be eliminated entirely as computers take over some aspects of their role and subordinates take over others. Those supervisors who remain will see their roles change from routine surveillance to focus more on training, helping to implement new systems and procedures, boundary roles, and dealing with ergonomic issues surrounding the new technology.....The number of middle managers is also expected to shrink because of a decline in the number of subordinates, computerisation of information flow and resource decisions, time savings from more efficient communication...A key issue is...whether managers will be permitted to use these time savings to improve the quality of their performance...Senior managers...will have unprecedented access to operational data...an impressive new set of tools to assist in strategic decision-making...the roles of some sub-units, notably the personnel/human resources and computer/information services departments may broaden in order to deal with the human and technical problems presented by the new technology...The hierarchy itself will likely become flatter and more compact, and coordinating mechanisms other than traditional bureaucratic control will become more feasible... (Long, 1987: p. 216).

Along similar lines, a survey of senior UK managers by Rajan and Pearson (1986) reported that larger firms expect to rationalize their management structures and remove or reduce some layers of management - but that this will be offset in the whole economy by a growth in managerial staff in smaller firms. In common with many other studies, they also noted a growing demand for IT skills among managers, whose job content is in many respects actually being broadened.

However, industrial relations issues (usually of a non-union kind) are liable to be vital here. Intermediate levels of management, while hardly as powerful as senior management, do possess considerable organizational resources, and are often in a good position to resist restructuring or displacement of their work. They are also often better informed about new IT than senior managers, and thus able to shape its application in ways that correspond more closely to their own interests.

Many studies suggest that IT can be (and has sporadically been) used to improve the quality of working life in offices. It does seem rather ironic that, at the same time that new technologies are heralded as meaning the end for Taylorist organization of work in factories, much service work is being transformed into work in 'office factories'. There is no guarantee that a neat parallel exists between the integration of previously fragmented aspects of office work and quality of working life. It seems evident that devoting all of one's time to a fragment of a production process, in such a way that one has little sense of the final product (or even of the relation between one's own work and final product quality), is alienating.

PRODUCTION WORK IN MANUFACTURING INDUSTRY

Perhaps for historical reasons, manufacturing production work has been the focus of considerable attention, although there is limited directly comparable cross-national evidence. Much of the survey research on the implications of IT for these workers has been concerned either with overall employment levels, or with the question of whether the use of IT tends to be associated with deskilling or upgrading of work. The results of studies we have already encountered as providing evidence on diffusion, such as the cross-national PSI-based surveys discussed above, and the German META study (Schettkat and Wagner, 1990), among others, tend to be fairly consistent. Employment levels tend to be maintained better, or even increased, in IT-using as compared to non-using establishments. On average an upgrading of skills is found, but this conceals some divergence: some groups of production workers are liable to experience less demand for their skills, and more simplified and routine tasks.

The Distribution of Demand for Production Workers

The implications of IT use for the structure of demand for various occupational groups will be strongly affected by existing national differences in occupational structure of manufacturing industries. Two major influences are at play here. First, the size structure of an industry has a strong influence on the occupational structure. National industries with a large proportion of small to medium sized enterprises tend to have a higher proportion of workers in the more highly skilled occupational categories. In general, large establishments employ workforces with a lower skill structure (see Ducatel and Coombes, 1989 for UK evidence on this).

Second, there are historic and cultural factors at play here. Of particular importance is the way that workers gain experience and qualifications for their jobs, and their opportunities for promotion (Maurice et al, 1980). For instance German manufacturing plants tend to have relatively low proportions of supervisory and staff grades in the workforce. Lutz (1981) found about 4.5% of German workers were supervisors of managers as against 9% in France. The reason for this difference is that German workers are invested with more responsibility than their French counterparts which allows for a flatter corporate hierarchy. For example a recent survey by ISF Munich found that the workforce in German machine tool engineering firms was typically made up of over 80% skilled employees. (Schultz-Wild, 1990).

A similar effect is seen with German *Meisters,* who are usually seen as having a much higher level of technical competence than French *Contremaitres* or British Foremen. The *Meister* has the role of troubleshooter in a technical sense as well as being a communication medium between management and shopfloor. This is seen as an important contributor to the flexibility, and productivity superiority, of German industry as compared to other European work organization structures (Bessant and Grunt, 1985). The German system fits more closely into the 'flexible' category, as it relies upon a more adaptive organization, where systems of control and supervision are not as formalized as for instance is the case in the more hierarchical French environment. As Lane, in a detailed discussion of these issues, points out in German industry:

> the high level of occupational skill possessed by employees at all levels of the hierarchy and its homogeneity mean that workers, technical supervisory and managerial staff see themselves as a professional community (Lane, 1989: p. 35).

These factors have important implications for the future structure of work organization, and demand for different occupational groups, particularly in the light of the Single European Market. We see here that Germany, with arguably the most efficient national industrial system within Europe, is already more advanced upon this road than its industrial competitors. As the barriers to direct competition between industries in each European country are rolled down it is a matter of urgency that we should consider the means by which the rest of Europe can follow the German lead. This will be less a matter of direct emulation, than one of building on existing national characteristics to develop towards more responsive organizational structures. Clearly, this requires not only a restructuring of current work structures, but massive efforts on the development of skills and training, which are issues taken up elsewhere in the book.

Organizational Flexibility in Germany

The impressive organizational flexibility of German industry is in part achieved through the idea of a professional community within the firm. As we have noted the flexibility of the German manufacturing industry's work structure bears parallels to the 'flexible specialization' thesis of Piore and Sabel (1984). This is no surprise given that new structures of work along these lines were identified by researchers from ISF Munich from the late 1970s (Lane, 1989).

The evidence for new work organization structures emerging in German manufacturing came primarily from the car industry (Kern and Schumann 1984, 1987; Heizmann, 1984; Jurgens et al, 1986). These issues clearly have implications for skill levels, which we do not discuss here, as well as for the nature of work conditions. For instance, through the effective intervention of unions, new forms of work have been encouraged at Volkswagen which reduce line work in components assembly from 90% detailed repetitive work to 15%. Here is an application of robots to enhance the quality of working life. It is in such medium-batch and larger production environments that robots can replace the repetitive work currently done by humans. However, to make robots work effectively, a high degree of expertise at all levels of an enterprise is increasingly acknowledged as necessary (Ebel, 1986).

New positions with greater responsibility have also been created such as *Anlagenfahrer*, the monitor of complex machinery. Similar attempts to upgrade the conditions of work have been documented at Audi. Audi has pursued the idea of production teams and job enrichment particularly of the assembly-line loaders who have been given more skilled tasks to reduce the monotony of their work. The fusing of functions, so that workers take up tasks which were previously of a higher skill, is an important indicator of changing work organization structures. The *Anlagenfahrer* position has also appeared in the chemical industry where the roles of process control and process regulation have been merged. These developments are important because they reduce the career barriers which previously existed between different levels of employee, making the organization less hierarchical and opening up promotion opportunities through flatter work organization structures.

Recent work by ISF Munich indicates the need to look at structural alterations to work organization due to the increased integration of manufacturing operations as CIM begins to diffuse through German industry. In particular, Bieber and Deiss (1990) point to the ability of major automobile firms to increasingly dictate market conditions for their suppliers. They point out that alternative market opportunities for suppliers are declining, there is a trend towards single sourcing of component, contractual conditions are being reinforced and so on. This means paying greater attention to working conditions outside the core industries, and the larger producers. The threat that these authors portray is one of a polarization of working conditions across firms linked in new telematic networks.

Thus we might concur with Lane's comment on the core manufacturers in Germany that 'investment in automated technology can only succeed if it is allied to investment in human resources, and that any automation strategy has to be combined with a work organization strategy based on upskilling and increased worker autonomy.' (Lane, 1989: p. 172). But that does not contradict the possibility that new challenges are arising outside the core, and in particular in the small and medium sized suppliers to the core producers.

Achieving Flexibility By Other Means: The British Case

There are other methods for achieving the ends of 'flexibility'- in particular through reductions in historic barriers between craft disciplines and by employing the workforce on less rigid contracts. The debate on flexibility in Britain is a particularly good example of how flexibility can be pursued other than through upskilling and increased worker autonomy.

The pursuit of flexibility in Britain takes a quite different form from the approach of German industrialists. Here the emphasis is far more on striving after workforce flexibility, than organizational flexibility. The debate centres on the seminal contribution of John Atkinson from the Institute for Manpower Studies (IMS, 1986, who depicts a model of flexibility that, broadly speaking, divided the workforce into functionally flexible and numerically flexible workers. Functional flexibility is the achievement of low demarcation barriers between craft disciplines. Numerical flexibility is enhanced by a greater use of workers on temporary contracts, part-time or variable hours contracts, and workers who are hired through outside agencies.

A recent large-scale study of these issues in Britain (ACAS, 1988) found that, whereas many employers have been trying to reduce demarcation between occupations, only about 25% have had any measure of success in introducing such changes. Similarly, whilst Batstone & Gourlay (1986) noted considerable change in demarcation systems in some IT-using large UK organizations, which was especially pronounced in sectors like food and drink, chemicals, and printing, there was little apparent change in civil service, finance, and production and electrical engineering jobs. In terms of numerical flexibility ACAS (1988) found that manufacturing industries were generally much lower users of part-time workers than private services or the public sector. However, whilst the number of part-timers had increased in 29% of cases, the number of temporary workers on fixed contract had increased by over 40%. Similarly, 90% of manufacturing firms sampled used outside contractors particularly for functions such as maintenance, cleaning, transport, catering and computers.

Flexibility and Production

Turning from the UK to France, a French enquiry into negotiations at the enterprise level between 1983 and 1984 indicated that temporal flexibility in terms of the length of the working day and new forms of time management were of equivalent importance to traditional wage negotiation (Belier, 1987). Even where attention has turned to developing polyvalence, multi-tasking, job enrichment and team-work these are not necessarily related to the need to create new forms of work associated with the introduction of new technology. Rather, for instance at Renault, the motive of management may be related to the struggle to reduce absenteeism and automation is merely accentuating the move to flexible patterns of work (GRAP, 1985).

In many ways we might see these approaches to building flexibility into the organization as starkly contrasting to the German example, which is aimed at an integrated product development, manpower and technological strategies. The original IMS studies found that British management often had no formal manpower strategy and were unwilling to devote the resources that the German approach would require.

OTHER SERVICE WORK

While IT has major significance for many production processes specific to particular manufacturing and service industries, it is also of general importance for a range of non-office (or only part-office) service workers throughout the economy. This may involve direct changes to their work, or indirect changes reflecting transformations of the products with which they deal.

For example, sales work (we refer here not just to shop assistants, but to occupations such as travelling sales representatives and sales office staff) and repair and maintenance work are being affected by product changes. This is nowhere more true than where heartland IT equipment is involved: microcomputer maintenance, for example, is being segmented into two types of job - simple repairs that can be executed by a sales representative with little training, and more complex jobs that involve transporting the computer to a warehouse, or simply replacing a whole section of it. In addition, some firms are offering viewdata systems for customer orders and queries (so the customer can use a computer-communication system to log an order or to explain about a problem...which saves the firm clerical work in recording orders and common faults) (Brady, 1984). Less marked trends are visible more generally, especially as microelectronics displaces older systems based on mechanical or electromechanical apparatus. Fewer moving parts tend to mean fewer physical breakdowns; and those problems that do occur require highly skilled attention to correct, and often are far cheaper to deal with by a replacement of a module. So, IT may be used to change:

1. the products being handled (be they goods or services like insurance policies);
2. the way in which products are physically stored, delivered and marketed;
3. the ways in which sales activities and after sales services are carried out.

Telecommunications (e.g. cellular telephones) can be used to relate mobile sales workers and transport workers to offices on a more efficient basis, and may be used together with simple computer activity management systems to provide better scheduling of visits and routes. Desktop publishing and videotape production may be used to provide better quality and 'customized' promotional, explanatory and training material; several firms are experimenting with more advanced interactive training materials (using interactive CD systems), and this too is liable to be used at the client interface.

Transport workers have experienced considerable change over the last few decades, although this has largely been due to non-IT technologies such as containerization, which has substantially affected handling and packaging functions, and shifts in the locus of employment between manufacturers, retail and wholesale firms, and specialized producer services. The changes here are more changes in the structuring of their activities than in the products they are dealing with; and the core tasks, such as driving vehicles, are unlikely to be substantially transformed by IT - perhaps more important will be regulatory change governing vehicle size, safety and hours of work. But a range of new devices are very likely to accompany and/or oversee drivers. These include portable computer-telecommunications devices to help with routing and scheduling. The management of physical transport is also liable to be transformed by efficiency-enhancing computer analyses, with rescheduling of operatives' movements becoming much more feasible as real-time information on their activities is available.

The related tasks of storage workers are liable to be directly affected much more obviously by the application of IT. Stock accounting and warehousing are likely to be transformed in a more visible fashion than is the physical delivery of goods from site to site. Automated warehousing, automated stock control and sorting and computerized transport planning are liable to mean substantial reduction of staff and changes in working conditions in these areas in the longer run.

Large manufacturing firms and some supermarkets and retail chains are moving toward integrating electronic cash registers with stocktaking, warehousing and ordering. Likewise some specialized warehousing firms (who may offer particular types of storage, e.g. low temperature storage) are using such integrated systems. Since the costs of installing such advanced equipment are very large, it is unlikely that smaller firms will move into the direct use of such technologies on any scale in the near future, though they may shift to using specialized producer services that do rely on such equipment. However, basic EFTPoS and EPoS systems are diffusing more rapidly, providing data capture which reduces requirements for data entry. Labelling and pricing systems reduce requirements for manual tasks in stores, and reduce the need for detailed visual inspection in stocktaking see Chapter 5).

Security occupations are experiencing rapid growth in demand, and security concerns have led to much IT innovation in this application area. IT is being applied to, for example, video surveillance of sites, a variety of intruder detectors and alarm systems (including fire, smoke and other emergency detectors, and with capability to alert emergency authorities), improved communications for guards and vulnerable staff, and other types of controls (such as computerized recording of the whereabouts of staff in sensitive installations). The use of electronic funds transfer and employee bank accounts may reduce the risk of traditional theft, but gives rise to fears of new types of computer crime, and thus to major investment in security against frauds and hackers. Just as some workers are employed to test hardware for reliability, and software for 'bugs' that might emerge in actual use, so the function of intruder-proofing sensitive IT installations against 'teleintruders' has become of considerable significance.

Cleaning and catering jobs have to date been little affected by IT applications, and the nature of the work would seem to insulate them to some extent from this in the foreseeable future. On large sites there may be exceptions, however: e.g. the Paris Metro has introduced automated cleaning equipment, and elsewhere in Paris street-cleaning vehicles are used which relieve workers of much of the unpleasant and physically uncomfortable tasks of stooping or wielding brushes to remove rubbish. As well as such immediate applications of new technology (not necessarily IT-based, but usually microelectronics-controlled), there may be indirect effects reflecting changes in the labour force and physical capital (in manufacturing and service industries) that they service. Changes in organization size and in their spatial location may be significant in these ways; for example if smaller branch sites result from 'flexible specialization', then large concentrations of these workers may be also common (and the relative advantages of contracting-out greater). There are some instances where technological change may also facilitate the shift to producer services in a more direct way: for example in catering, where more industrialized preparation of food at central sites may no longer be synonymous with poor quality meals.

CONCLUSIONS

This section has extended the earlier discussions of how work organization is changing in respect of the diffusion of IT into a variety of occupational groups and how new organizational structures are emerging. We have pointed to a number of challenges and implications of these developments.

It is apparent that, on the whole, office workers are liable to encounter greatest change in their working environments through the application of new IT. The major diffusion of office IT which gathered pace in the 1980s is more likely to be the beginning of an ongoing process, than a one-off development. Challenges will be faced by occupational groups as yet little touched by new IT - and this will extend beyond the office to many other parts of the workforce, as discussed above.

But the fundamental issue will concern the ways in which new technologies are used, the managerial strategies for realising the potential and for dealing with the competitive challenges of the 1990s. If the evidence of technological change in manufacturing is anything to go by, there is liable to be considerable diversity across firms and countries. Unless best practice is diffused more rapidly than heretofore, this looks set to reinforce divergent trends in competitiveness and in working conditions. Management awareness and training therefore emerge as critical issues for enhancing use of IT systems. Having provided the framework within which these topics can be addressed, it is to the dimensions of working conditions that we turn in Chapter 10.

NOTES

1. The industrial sectors are based on the Standard Industrial Classification, and elaborating on classifications found useful in previous studies, see Miles et al, 1988.

Primary:	extractive industries (mining, etc), agriculture, fishing and forestry; construction.
Process Manufacturing:	chemicals, pharmaceuticals, mineral processing, metalworking, etc.
Assembly:	typically large-batch production - more than a thousand units - such as consumer electronics and household appliances industries, automobile manufacturing, food and drink industries.
Variable:	typically small batch or highly complex products as in specialized engineering, certain capital goods industries - including some IT industries.
Material/Physical Services:	services involved in transporting and storing goods and in transporting people, retail and wholesale, catering, warehousing, transport, sanitation.
Social/Human Services:	services mainly effecting biological or psychological transformations in persons, and mainly organized through state institutions: education, health, welfare - but also public administration and defence (and arguably such consumer services as barbers and beauticians).
Informational Services:	services mainly involved in processing information and knowledge, including the symbolic forms of property rights: banking, finance, professional and technical services, media.

10. Information Technology and the Quality of Working Life

Ken Ducatel and Ian Miles

STRESS, HEALTH AND SAFETY

The European Commission has been energetic in its attempts to ensure adequate standards of health and safety for European workers. For instance, in the Action Programme for the Social Charter, Health and Safety issues generate most of the legislative action on working conditions. There are 10 directives extending protection to workers in the high risk extractive, construction and transport industries (Teague, 1989). There were also plans to set up a safety, health and hygiene agency to organize and co-ordinate health and safety programmes (Wedderburn, 1990).

These initiatives are harbingers of a system of consistent and harmonized health and safety legislation across the EU. At the moment there is a wide divergence in national standards. For instance, only two countries, Britain and Denmark have a central national body to administer health safety policy. France has a complex and overlapping system, in which the major responsibility for health and safety as well as other labour relations issues falls to an inspectorate within the Ministry of Social Affairs. In Germany each *Land* has its own inspectors (*Gewerbeaufischt*), whilst at the regional and sectoral level a system of employers' mutual insurance bodies (*Berufsgenossenschaften*) draw up binding systems of regulation and standards. On the other hand countries such as Greece have only recently (1986) been able to enact health and safety legislation which is partial in its coverage, as it excludes the rapidly growing tertiary sector (Valavanidis and Sarafopoulos, 1989).

The prospects for effective legislation on health and safety on a European level are good given both the strong ethical arguments in favour of adequate employee protection and its undisputed inclusion within the qualified majority voting system. Such initiatives, however, provide protection for only a small proportion of the workforce, and generally exclude any reference to occupational risks associated with the introduction of new technology. This may seem to be reasonable, after all it is generally

believed that the overall trend is towards increased occupational safety with
the introduction of new technology. Certainly, workers are less likely to be
engaged in extreme physical exertion. Also, in many areas they will be less
likely to be directly working with hazardous substances. Agervold (1990)
reviews studies carried out for the European Foundation which suggest a
general reduction in physical nuisances as being associated with new IT, but
with some exceptions - e.g. more highly automated NC equipment in
Germany evoked more complaints on a number of scores. This was
attributable to work organization rather than to the IT itself; the jobs were
more highly rationalized and fragmented, with higher intensity of work and
fewer interruptions in the work cycle.

Two areas of growing risk are more systematically associated with the
introduction of new IT in the workplace. The spreading use of computers
at work exposes more and more of the workforce to the potentially
deleterious effects of VDUs and the musculoskeletal problems associated
with the fast inputting speeds which can achieved using computer keyboards.
These direct physical risks are complemented by psychological damage
which can result from employee stress associated with the faster pace and
responsibility of automated work environments. We shall discuss these
issues in the following subsections.

First, to review health and safety issues in the EU, let us turn to a recent
overview of trends in working conditions across EU countries, carried out
for the European Foundation (Schuh, 1990). This reaches a number of
interesting conclusions. In terms of sectoral issues, a number of summary
points are made.

1. Agriculture: self-employment prevails; work organization is very much
   dictated by nature; accidents and diseases related to unsafe equipment and
   chemicals, or inappropriate use of the same, are major work hazards.
   (However, we would add that some countries feature large-scale farm
   organization and factory farming conditions, where the first descriptive
   comments need to be substantially qualified.)
2. Manufacturing: conditions vary with sector, company size, occupational
   group, etc; working conditions changes lag behind technical changes.
   Gains and losses often go hand-in-hand, for instance reduced working
   hours can often be combined with the intensification of work. Large
   sections of the work force are subject to fatigue and high workloads.
3. Services: these can also be stressful, and here both private and public
   sectors are being strongly influenced by the use of IT. Repetitive Strain
   Injury from keyboard work is the obvious issue here: other problems
   associated with use of keyboards and VDUs are less convincingly
   documented, and may well reflect general work stresses more than the

technology by itself. Public services are under particular pressures to increase efficiency, and are under financial constraints, causing stress for workers.

4. In all sectors there is a tendency for more use of industrial chemicals, some such as photocopier and printer chemicals can be associated with IT use. The noxious effects of these chemicals are often poorly understood, and typically workers are unawareness of dangers. IT use itself is becoming familiar, but there is little global difference in working conditions between users and non-users at present. Overall, there is a tendency to decreasing physical workloads, but 'multifactor' and 'psychomental' workload are often increasing, perhaps attracting less attention than traditional safety problems, but resulting in psychosomatic illnesses and self-destructive behaviour. (based on Schuh, 1990: pp. 3-9 *passim*)

Schuh cites French surveys on workers' exposure to risks from the physical environment (Tables 10.1, 10.2), demonstrating a number of trends that are likely to be common in broad outline across the EU. The overall conclusion is that the exposure to hazards is closer between white- and blue-collar jobs than might be assumed. Even so, working conditions are systematically worse in terms of these physical hazards for blue-collars. Trends over time are by no means all positive. For example, all categories of worker demonstrate increased likelihood of handling toxic materials, even though the safety precautions associated with this might have improved. There is little evidence, over the admittedly limited time-period, of rapid improvement or deterioration of conditions.

These studies provide valuable background to our analysis of the implications of IT, by displaying broad features of the occupational incidence of health and safety problems. One further point should be made before turning to the topic of technological change. This is that not only government regulations and awareness programmes influence occupational health and safety. Unions and other groups (for instance, concerned scientists and medical workers) have also played a prominent role in several countries (see Chapter 11). A study of Dutch occupational health and safety activities outlines the role of employees as initiators of change (Buitelaar, 1989). The sophistication of workers' investigations into health and safety conditions was found to have evolved over time. Improving the quality of work and shaping technological change are more frequent features of recent initiatives; investigations have grown in scope to cover entire companies and sectors, and to involve inter union cooperation; and external sources of research support are more likely to be used. Buitelaar concluded that such action should be a part of strategies for improving working

Table 10.1   Risks in the working environment, France 1984
             (per cent of wage earners)

Source of risk	Blue Collar		White Collar	
	Men	Women	Men	Women
Inhalation of gas	24	10	19	8
Inhalation of dust	51	48	34	18
Inhalation of toxic substances	25	46	17	7
Handling toxic substances	25	15	18	10
Handling explosives	7	2	6	2
Falls	31	10	20	5
Electric shocks	18	7	14	3
Burning	21	12	15	6
Machine injuries	34	33	20	6
Walking around	27	4	26	5
Falling materials	32	9	21	3

Source: Schuh, 1990: p. 23

conditions, and that it can facilitate innovation.

HEALTH HAZARDS OF IT

One recent summary of research findings on IT and stress, based on a series of studies conducted for the European Foundation, is summarized in Table 10.3. This sets out features that apply to both the introduction of the new technology, and to ongoing use.

We shall pay attention to these two areas in reverse order here, first considering implications of the use of IT, then issues arising around its introduction. It is necessary to treat this summary in a very qualified way: not only do different generations of IT take distinctive forms, but also there

Table 10.2   Trends in physical hazards, France 1978-1984
(per cent of wage earners at risk)

Source of risk	Farm workers		Blue Collar		White Collar		Service workers	
Year	'78	'84	'78	'84	'78	'84	'78	84
Inhalation of gas	10	10	20	22	6	11	7	13
Inhalation of dust	42	41	48	50	12	13	17	20
Inhalation of toxic substances	23	27	23	23	4	4	8	10
Handling toxic substances	31	45	21	22	3	4	13	16
Handling explosives	2	1	6	6	1	1	2	1
Falls	30	26	30	27	6	5	10	8
Electric shocks	9	6	19	17	3	2	6	5
Burning	8	3	24	20	2	3	9	12
Machine injuries	31	35	33	33	3	3	1	3
Walking around	27	19	22	24	11	9	6	6
Falling materials	-	16	-	28	-	4	-	4

Note: figures rounded up

Source: Schuh, 1990: p. 24

is considerable managerial latitude in the forms of work organization around, and the patterns of introduction of new technologies, and different groups of workers are liable to experience divergent outcomes.

Provision of information hazards associated with Visual Display Units (VDUs) have been recognized since the middle 1980s (ILO, 1986). They include headaches, 'dry eyes', eye fatigue after 2 hours or more, and (most controversially) have been associated with skin diseases and miscarriages. A study of office automation (CEC, 1984) drawing together experiences from around Europe, found: in Denmark, 95% of operators reported some kind of health problem, with 73% having strained eye muscles or visual discomfort; in Germany there were 'alarming' figures of problems with VDUs. Similar results were found in the Netherlands in a study by the *Stichting Toekomstbeeld der Techniek* (STT, 1983). In France recognition

Table 10.3   Research results on technological change and stress

Phase	Situations	Risk Prevention	Reactions
Planning	Fear of change in working conditions and/or of job loss	Provision of information, participation, job security, protection of working conditions	Dissatisfaction, stress & illness, Or: confidence and motivation
Introduction	Insufficient training, low use and maintenance of skills of older employees, etc	Training and retraining	Job change, lack of routine, stress and cognitive overtaxing Or: efficiency competence, cognitive development
Operational	Work pressure, low work quality, lack of participation, isolation, fear of equipment or its breakdown, responsibility for people or machines, cognitive overtaxing, software problems	Organizational changes, psycho-social changes, software, ergonomics, coping	Psychological stress reactions, psychosomatic stress reactions, effects on family and leisure Or: growth and development

Source: based on Agervold, 1990, Table 5.5

of the dangers of VDU use led to *l'Association Française des Banques* and the five biggest unions establishing an outline agreement on the introduction of VDUs which specified that new ways of working should not lead to monotony or nervous tension, and should be intellectually and psychologically satisfying (Lemaitre and Teyssier, 1987). In the UK white collar unions such as APEX and NALGO produced guidelines on the ergonomic design of work environments (see for instance APEX, 1985).

The same problems with VDU were also been noted in Spain (Manzanares, 1985), with 72% of users surveyed complaining of tired eyesight, 64% itching and aching, 54% pain when they close their eyes etc. Recent physiological research has indicated that many of these problems are related to the flicker of cathode ray tubes and, unfortunately, the backlit liquid crystal displays found on laptop computers. This increases levels of involuntary eye movements, with consequent eyestrain and headaches. Given the widespread and long standing acknowledgement of these problems it is perhaps surprising that it was only relatively recently that an EU directive on the use of VDUs was passed. For instance, Council Directive 90/270/EEC - Official Journal of the European Communities, June 21, 1990 came into effect on December 31, 1992, and concerns the design of VDU equipment and its associated software, and its use in the workplace. Even now this directive does not extend to cover the range of occupational groups which are likely to experience extended periods of use of VDUs during their work, such as some checkout operators, drivers using on-board computers and so on. Even so the directive is far reaching in calling for software to be 'easy to use' and 'adaptable to the operator's level of knowledge' which echoes our earlier comments on the need for organizations to adopt a more flexible organization approach in order to gain the most from the generality of IT.

Office activities, which are by tradition considered to be 'safe jobs', as compared to more physically taxing manual work, will become a key focus of attention for management as the use of personal computers extends into a wider range of occupations and becomes more intensely used by some groups of workers. More recently recognized dangers of the automated office include issues associated with white collar workplace design such as 'sick building syndrome' and the exposure of workers to ozone emissions from laser printers and photocopiers and increased musculoskeletal problems.

Considerable concern has recently emerged around a class of musculoskeletal problems known as Repetitive Strain Injury (RSI) or tenosynovitis. Such problems have long been known to affect specific occupational groups, such as power drill operators, but may now gain a higher profile given that it now afflicts more vocal groups of workers, particularly the recent cases amongst journalists (Los Angeles Times, Financial Times) and other professionals newly introduced to large-scale keyboard use. This painful condition can take various forms, resulting in anything from mild irritation to major disability - although there is still controversy about the biological processes involved (Bird, 1990).

Among occupations most frequently affected by upper-limb RSI are, reportedly: secretaries, VDU operators, and supermarket checkout staff (Burns, 1990, reporting on a study for the UK Health and Safety

Executive). However, there is widespread agreement that it is job design rather than technology itself that is responsible for problems: lack of task variety, frequent breaks, and attention to posture, together with other elements of the job seem crucial:

> people are more likely to recover if the symptoms are mild when they first visit their doctors. A change of technique at work may alleviate symptoms just as well as stopping the precipitating activity completely (Bird, 1990: p. 51)

One reason for mounting concern about RSI - over and above the disputed, but widely asserted claim that its incidence is rapidly increasing - is the growth in claims for industrial injury compensation on account of RSI-type problems. This has led to particular attention in Australia, due to that country's health and safety legislation. This is, however, an indirect way of responding to problems - after the damage is done.

The ineffectiveness of action on the problems of VDU and keyboard use so far is partly due to the difficulties of isolating the effect of the technology from the way in which it is used. In particular what must be avoided are occupational structures which require workers to spend long periods engaged solely in one activity. Again, another argument against Tayloristic approaches to job specification, is that to use the workforce in a way which limits the range of tasks they perform is only viable where the employees remain in those posts for a short duration. Given the ageing demographic structure in Europe, there are strong social benefits in maintaining the labour pool in good physical and mental health. These issues are likely to affect personnel management in the near future as the labour market tightens, and high labour turnover strategies of management become difficult and costly. All these factors point to a basic need for managerial training and awareness of job design factors which gain the benefits of good ergonomic design.

WORKFORCE ATTITUDES

One way of approaching the issue of technological change and the quality of working life is enquiring as to workers' views of new IT. Cross-national surveys have to be treated with some caution. National differences in response bias (answering in a way thought to please or impress the interviewer) and linguistic differences which may give translations of the same questions different emphases can affect results. Nevertheless, treated with due caution, well-designed studies can be illuminating.

One study, results of which are represented in Table 10.4, is often interpreted as being about IT-related change at work. The questions used

*Table 10.4   Perceived effects of technological change, 1982 (percent
of those with experience of technological change)*

	USA	Ger	Swe	Jap	Total
More monotonous	22	25	25	41	-
Greater loneliness	18	19	31	31	39
More psychologically taxing	-	35	40	62	56
More difficult	38	48	45	69	46
More dependent on others	38	38	44	30	51
More responsible	-	57	66	74	78
More interesting	74	61	74	59	72
Cleaner	42	52	53	51	61
Less physical strain	35	58	60	42	64

Source: Yuchtman-Yaar, 1989

are not actually so specific (Yuchtman-Yaar, 1989).   Those who
experienced 'technological change in work in last 10 years' - about half of
the total sample (2344 of 5957) were asked the questions reported here. It
is noteworthy that attitudes towards technical change at work emerged as
generally positive, or at least with the frequency of positive judgements
outweighing the (not negligible) number of negative ones. This echoes our
earlier discussion of Finnish results suggesting some polarization of the
experience of IT among different groups of workers.   Here blue-collar
workers report reductions in the unpleasant physical features of work, like
pollution and physical strain; but increasing loneliness and monotony.
   Another study (Vine, 1985) involved surveys in six European countries,
Japan and the USA.   Again workforce attitudes are compared, this time
specifically to IT (Table 10.5). Despite fears about the labour displacement
consequences of IT, Vine's study again demonstrates generally positive

Employment and Technical Change in Europe

Table 10.5   Comparative data on attitudes to IT , 1985 (percentages)

	Fr	Ger	UK	It	Nor	Sp	US	Jap
Experience of IT[1]	26	11	28	7	21	12	37	14
Interest in using IT[2]	37	23	22	29	29	41	32	41
Willing to retrain[3]	60	37	58	46	57	53	65	28
IT worsens unemployment[4]	47	53	63	48	45	63	43	47
IT helps create jobs[4]	23	12	22	19	25	13	50	24
IT reduces tedious tasks[5]	65	38	79	63	74	75	77	39
IT solves problems[5]	44	27	52	42	46	64	63	47
IT invades privacy[5]	71	51	75	37	56	69	68	50
The government should prioritize modernization[6]	38	18	43	21	24	40	35	14
The government should protect jobs[6]	46	67	46	60	57	54	60	63

Notes:
1 'I have already used an information processing system such as a computer or word processor'
2 'I have never used one but it would interest me'
3 Percent responding 'absolutely' or 'probably' to the statement 'Some think that in order to keep their jobs in a world of rapidly expanding modern technology, such as the use of information processing systems, people should undergo special training. Would you personally be prepared to undergo such training?'
4 Respondents asked to state which opinion comes closer to their view
5 Data represents percent agreeing with respectively: 'In the workplace information processing systems will cut down on the more tedious tasks', 'these systems will help people like me solve everyday problems', 'it will be increasingly possible to use computer data banks to infringe upon personal privacy.'
6 Respondents asked to state which opinion comes closer to their view: 'it is essential that we modernize the outdated sectors of the economy as quickly as possible even if this will make unemployment worse,' 'it is more important to preserve jobs even if this means slowing down the modernization of industry.'

Source: Vine, 1985

attitudes toward working with IT, and to undergoing retraining where this is necessary. Resistance to technical change from the workforce does not seem to be a major problem for the diffusion of IT. Surprisingly, Germany and Japan are the least positive in terms of expressed attitudes to IT. The reasons for this can only be speculated about: perhaps higher rates of innovation have fostered more negative attitudes? Or perhaps, as Yuchtman-Yaar argues, cultural factors are playing a role in determining responses. This seems be more plausible than the hypothesis that the results simply reflect actual experience with IT. As well as cross-national comparisons, these studies allow for contrasts to be drawn among groups within countries. Younger respondents tend to express more positive attitudes than their elders, suggesting that the acceptability of IT is liable to continue to grow. The overall impression is that, in terms of workers' own evaluations, experience with IT is most often rated positively.

Turning to studies of actual work places, we can return to the UK study by Daniel (1987). He used the 1984 Workplace Industrial Relations Survey of over 2000 establishments (we have already encountered this as a source of diffusion data - and they include information from shop stewards as well as management respondents, see Millward, 1986). This study contrasts IT-based technical change - the use of microelectronics on the shop floor, and of computers and word processors in offices - with 'conventional' technical change and with organizational change. High levels of technical change were found, and these were generally accepted by workers; there was no evidence suggesting that trade unions inhibited the rate of change. (Indeed, shop stewards and union officials tended to be particularly supportive of new technology.) Manual workers supported the introduction of IT in three quarters of cases, according to management respondents, and strongly resisted it in only 2% of cases; office workers tended to be even more strongly supportive.

On the wider European scene, similar results are reported in studies conducted for the European Foundation (Butera et al, 1990). Almost all of these studies date from the early 1980s - as does Daniel's work, along with many of the diffusion studies reviewed earlier. It seems that there was a wave of concern about the implications of new technology - and possible resistance to it from workers - in the early 1980s.

PSYCHOLOGICAL ASPECTS OF IT USE

From the results on workers' attitudes to the introduction of IT, it is important to examine a second type of occupational health and safety issue: stress and psychological problems. Again, it may be helpful to begin with Schuh's (1990) overview of recent research evidence on developments across the EU. Schuh notes that "all highly industrialized member countries report a general increase of psycho-mental stress or even of psychosomatic illness' (Schuh, 1990: p. 25). While it is difficult to untangle the extent to which these are due to events at the workplace, to changing expectations of what work should offer, or to external social factors altogether, many experts relate these developments to changes in working conditions: some of which are encompassed in other items on Schuh's list.   While to the outside observer increased levels of attentiveness are frequently visible aspects of IT work (presumably related to the more rapid responses of the equipment and generally higher levels of interactivity that it implies), hidden workload may remain important. Schuh cites instances of workers needing to stand for hours at CNC machines, of keyboard operators sitting motionless in front of screens. Also, the quality of work has changed in terms of its becoming less tangible as it is more computer-mediated: instead of direct sensory information, the operator is often fed information on a rather abstract model of the process in question.   Finally, workloads often combine in a multifactorial way - stress with time pressure, with night work, with dangerous materials - with unknown implications: although it is unlikely that different stresses will very often cancel each other out, leaving an unstressed worker!

Because IT can report on how a job is being done, as well as carrying out the job, installing IT into the workplace can create opportunities for management strategies involving more highly paced and closely monitored production work. The increase in intensity can take a number of forms, according to the nature of the work environment and the manner of implementation of technology. Although IT might contribute to a climate of greater organizational flexibility, the general effect of these movements may also increase the intensity and therefore stress associated with automation.

In contrast to much economistic thinking, which tends to assume that the dominant rationale for applying IT is to increase productivity and efficiency, in practice innovation may be motivated by quite different purposes. Fortunately, there is some empirical evidence which bears on this theme. A study of German manufacturing (Ewers et al, 1990) shows that among firms adopting computer-aided systems in 1985/6, the main motive was indeed reported as being reduction of production costs. But this was closely followed by improvement of product quality, and then by reduction of production time. Further down the rank ordering were positive sales expectations, improvement of production quality, and overcoming capacity bottlenecks. Further down still were overcoming personnel bottlenecks and testing new techniques - and no less than five more motives were also noted. Furthermore, over time, studies of investment in German industry demonstrate that the salience of different motives is liable to vary, with some factors becoming more important, others less so. Since firms display different motives for, and strategies in, IT use, it is unlikely that we will always find productivity improvements as a result of new technology.

Nevertheless, it is fairly often the case that new technology can be introduced for a variety of reasons but that thought for the humanization of work is often an afterthought (e.g. Ebel and Ulrich, 1987). When the management of production is broadly Tayloristic a high priority is placed on the elimination of human discretion in the act of production. Thus, work reorganization inherent in the introduction of IT would be expected to reduce either the amount of human intervention in the labour process or the autonomy of line workers. Sometimes this is called the American model of automation, which attempts to move to a workerless environment (Ebel, 1989). In such cases, the remaining human involvement is paced by the machines and is increasingly degraded to the level of machine minding and feeding. However, such approaches are in practice restricted to mass production of large-batch environments (Warner et al, 1990)

In other environments, as we have seen from the example of the West German automobile industry, there has been an increasing shift of emphasis in managerial style towards the development of human know-how as a key organizational resource (Drucker, 1983). In these writings, and in the efforts to create anthropocentric and human-centred systems (especially in Germany and Scandinavia), labour is seen as an active participant in organizational efficiency and skills are seen as resources to be built on rather than problems requiring removal.

In many modernized work environments, particularly in manufacturing, labour costs are only a small proportion of operating costs. The increased integration of complex and highly expensive high technology equipment means that an essential ingredient in maintaining good rates of return on investment is keeping the machines running at high capacity. This requires skilled workers who are willing to take responsibility for their machines and who identify with the performance of the company, which in turn requires management to have a more conciliatory attitude towards labour.

As we saw earlier, this type of development is exemplified by research in the German automobile industry, here:

> the new worker is a sort of scout - sensitive to breakdown with quick reactions and the ability to improvise and take preventative action. (Kern and Schumann, 1987: pp. 162-3)

Some analysts see in these developments, often portrayed as Post-Fordism, a more fulfilling system of work organization which is already emerging. But fulfilling in what sense? The flexible specialization thesis contains a well-articulated example of an argument which pervades the literature concerned with the introduction of new technology into the workplace. This argument runs along the lines that we cannot, *a priori*, say that IT is good or bad for working conditions, but if it is implemented in the most effective manner possible it will lead to a greater incorporation of workers into the labour process, and the new styles of management which use labour as a resource and employ information technology to maximum effect lead to a reconstitution of skill.

This trajectory, if it exists, therefore, would seem to create a new common purpose between management and labour which enhances skill and makes the enterprise more competitive. As with all industrial developments, however, we see new challenges emerging from the potential reorganization of working conditions. It is stressed time and again in the literature that the benefits of reskilling associated with new technology have to coincide with a reorientation in management attitudes. The flexible technology has to be introduced alongside both more flexible working practices and more flexible definitions of the role of managers. To some degree this requires more industrial democracy, a greater degree of participation by the workforce in the process of technological change, to which we turn below. It also puts a greater onus upon the ability of managers not only to respond to the logic of production but also to the needs of the workforce as human beings.

To exemplify this issue we might invert one of the tenets of the working conditions literature, which is that a more skilled job is better than a less skilled job. In general higher skill levels may be desirable - but only if they are appropriate for the workforce and the organization. Skill can be measured in a variety of different ways, but its basic constituents are the degree of training required to carry out a task, the number and complexity of the tasks a particular job entails and the degree of control the worker exercises over the labour process.

Job enrichment programmes try to increase job satisfaction by increasing the number of tasks involved. Practical evidence indicates that such programmes tend to increase the range of tasks in a horizontal sense rather than vertically. That is, they increase the number of different things the worker has to do without substantially increasing the worker's control over the way in which the work is carried out (see for instance the review in Buchanan and McCalman, 1989 and the less sanguine analyses in Shaiken, 1984 and Beynon and Nichols, 1977). As many job enrichment programmes have been aimed at increasing the range of tasks carried out by assembly-line workers, the possibilities for a substantial improvement in the quality of work are limited by the external constraints of the position of the worker within an overall production process. The pace of the work is externally determined, and more productivity will almost certainly mean a greater intensity if not a higher pace of work.

Job redesign associated with new technology can also lead to an increase in skill in the sense of more complex combinations of tasks. (An obvious example is machine operators taking the role of carrying out first-line maintenance and repair duties.) But again, such job enrichment strategies could equally be part of a programme of work intensification. The gains in job interest of operators being responsible for the smooth running of their machines has to be offset against the extra stress of that responsibility, particularly in an organizational environment which is stressing high productivity from high technology machinery.

The idea of teamwork, perhaps in the form of quality circles, has been widely advocated as a way of dealing with the stress and boredom of assembly-line manufacture. As an example, quality circles in France grew from a few dozen in 1981 to 15,000 in 1985 involving 150,000 workers (Belier, 1987). Jurgens et al (1988) in the case of General Motor's Germany's experiments with teamwork, point out that management is allowing greater self-autonomy to the team, but only within a framework of tightly controlled time standards, and with higher levels of electronic monitoring in order to achieve a higher number of productive actions per working day.

Experimental results from social psychologists are relevant here. These results indicate that work situations which have 'tight coupling' or the sort of technical system in which levels of inventory are minimized, with a close integration of one part of the labour process to another, (highly likely where maximum use of the capital investment is desired) are likely to lead to low levels of job satisfaction and psychological well-being amongst workers (Corbett, 1987).

The stresses of greater responsibility would be compounded if managers were attempting to introduce new technology and new practices 'on the cheap', by supplying insufficient support and training for workers moving into their new roles. Studies show that stress from work often comes from the workers feeling out of control because they are not well-trained for their new work roles or for the technology. The complexity of IT systems means that they are prone to bugs and running-in difficulties during and after installation, possibly increasing still further the anxiety and helplessness of workers.

There is a further specific challenge to improved working conditions with IT, which is the possibility that it might be used by management for surveillance - the 'spy in the sky' syndrome (Shaiken, 1984). The shift to a system of management which stresses the importance of having workers identify with their company is seen, particularly in some Italian and British contexts, as compatible with a system of closely matching employee rewards with performance. Information technology provides a potential means of close, detailed evaluation of employee performance through electronic monitoring systems. Again, however, the stress on the worker is increased. These systems are not compatible with high standards of employee health and safety. If surveillance is overlain by the other potential assaults on good working conditions, we might argue, contrary to the standard position that increased skill is of itself good, that skill increases associated with new technology are only as good as the working conditions that result.

THE INTRODUCTION OF NEW TECHNOLOGIES

Technological change introduces uncertainty to working conditions, and the threat of loss of control over important features of one's life. Adaptation to new technology is often a protracted affair - and if working conditions have deteriorated, as they may sometimes do, long-term difficulties can be experienced.

Much IT-related change comes without preparation and participation of the workforce. And even when users are involved in technological choice, five factors can give rise to problems. (See the discussion in Agervold, 1990, based on studies carried out for the European Foundation.)

First, IT is seen as threatening by many potential users: they are daunted by the idea of having to acquire new skills, are unsure of whether they have the cognitive abilities to do so, and often suffer misapprehensions as to the specific abilities required (frequently computers are associated with mathematical competence). Furthermore, 'technofear' is supported by the fact that IT systems are highly interactive, apparently behaving in a volitional way; computers can respond to users verbally in such a way as to make it clear that one has made a mistake, or badly designed user-computer interfaces can be recalcitrant, refusing to carry out a basic task without clearly explaining why.

Second, and related to this, is a set of features of the work itself. As well as the shift from manual to mental work, and the reduction of exercise that may be associated with this, there is also frequently a socially-imposed intensification of the pace of work. Users are reluctant to leave IT systems in the middle of a job, for example, when they would have been quite prepared to set a typing task aside. This may be associated with perceptions as to the high cost of the system, of the immaterial (and therefore vulnerable) nature of the product, or even with suspicions that an unwatched IT system will get up to unpredictable tricks! Importantly, there may also be ambiguity as to responsibility when system failures occur (and this is quite liable to increase with the move to networking).

Third, there are frequent mismatches between technical performance and user requirements. Ironically, IT is plagued by poor communication between engineers and software writers, on one hand, and end-users on the other. This is felt by companies, who acquire systems that do not meet specifications; and by individual workers, who encounter frustration and awareness that they are working in suboptimal ways. The writers of manuals do not always succeed in bridging the supplier-user gap, even when systems are in principle adapted to user requirements.

Fourth, technological change is sometimes feared precisely because it is suspected that job loss will occur, or that one's own position will be undermined by failure to cope with the new systems. In Chapter 11 we shall see that the generally positive welcome workers give to IT systems, even when they are introduced with little consultation may be a result of the impression that, at least, if one's firm is bothering to spend money on new equipment, it is unlikely to intend closing one's workplace down in the near future.

Fifth, training for IT is often quite inadequate. Agervold (1990) notes that Danish, German and Irish workers experiencing new IT all reported that training was regarded as too theoretical, as paying too little attention to practical problems that arise in the actual work. Often formalized training programmes are used when IT is first introduced, but workers joining at later stages are given only informal training - and though this may be more problem-oriented, it is often felt to be inadequate too. There also seems to be:

1. widespread failure to recognize the need for training associated with new IT - the idea is that the worker can simply pick up the skills on the job or from reading a manual (very common in office work)
2. little recognition of the need for ongoing training as hardware and software is updated and as applications and demands for quality output increase.

11. Industrial Relations and Participation in Technological Change

Ian Miles and Ken Ducatel

INDUSTRIAL RELATIONS REGIMES

Industrial Relations and Employer Strategies

An important effort to map out characteristic industrial relations and workplace regimes in three of the major EU countries - France, Germany and the UK - has recently been made by Lane (1989). While rather schematic, and deriving mainly from studies of manufacturing industry, the approach adopted is enlightening, not least in displaying the diversity of situations in the three countries which form the EU's largest pool of IT use.

The first point to note is that of the three, Britain had, in 1985, the highest level of union membership (50%) followed by Germany (40%), with France trailing at 22%. There are strikingly different structures in each case. In Germany the central control over unions in the *Deutscher Gewerkschaftsbund* (DGB) is strong, whereas the British TUC, and the multiple French union federations are weak at getting constituent unions to agree joint policy. The style of unionization also varies markedly. In Germany unions are organized by industry. British unions tend to be craft or occupation based unions. And French unions tend to have a strong political complexion. The effect is to ease the creation of collective agreements in Germany, where regional level industrial agreements are well policed and considered binding on both sides. British trade unionism has been plagued by conflict (reflecting differences of interest at plant level) between the, sometimes quite large, number of unions existing in many major plants. French trade unionism operates at a number of different levels above plant-level, and tends to concentrate on setting minimum standards of wages at industry level and on social issues negotiation has tended to be at national level.

Figure 11.1 Centralization, unionization and the level of bargaining

Centralization of structure
and level of bargaining

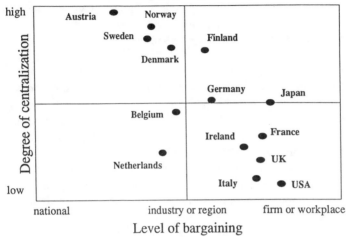

Unionization and level
of bargaining

Source: Bean, 1985

The flexibility of IT, however, creates pressures for local level negotiation, because it is hard to predict in detail the type and scope of application which is going to be developed. Thus, notwithstanding the general pattern of French industrial relations, technology agreements are most often negotiated at plant level. A 1986 evaluation of French collective bargaining in France resulting in new technology agreements showed that, of 20 agreements from 1983, 5 were concluded at branch level and 15 at firm level. (Bachet and Duchemin, 1989).

We can generalize this account of union structure to more countries in the community by reference to Figure 11.1. As Vickery and Campbell (1989) point out with the aid of this figure, there is an association between the level of bargaining and the degree to which labour and management negotiation are centralized. More centralized systems deal with issues such as the impact of IT at a higher level, and quite possibly in a more strategic manner than the more decentralized structures. Trade unions in the decentralized bargaining context are liable also to have fewer resources to call upon at local level, and may be less prepared to anticipate the range of effects of IT implementation. Moreover, discussion at national or industrial level between employers and labour is likely to aid an effective learning process for industrialists about problems, other than manpower issues, associated with the introduction of specific new technologies, if only because the process of negotiation opens a debate which may otherwise be privatized through the competition between firms on issues of technological advantage.

A related account is given by Della Rocca (1986), who distinguishes three main industrial relations regimes within which IT is introduced, proposing national exemplars of each.

1. Taking as an example the UK, confrontation with technical change is mediated via occupational and craft traditions, with high levels of informality surrounding rights and procedures (called into play in management-worker and worker-worker interactions). The trend is toward central negotiations, but slowly, through multiple channels, and via reduction of multiple unions; with efforts to establish procedural structures for IT introduction at local levels. There is also a trend to more formalized procedures, with competition among unions as well as between unions and employees in establishing conditions.
2. In Scandinavia and Germany, rights and responsibilities are regulated by external institutions which define working conditions and negotiation systems (even so local negotiations may not always be consistent with national positions). In such environments, the trend is toward decentralization (greater freedom of movement at local levels) together

with efforts to extend and reinforce procedures for dealing with IT-related change and the aspects of working conditions that these cover.

3. In Italy control of working conditions occurs at workplace level, with frequent recourse to industrial action within the context of politicized industrial relations and plurality of unions. Trend towards centralization via institutional channels (i.e. more agreement with state and employers on national frameworks for technical change, training and employee rights). However, trend away from formal, detailed arrangements (except in areas like job protection) toward more flexibility with respect to, for instance, allocation of staff, demarcations, etc.

The picture that emerges is one of Northern European countries tending towards more corporatistic or legalistic systems of industrial relations, with relatively high levels of consensus, as opposed to more voluntaristic and confrontational systems in Southern Europe and the UK. Governments, then, have tended to vary in terms of their levels of involvement in regulating working conditions. Where regulation has been most active, it should be noted, this is generally in terms of standards (e.g exposure to noise, to hazards, hours of work, training opportunities, etc.). There has been little involvement in legislating on more subtle features of job design, or on union rights *vis-a-vis* job design. The more elaborate systems of regulation do lay down rules about providing information to employees about change in technology; later we shall consider how far this goes toward facilitating participation in managing IT-related change.

The European Foundation (1985) also provides data on comparative industrial relations regimes associated with new IT. Its study is not as focused on manufacturing as those discussed above, though the analysis is broadly similar. Table 11.1, elaborated from a number of tables in European Foundation (1985), presents an overview of unionization and systems for dealing with the circumstances of the introduction of IT in five EU countries. Again the account is schematic, and the author stresses that traces of all of these features are found in all countries in practice.

Trade Unions and Technological Change

It has long been acknowledged that IT presents a large challenge for unions and workers in their struggle to gain better working conditions (Willman, 1986). The challenge to worker representatives is all the more serious given the large-scale restructuring of the European industrial basis in response to the economic difficulties of the 1970s and 1980s. The two effects cannot successfully be separated one from the other as the job losses associated with recession and technological change have both contributed to the 'new

Table 11.1 Unions and IT in Europe

Country	Union Density	Bargaining level	Technology agreements
Denmark	very high (>70%)	National mainly, some at company, little at plant level	Found at national/sectoral, company/plant levels as well as general agreements
Germany	low (<50%)	National mainly, some at company, little at plant level	Found at national/sectoral, company/plant (mainly on VDU use) levels as well as general agreements
Ireland	high (>60%)	Takes place at country and plant level	Mainly general agreements with few at company/plant level
Italy	low (<50%)	Mainly at company level, although bargaining does take place at national and plant levels	General and company/plant level agreements
UK	moderate (>50%)	Mainly at plant level with some company level bargaining	General and company/plant level agreements

Source: European Foundation, 1985, Tables 2-4

realism' of union organizers (Evans, 1984; Lane, 1989). The approach of unions in many European countries now stresses 'damage limitation' rather than militancy, and co-operation with management plans to create more efficient enterprises by reorganizing working patterns.

On the other hand, managers have had their hand strengthened in their attempts to exercise 'the manager's right to manage'. Thus, whilst there are attempts by the Commission to create a standard level of practice on industrial democracy, including employee rights to disclosure of information on impending technological change, the trend in some countries has been away from industrial participation (see for instance Treu and Negrelli, 1987). In many cases the process of technical change and particularly the associated capital investment strategies are seen as an area of sovereign managerial authority.

Research indicates that major investment decisions are taken centrally within an enterprise. Decisions on IT investment are, furthermore, more likely to be informed by a technocratic perspective than one which is responsive to human needs. That is, whilst senior management are likely to take opinion on the technical merits of the investment from internal experts or external consultants they are unlikely to hire external advisors for information on the work organization effects or to approach the union or works council until after the decision to invest has been taken (Deery, 1989; Fröhlich et al, 1990; Willman, 1986). We consider these empirical studies of participation in the following subsection.

Trade unions have found IT a considerable challenge. It is seen as providing new jobs and an end to some forms of drudgery; it is seen as threatening employment and as deskilling labour. The challenge has had technical aspects: unions, often under pressure on the economic climate of the 1980s, have often found themselves at a disadvantage in comprehending the implications of new IT systems. Their attention has often been centred on traditional issues of health and safety and ergonomics - and of course, job loss and training - and questions such as job design have been relatively neglected. As IT has been introduced in occupations which are poorly unionized and have little experience of using advanced technologies, the technical resources of unions have often been strained.

This is illustrated in a detailed review of UK trade unions' policies concerning new technologies (Dodgson and Martin, 1987). Analysis of settlements achieved in UK manufacturing over 1980-84 shows that the great majority included the introduction of new technology. But even in manufacturing, trade unions' research efforts on new technology were found to be low, implying a reactive approach to new technology, and strategies with at best limited success. UK unions may be more disadvantaged here than those in most Northern European countries, nevertheless the diagnosis may apply with force to much Europe.

A major part of union strategies in the UK was the establishment of New Technology Agreements around IT. Williams and Steward (1985) surveyed some 240 such agreements adopted in the UK over 1977-83. 1980 seems to have been the peak year of adoption; white collar unions were responsible for most agreements. Sectorally, engineering industries - especially 'high tech' firms - and public services dominate; occupationally, white-collar jobs predominate. In practice, both the adoption and content of new technology agreements fell well short of trade union objectives. Unions tended to be involved at relatively late stages in the introduction of new technology, and the agreements tend to be defensive and reactive in character. While fairly tight standards are often achieved over, say, health and safety, there is little progress (from the worker viewpoint) in terms of job design and reductions in working time.

A large-scale survey (Batstone and Gourlay, 1986) drawing on a sample of over 1000 UK shop stewards, mainly from large firms, concludes that the 'effects' of new technology are in large part a product of management and union strategies. The main consequence for union organization was not so much a weakening of union structures - indeed, stronger union organizations tended to be strengthened, weaker ones weakened. Rather, the result tended to be increased union awareness of the need to understand the broad context of management policies.

Can such results be generalised to other EU countries? In large part, they would seem to be. Deery (1989) reviewing recent literature, concluded that:

> in most industrialized countries trade unions have sought to establish the right to participate in decisions involving the introduction of technological change...During the late 1970s and early 1980s there was a gradual, although uneven evolution of these participative rights established by way of collective bargaining or through statutory means. In spite of these developments there is almost universal agreement that trade unions have exercised little influence over the process of technological decision-making and the subsequent organisation of work (Deery, 1989)

New Technology Agreements were pioneered in the UK, Germany and Scandinavian countries, but have been adopted in other Northern European EU countries, as Albertijn et al (1990) note in their study of Belgian agreements. This makes an interesting comparison to the UK case, since Belgium in the 1980s was more attached to a notion of consensus between social partners, trading-off economic and social concerns, than was the UK. With a national system of collective bargaining, Belgium established a national interprofessional technology agreement, covering the whole of the private sector, in 1983. Despite wide awareness of the agreement, a survey of shop stewards concluded that its impact in practice was marginal: a detailed study of nine companies revealed that the provision of information to workers under the agreement typically happened only after key implementation decisions (and often further steps in implementation) had been taken. The national agreement, furthermore, proved hard to apply within existing company information and negotiating frameworks, while one result of its introduction was to almost halt the formulation of company-level technology agreements.

Christis et al (1985, as summarized by Albertijn et al, 1990) compared technology agreements in Germany, the Netherlands, Sweden and the UK. While differences of nuance were found in the form of technology agreements in the different countries, it was concluded that the key factor in a union's role in technological change was not the existence or otherwise of such agreements: rather it was the degree to which the union's organization is able to cope with questions of technological change. (Similar conclusions are reached in Deery, 1989.) The agreements may be useful in securing release of information, but typically leave unions dealing with the consequences of IT implementation rather than participating in the choice of technology and the design of work.

Stepping back from these studies for a moment, Cressey (1990) makes an important distinction between strategies which can be used by unions and workforces in respect of IT-related technical change. Control can be exerted:

1. prior to change, influencing decisions on the type of change contemplated;
2. during introduction of IT, influencing how change is introduced;
3. after the event, reacting to change, seeking to control its 'effects'.

Contrasting different case studies conducted for the European Foundation, Cressey notes that control prior to change is most likely within frameworks such as exist in Denmark and Germany providing for roles, rights and responsibilities about workplace change - and which command a degree of consensus. (Austria and other Scandinavian countries with what are sometimes called 'social democratic corporatist systems' are also characterized in this way.) The main focus for influence during the change process is the enterprise; procedural conditions at this level (usually in the form of new technology agreements) were relatively rare. The most common union role was control after the event. Here the typical foci were conditions such as job security, retraining and redeployment, regulation of the pace of work, wages, etc. Again we see trade unions constrained to following traditional objectives, despite wide-ranging changes associated with the introduction of new IT.

'Traditional objectives' may vary from country to country. Tallard (1989) sees both French and German unions as typically dealing with the consequences of new technology, with employers seeing involvement in investment decisions as an infringement of their rights. But the national vocational structures lead to very different emphases:

> In Germany the main national agreements have sought to protect the skilled worker; the cost of deskilling has been made so high as to affect the employer's choice of technology. The German system is designed above all to protect 'job property rights': job classifications, use of skills and pay levels...In France the main agreements at both national and company level have concerned grading and training. Because of the limited importance of formally certified qualifications...occupational status owes more to the worker's classification within a relatively rigid grading system...Training is the central focus of [IT] bargaining: it has been the basis of a national multi-industry agreement and of a law requiring negotiations at company level...[IT] bargaining in Germany centres on the flexibility of the main rules of the system; in France, on structural; changes to the rules...In Germany, because rules are flexible, change can occur organically; but in France, because rules are rigid, they themselves must be altered (Tallard, 1989: p. 294).

From a survey of trade union secretariats in Western Europe, Bamber (1989) reached broadly congruent conclusions concerning international and sectoral differences. He summarizes the results to date:

> [In] countries with adversarial traditions of industrial relations (most English-speaking countries), unions are less likely to cooperate with technological change than their counterparts in countries with recent traditions of social partnership in industrial relations (West Germany and the Scandinavian countries)...differences in union behaviour reflecting contrasting legacies of employers' habits...British unions have traditionally placed more emphasis on bargaining after decisions have been made, rather than on participation in making decisions, in contrast with many of their German and Scandinavian counterparts, which face more paternalistic employers...Even in countries with adversarial traditions...many managers are aiming to introduce quasi-paternalistic programmes which may be called employee involvement..or quality circles...
>
> ...we can begin to predict union responses by posing or answering four questions. First, is it a craft or an industrial union? (The former generally oppose change which destroys the basis of their craft.) Second, what is the state of the product market? (Unions are more likely to accept change when there is a high degree of competition and an expanding market.) Third, what is the type of technological change (...number of jobs affected...skills required...)? Fourth, at what stage is the innovation? (Union opposition is most likely at an early stage, when there is considerable uncertainty about the change.) (Bamber, 1989: pp. 212-213)

Della Rocca (1986), summarizing studies carried out for the Olivetti Foundation, makes the additional points that, partly in response to the blurring of occupational demarcations in IT-using work organizations, the role of informal consultation and negotiation has grown. (He contrasts this with a union view that this growth is due to improved quality of bargaining.) This reflects the problems and disputes that arise regarding work allocation and demarcation lines between functional groups.

Figure 11.2   Modes of participation

No Involvement	management planned and executed schemes
Information Provision	briefing sessions information agreements group forums on change
Consultation	advisory committees project groups new technology committees steering groups
Negotiation	productivity agreements protective clauses in general agreement planning agreements new technology agreements
Joint decision-making	veto powers status quo clauses joint decision-making bodies

Source: Cressey, 1990, Table 4.3

PARTICIPATION IN TECHNOLOGICAL CHANGE

Quantitative Analysis

This section will mainly refer to workplace level studies of participation in technical change before moving on to a series of further-reaching questions about IT and trends in participation.   There are a number of other important levels of analysis, especially detailed qualitative case studies of participation at plant level.   Cressey (1990) provides an overview of such research, in addition Cressey gives a useful guide to the wide variety of forms which participation can take.   He places it on a scale from no involvement of workers at all to joint decision-making of workers and management (Figure 11.2).   This chart does not, it should be noted, readily accommodate the legal dimension of such participative mechanisms - e.g. whether new technology agreements are legally enforceable.

Perhaps the most ambitious, and certainly the most extensive cross-national survey study of these issues, is that presented by Fröhlich et al (1990) for the European Foundation.   This involves surveys of over 2000 each of managers and worker representatives, drawn from in five IT-intensive sectors (mechanical engineering, electronics, banking, insurance and retailing), in five countries (Denmark, France, Germany Italy and the UK), in early 1986.   No involvement of the workforce at all in IT-related change was reportedly rather rare. However, involvement mainly centred upon disclosure of information. More participatory forms of involvement were extremely limited, consultation and negotiation and joint decision-making. Furthermore:

> The extent of involvement is distinctly higher in...operational phases. According to management the percentage of 'no involvement' is about 35% in the planning phase; it is 41% according to workplace representatives. The percentage increases in the selection phase to 41% and 57% respectively. Thus, in both strategic phases, 'no involvement' and weak forms of involvement were dominant. This pattern looks distinctly different in the two operational phases: 'no involvement' decreases sharply, while the share of 'consultation and negotiation' sharply increases. In the introduction phase managers report nearly 30%, and worker representatives roughly 25%, of 'consultation and negotiation'.   In the post-evaluation phase ratings of 35% can be observed. However, 'joint decision-making' has a different pattern; it lies between 5 and 12% in all phases of technology introduction...it is   found only in a small minority of companies in the five countries studied. In Germany and Denmark the percentage is significantly higher   (Fröhlich et al, 1990: pp. 12-13).

Intentions as to future involvement were also explored in this study, whose authors conclude that changes in attitude are occurring which may well change this general picture of low participation (Table 11.2). Nevertheless, only around 30% of mangers actually favoured more workforce involvement, as compared to 55% of worker representatives. Among these are managers prepared to promote employee involvement in strategic as well as operational phases of innovation, although it is apparent that the enthusiasm for more participation is stronger in the latter phases.

More detailed studies have been carried out in various individual countries. Apart from the studies of technology agreements, one of the most detailed studies is Daniel's survey across all sectors of the UK economy in 1984 (Daniel 1987) which reports, in line with the results discussed earlier, a relatively low level of union involvement in managing technical change -

Table 11.2   Intentions on worker involvement

Phase	Managers		Workers' representatives	
	Past	Future	Past	Future
Planning				
No involvement	35	15	0	8
Consultation/negotiation	15	37	15	45
Joint decision making	5	9	5	25
Selection				
No involvement	47	22	55	13
Consultation/negotiation	12	30	10	40
Joint decision making	5	10	5	25
Implementation				
No involvement	20	10	25	5
Consultation/negotiation	30	45	30	45
Joint decision making	10	15	5	30
Post-evaluation				
No involvement	22	8	25	2
Consultation/negotiation	35	50	32	50
Joint decision making	10	15	5	30

Source: Fröhlich et al, 1990: 18-23, drawn from text and a series
of graphic representations

even in sites where unions are recognized, only around 50% of shop
stewards were consulted at any stage of the introduction of IT affecting
manual workers. A similar proportion of cases involved no consultation (or
even discussion with individual workers) about the innovation where there
was no union recognition. Consultations were more prevalent when office
workers were involved: this appears to generalize to other countries,

according to Cressey's (1990) review to be discussed below. Northcott and Walling's (1988) study of UK manufacturing likewise concluded that worker resistance to IT is a relatively insignificant factor (despite a few well-known areas of conflict). Only some 8% of managers surveyed saw opposition from unions or shopfloor workers to be a very important problem - as compared to 7% regarding opposition from senior management as a serious obstacle! These figures pale in comparison to those for other problems: 51% cite skill shortages, and over 20% each of a range of other (mostly financial and technical) problems.

Research has repeatedly demonstrated, then, that usually it is only once the decision to adopt IT has been taken that working conditions are considered. This means that the ability of unions or workers to influence the initial decision is often extremely limited. This applies even, for instance, in Belgium where notification of such decisions is required 3 months in advance - but where planning which strongly bore on social dimensions of the technological change was often taken long before notification was required (Albertijn et al, 1990). This confirms the point made in the discussion of health and safety aspects of IT: legislation by itself may be insufficient to improve conditions thoroughly (though this does not diminish its necessity).

Further evidence on this topic comes from Cressey's (1990) review of case studies carried out for the European Foundation. Across a range of IT and countries, it was most common for simple notification of the workforce to be the only approach to worker participation used; there was a move toward more notification and consultation when the phase of selection of technologies was entered, though consultation was local and based on specific problems, with little notification; bargaining, consultation and joint decision-making were used more extensively in the implementation phase. Cressey notes that in the selection phase higher degrees of involvement were observed with NC and WP equipment, where scope for choice had not been foreclosed in the planning stage; and white-collar groups were consulted more often.

This study suggests that participation is likely to be concentrated at upper reaches of the company hierarchy in earlier stages of the process of technological change, opening up to less senior groups the further towards or into the implementation phase one proceeds. A NEDO (1983) survey of plants in the UK electronics industry likewise found consultation to be much more prevalent at later stages of technological innovation (implementation) than at earlier stages (planning, choice of equipment). This survey also assessed views of consultative arrangements - while management and unions report different benefits, both groups tend to be positive. Cressey (1990) similarly found that when participation did occur, it tended to be rated positively:

1. it helped to improve the quality of working life, work environment, training arrangements, safety conditions, job security and in some cases there were gains arising from increased productivity;
2. participation also allowed for the expression, adaptation and resolution of conflicting interests as change emphasizes the need for problem resolution;
3. it contributes to improved industrial relations founded upon trust.

Cressey's conclusion is that participation in the introduction of IT, while limited, does take place in various forms. Management, trade unions and workers themselves do not form monolithic blocs in their views of participation; each is liable to perceive some utility when participation is relevant to the outcomes they seek.

Innovation may actually be facilitated by technological choices that are clearly beneficial to their users; and innovative ideas may be more readily forthcoming from workers who are not alienated from, and ignorant of, the technologies they are using. Technologies that support skilled workforces and humane work environments may even have an edge over others in international markets, as more groups of workers demand greater levels of participation in IT decisions.

Determinants of Participation

Management staff are relatively advantaged in terms both of technical understanding and influence. Some professional groups, of course, like doctors and engineers, may have particular expertise that gives them a measure of autonomous control over the direction of technical change: they are in close contact already with the design process, it is they, rather than management, that are listened to as users. Such groups, too, may be interested in preserving their own realms of decision making (and their control over subordinates). The strength of their professional organizations could well prove an important influence on the rate and direction of technical change. But 'information workers' in general seem better placed than some other components of the workforce; most of the New Technology Agreements introduced in Britain, for example, involved 'white-collar' unions.

To add to the structural inequality in the relative position of management and labour in decisions about new technology, is the general problem that unions rarely have the resources to call upon technical expertise in support of technological systems which are more in tune with ameliorated workplace design. Sometimes a programme of education for union officials might be necessary to create an integrated market of information about issues which other unions have encountered, and to create the opportunity to form good standards of practice, through one national union system interacting with another. French unions, for example, have been typified as having a much lower awareness of issues such as personal liberties in the modernization process than their German or Scandinavian counterparts (Lemaitre and Teyssier, 1987) and may benefit from direct exposure to German union experiences. This is partly due to the speed of technological advance and the associated high cost of expertise in the area. It is also a consequence of the flexibility of IT. The array of different combinations of hardware and software which can be put together is vast, and consequently unions are unable to establish any more than (very) general guidelines on how technological systems should be established. Unlike management they cannot produce a guide to technological implementation on an enterprise by enterprise basis.

The possibilities for industrial democracy in the initial stages of IT implementation are therefore structurally restricted. The review of empirical studies of participation above suggests that this remains true even when unions are supported by some of the most protective industrial democracy legislation to be found anywhere in Europe. Unions cannot hope to anticipate, centrally, the technical trajectories of each individual management, and if they had the resources to construct a plan for each workplace, they are unlikely to be given the information in sufficient time to provide an adequate response.

In contrast, however, there are more immediate possibilities for worker representatives to take an active role in the process of introducing new technology into a specific workplace. At this level, the management often require the staff to adapt to the new technology and to aid in the process of debugging the new hardware and software as it moves out of the implementation stage into full use. Successful reports of programmes and experiments to incorporate workers into these stages of development are quite common (e.g. Mumford, 1983; Piganiol, 1989; Kern and Schumann, 1987, CAM, 1986), and can lead to substantial improvements in working conditions in concert with the introduction of new technological systems.

To date, negotiations between unions and management concerning the introduction of IT have very largely focused on the specific conditions under which a technology chosen by management will be introduced. These include issues of training and retraining, work pacing and supervision, health hazards and ergonomics, hours of work and job loss. Though these are important issues, there is scope for exploring job design and choice of technologies beyond the protection of existing skills and occupational categories. Intervention into job design requires capability to debate about technical choice and, indeed, the design of technologies and technological systems. It means moving beyond simply transcribing traditional (and vitally important) union concerns like pay, grading, hours, and health and safety into the analysis of new IT. As the discussion earlier implies, there are both technical reasons (lack of access to expertise) and ideological ones (fears of unions being seen to be too close to management if they get involved in designing conditions of work) which make this difficult, especially in countries with a traditionally combative industrial relations system.

It is hard to take up new issues, and pursue new strategies, at a time when unions already feel under attack from many sides, and are often forced to focus on bread-and-butter issues of protecting jobs and wages. But this arena may well play a great role in determining future occupational structures - and unionization prospects - and work quality. Deery (1989) identifies four circumstances affecting participation, and two classes of factor affecting influence. These are summarized in Table 11.3, and provide a convenient overview of many of the topics discussed above.

The factors as listed here are abstracted from the broader social circumstances in which industrial relations operate. Certainly such features of the national regime as the degree of support given for union education activities and access to company information will be important. Likewise, the degree to which different unions are competing for membership from the same occupational groups, or have a tradition of liaison and coordination, will be a significant determinant of their scope for action.

The most common conclusion on the possibilities for greater industrial democracy in the introduction of IT seems to be that unions should aim to develop general guidelines to suit a variety of potential technological systems, whilst aiming to educate worker representatives at the local level to take the maximum benefit to working conditions during the actual implementation process at the level of the workplace (Deery, 1990). This means organizational change overcoming three major problems experienced by unions:

1. poor communications between their central office and the shop floor undergoing technological change;
2. poor inter-union communications, even where the same company and workplace is involved;
3. difficulties associated with laying down standards in the abstract, which lead unions to respond on an *ad hoc* basis to many proposed changes.

Table 11.3   Influences   on   union   involvement   in   technological   decisions

	Favourable	Unfavourable
Affecting participation		
Technological Objectives	Quality/performance enhancement, with problem-solving skills integral to success	Cost reduction, with little technical or operational dependence on workers
Management Style	Collaborative & open approach adopted throughout organisation	Conflictual & closed with different & competing management interests
Type of Innovations	Incremental changes with moderate workplace implications	Radical changes initiated at the top with major organizational implications
Union Power	Members strategically placed, highly unionized, and facing common and recognized technological threat	Members marginally located, lightly unionized, and faced with variable or uncertain 'effects' from technology
Affecting influence		
Organizational Expertise	Union organisation: united & cohesive; technically knowledgeable & skilled membership; internal & external assistance; strategic policy orientation; ability to obstruct change & force consideration of own proposals.	Inadequate internal coordination & communications; work groups unable to design organizational alternatives; lack of research resources; short-term & tactical policy orientation; difficulty in using sanctions where disagreements arise.
Organizational Structure	Robust at key levels where management decisions made & implemented; single union, or coordinated approach by several unions.	Gaps in intra-union organization at company or workplace level; competitive multi-union structure.

Source: Deery, 1989, Table 1 and 2

This pragmatic approach, however, is inadequate from the unions' point of view not only because it implies the acceptance by workers of the overall technological strategies of management, but because, as we have argued, a major issue in the development of IT is the trend towards networked workplaces.

INDUSTRIAL RELATIONS IN THE INFORMATION AGE?

Various developments suggest that industrial relations practice will continue to evolve. Disillusion has grown with many of the strategies pursued by trade unions, as their limitations in terms of achieving better conditions of work have been revealed. This even extends to more adventurous strategies such as those (notably in Scandinavia, with some German efforts) involving workforce participation in design of IT systems. For a review, see Læssøe and Rasmussen (1989). These strategies are important ones in that they draw on workforce skills, both in identifying potential innovations and in avoiding designs which overlook user requirements. They also have the capacity for stimulating much greater interest in and awareness of the process of technical change, and of raising the level of understanding of the operations of one's organization considerably. The approaches being developed to facilitate this sort of involvement are novel and evolving ones. Thus while a number of problems can be cited with this approach, these should not be seen as reasons to curtail experiments of this sort:

1. Even if one group of workers is involved, this is no guarantee that a successful product will not be diffused by conventional means to other workplaces - and management can quite legitimately claim that the same system should not need to be reinvented every time it is needed;
2. The time taken to acquire relevant expertise and to disseminate awareness among the workforce can be extensive, making the innovation process longer than that in competing firms;
3. It is not always clear that the product eventually emerging is notably different from alternatives available in the marketplace;
4. Treating the innovation (and thus the participation process) as a one-off affair is inadequate, since technical change is liable to be an ongoing process.

These are relatively rare experiments: as we have seen, much more widely-diffused strategies for worker involvement in technological change have been new technology agreements. Here too, there are signs of disillusionment; a slow-down is widely reported in the formation of technology agreements. For instance, no-strike agreements have replaced new technology agreements as the main focus of union debate in the UK. No-strike arrangements are widely touted by some commentators as the way forward for industrial relations in the information society.

However, these no-strike deals are only relevant to IT in a limited way. They tend to be, more than anything else, about the organization of greenfield sites. The establishment of greenfield sites is part of the process of economic restructuring in which IT plays a part, to be sure, and attention has been focused on the use of these deals by high-tech (often US or Japanese) multinationals. But they are a feature of these specific conditions, where there are new sites and typically unorganized workforces - sometimes drawn from groups of the population that have never been unionized, sometimes from skilled workers caught in areas of industrial decline. Often unions have been only too happy to enter into these agreements to secure work in the area, or to give one particular union a key foothold in what is seen to be a sunrise sector. As such features are not all that common, these arrangements have not developed more generally to any extent. Perhaps the main development here is efforts to increase the scope of no-strike deals in key parts of the public sector, typically in countries where neo-conservative parties are in power.

Managers across Europe have been seeking to reduce union prerogatives, often under the banner of increasing 'flexibility'. During the 1980s a measure of success has been achieved here, with unions typically on the defensive, having a great deal of accommodation to do to cope with changing economic circumstances. Among their problems have been declining membership (related to the growth of non-unionized sectors and the erosion of their manufacturing base), shifts in public opinion and political climate (especially neo-conservatism), and relatively high unemployment. Many of these pressures will continue in the 1990s, but demographic factors are to some extent working in unions' favour in most EU countries. Shortages of new entrants into the labour market, unless compensated for by new immigration (from Eastern Europe?) on a scale that is unlikely to be welcomed in most countries, will probably reduce the threat of unemployment and lead to more concessions in the way of union recognition and power.

In this light, we might expect greater union influence over working conditions, and an emphasis on protecting working conditions at the local level, probably by participating in the process of implementation of new IT. But, this is to ignore one important trend. As we have stressed, the 1980s tendency for local level workplaces to increasingly become merely components of the overall technological strategy of the enterprise is liable to increase in the 1990s.

This has considerable implications for working conditions and union strategies concerning them. In the future, many more enterprises will cease to be a series of separate workplaces linked together solely by their respective functions in the organization as a whole. Instead the enterprise will be a much more fluid system of technical, informational and manual resources, which are coordinated and directed through the organizational information system. This is liable to effectively undermine traditional models of a fixed workplace and labour process, with its associated and co-located technological structure and labour force.

To be sure, a great deal of technological hardware will still be situated in specific locations, and will be associated with certain stages of the labour process. Such rigidities imply that workers will maintain greater or lesser capabilities of acting collectively to influence the nature of working conditions. However, one can imagine extreme cases where the use of highly flexible information technology, such as the simple personal computer, can be used to create extremely fluid job descriptions and work environments. An extreme example of this is telework - whether of the much-discussed but little-realized telecottage variety, or as part of the more immediately significant creation of remote 'back office' environments. In either case, the important point is that the employer has the ability to rapidly alter the nature of the work being done, by switching different components of the labour process from place to place, or workstation to workstation. This is liable to be a major element of 'flexibility' at the organizational level.

Such an integration of workplaces could operate between regions, between states in Europe, and across continental boundaries. The prospect, for instance, of applying labour resources in one country, to the database resources of another, using technological capital located in a third, is not unrealistic: major financial companies are already pursuing such strategies. Yet it fundamentally challenges the ability of both workers' representatives and legislative bodies to provide an adequate system of protection for workers and their working conditions.

In the case of widespread application of the networking potentials of new IT, therefore, the ability of worker representatives to effectively intervene in the decision to implement new technology is likely to be limited. This need not even be an explicit form of managerial resistance to union activity: it may be more of a by-product of networking strategies than a central goal. But, the evidence seems to show that with relatively few exceptions, managers seek to place limits on worker involvement, and to maximize their own freedom of action, (the bright spot is that if survey responses are to be believed, the number of these exceptions will grow). Even where there is national legislation which requires that information be given to worker representatives on impending technological change there is a significant problem of non-compliance. Unions and workers have been more effective at ameliorating the way that new technology is applied, than in affecting the decisions on the overall technological system design.

Despite the disillusionment with strategies of active participation, our analysis of technological trajectories suggests that, given the increased scale of operation of European firms, and the important role of IT in the transformation of traditional concepts of the workplace-based labour process, greater involvement of workplace representatives in technological change must continue to be an objective. There may well be scope for exploring new modes of securing such involvement, learning from the partial successes of technology agreements and other mechanisms. In particular, it will be necessary to find ways of articulating enterprise-wide and local involvement. The localization of effective union action on industrial participation in the development of new technology is liable to neglect the increasing importance of firms which are managed as networks, rather than as a set of separate plants.

Again the issue of management awareness and training emerges as an important one. There is some evidence of increasing willingness to admit workforce participation in determining the trajectory of technological change. Efforts to further these trends, and bring them into harmony with new network structures of industrial organization, are required. Attention will need to be directed at the threats posed by managers 'externalizing' problems of industrial democracy and poor working conditions to sub contractors and suppliers in new network structures.

12. Afterword and Policy Conclusions

Luc Soete and Chris Freeman

The analyses presented in this book point to the overriding importance of the diffusion process of new information technologies. This diffusion is important not only for economic growth and employment but is important to the performance of the IT sector itself. It must be underlined that this diffusion process is ultimately a *social process*. Information technology clearly represents a potential increase in productivity and growth. In Europe, much of the policy has concentrated upon technological potential, with rather less concern for the social process. An approach to IT policy which balances the social and the technological is particularly important given both the often disappointing realization of the potential benefits of the use of IT and the disappointing performance of IT and IT intensive industries.

The completion of the Single European Market in 1992 is a significant contributor to the range of pressures which are leading to significant rationalization and increased efficiency in European industry. The studies represented here support findings elsewhere that the successful transformation and growth of European industry crucially depends upon its interaction with the social environment of Europe. The integration of structural changes associated with the introduction of new IT could represent a basis for long lasting high growth in Europe well into the 21st Century, generating new job opportunities. Reaping the long term benefits and advantages from new IT therefore is a crucial challenge for all European countries, with significant implications for their international competitiveness.

The importance of the social and organizational 'incorporation' of such structural changes is not surprisingly at the core of the findings of this book. This has emerged quite consistently from the management of innovation literature where successes and failures in innovation are generally more closely related to organizational and social factors than the quality of the technology. When dealing with a pervasive set of technologies, as is represented by IT, with a significant effect throughout the economic system, it soon becomes obvious that far from being imposed on society, the technology has to be imposed through a process of social and institutional

217

change, negotiation and interaction.   As these chapters show, there are various bottlenecks, shortages of adequately trained manpower, lack of retraining and educational provisions, work organization problems that will significantly impede the realization of the potential output and productivity gains associated with IT.   This is also true of institutional and regulatory barriers to IT-related demand, where the fragmented markets of Europe might prevent demand reaching a   sufficiently large scale to make it profitable for European producers to invest.

The policy recommendations which we put forward, following the research programme of which the chapters in this book were a substantial part,   fell into three distinct groups.   First, we were concerned that there should be major efforts to reduce the diffusion bottlenecks   in work organization, skills, education and training areas.   The aim should be to unleash the growth of efficiency of the more rapid diffusion of IT in the context of the larger European Single Market.   We were also concerned to reduce the negative social externalities' of very rapid diffusion of IT - particularly the danger of an increased duality in the labour market, with increased unemployment amongst the primarily unskilled workforce concentrated amongst ethnic minorities, school drop outs and hard to train individuals.   There was also the danger of heightened regional growth inequalities emerging across Europe.   The greater mobility of labour in a Single European labour market, particularly the more highly skilled workers, will raise severe social and internal cohesion problems going well beyond the need for retraining, labour adjustments, etc. Conventional Regional Fund provisions from this may prove to be insufficient.   There is nothing in the diffusion of IT so far which promises a harmonized, well distributed development pattern.   If anything the reverse is true.

Second,   recommendations can be aimed at improving the general environment for the diffusion of IT across Europe.   By increasing the ability of the IT producing industry to respond to new demands at home and abroad and by policy actions which increase the demand for such products and services, new areas of employment and growth may be generated. One of the major bottlenecks here relates to the urgent need for an integrated, but not monopoly provided, telecommunications infrastructure across Europe. There are indications of a need for European technology policy to become more demand led, so that the increased technological capabilities can be enhanced through direct feedback from learning and experience.

Third, the policy making bodies at national and supra-national level need to facilitate the coherence of micro-economic policies on technology, employment, work organization, training and education. In particular, and as demonstrated even in the qualitative studies represented by this book, the near absence of adequate employment monitoring research tools represents a major gap in our ability to talk with authority about trends in the employment and technology.

It is not so much the IT itself, the hardware, which should be the focus of attention, but rather the social integration of such technology. Particularly in the case of a pervasive set of technologies such as IT, this argument has crucial implications. It means that technology cannot be imposed on society, it has to be mediated through a process of institutional change and negotiation.

The development of human resources is a complex system involving a number of different national and local institutions and authorities. Furthermore, firms play a leading role in determining the nature of demand for labour and in fashioning enterprise-based training and utilization of labour. Finally, the participation in the labour market is not only influenced by education and labour market policies but is also influenced by the interface with policies aimed at social protection. Similarly, tax policies play an important role in determining attractiveness of investment in human resources relative to physical and other investments. Policies aimed at human resources need in other words to consider action on the part of a number of actors. Given the range of different actors, the co-ordination of policy-making is absolutely critical. As the chapters on training show, there is therefore and explicit need for better co-ordination between education, the traditional preserve of education ministries and training, where labour market authorities and the private sector play the dominant role. As for the level of demand for labour, changes in management practices are likely to have a fundamental impact on the development and utilization of employees. Here the diffusion of IT opens up new directions and possibilities, thus we begin our discussion of policy recommendations by looking at issues of management practices and work organization.

WORK ORGANIZATION AND MANAGEMENT PRACTICES

Social Policy and Technology: a New Priority

The detailed analysis in this book points to a number of crucial areas for policy action both at the Pan-European and the national level. At the European level, as with technology policy, the main goal has been to strengthen European infrastructure. Here the social infrastructure, particularly as represented by the Social Charter, has concentrated on the development of a number of minimum basic social rights. In the words of the European Commission 'ensuring a minimum of consistency', between various employment contract forms 'in order to avoid the danger of distortions of competition and increase the transparency of the labour market at the Community level'. In doing so, we believe the Community has taken a crucial and essential initiative, by setting out the broad social infrastructural framework within which different countries' social policies can in the long term be further harmonized, given the widespread diversity in existing social legislation between member countries. However, just as in the case of technological infrastructure, to limit European social policies to the development of a minimum set of harmonization rules on employment contract, social security and health and safety at work is to dramatically underestimate the importance of the social environment in the structural change processes associated with the single market, and particularly the diffusion of IT.

In our view, the advantages of the harmonization and strengthening of the social infrastructure within the EU will only be realized if they are accompanied by the development of policies aimed at improving the 'social' integration of new technologies both at the private and public sector level. Alongside the Social Charter the interaction between technology, labour and organization is an essential and urgent domain for policy research and action. There is now a significant need for research and policy advice on the issue of how to improve the competitiveness of enterprises *at the social level*. As this book illustrates, the latter is one of the most essential issues in the long term determination of European competitiveness.

The implication which we draw is that there is an existing gap at the European level in the integration between technology and social policy. The organization of work, which lies at the intersection of these two policy frameworks, because of its influence to European competitiveness is as important an issue as progress on the Social Charter.   Also, given the involvement of many actors, policies aiming at institutional implantation of education and research in technology, labour and organization have implications at supra-national level and so require supporting policies and institutional infrastructures.

Workforce Participation

Effective implementation of IT requires a firm positive commitment by the workforce. It is not just a question of passing information down from the upper layers of management, although this is also essential, but of responsible involvement at all levels, which requires more active forms of consultation and joint decision making including social dialogue on initial training.   The European Commission has tried to promote such wider participation, particularly through studies supported by the European Foundation for the Improvement of Living and Working Conditions reviewed here. The findings indicate that the countries which have experienced more advanced forms of participation tend to have better industrial relations and firmer decision making. It seems the case that changes in the relations between managers and trade unions should seek to enrich participation in technological change.

Trade unions are often ill-prepared to cope effectively with technological change, and the implementation of new technologies and related aspects of working practices. Appropriate programmes for raising awareness, knowledge and skills and for facilitating the development of social networks which can relay learning experiences are required. The Single European Market requires going beyond existing trade union structures, so that information can be shared across union and national boundaries and between unions and other groups, such as researchers, education and health services.

Improving the Quality of Technology Management

A recurring issue in the book has been the need for more professional management of the implementation of new technologies. This requires a move away from traditional technocratic orientations, within which 'systems' are selected and implemented, with ergonomic and job design issues entering at a late stage, to one in which managers are trained to be more effective in developing the synergies between human and technical resources. Such developments depend upon more direct formal training of managers in the disciplines of technological management, which is so often marginalized within the training of higher level technical and professional staff and even within specialist management higher education, such as Master of Business Administration courses.

One potential advantage of a Single Europe is that there should be more opportunity for comparison between 'best practice' in technology management. As we have seen, new IT is implemented in very different ways in different firms and countries even though engineers and consultants often start out with what constitutes 'normal best practice.' Whilst we do not claim that this is solely a matter of voluntary choice (corporate decisions are based on a mix of factors including skill, organizational structure, and pre-existent patterns of investment), management competence and the cultural predispositions of management clearly are important. These variations lead to stark differences in prospects for working conditions in different European countries. In order to further develop and spread best practice there is a clear need for mechanisms to transmit new institutional practices, such as; staff secondment schemes, international workshops, cross-national training schemes, etc.

Whilst European Commission sponsored measures such as the Human Capital and Mobility scheme are a move in the right direction, it is necessary for all these efforts to achieve legitimacy in the eyes of management. For instance, the dissemination of new information about management practice has to be visible in the literature and in the conferences attended by senior management personnel. These approaches cannot simply be constrained to an information programme on the potentialities of new technologies. The information needs to extend abstract intelligence into practical know-how and action. Such programmes are important as part of establishing a demonstration effect which could aid the 'transfer of technology' (in its widest sense), from more advanced sectors and regions to the lagging areas and industries.

SKILLS, TRAINING AND RE-TRAINING

A large proportion of the training and retraining which takes place in Europe is and will remain at enterprise level. Obviously, firms are in the best position to assess the specific requirements of their own product and process innovations or their organization's reforms. Such changes are related to their own strategies for research and development and new investment, which cannot be known or integrated by government. Such strategies are often related to programmes affecting company personnel policies, including promotions, recruitment, retirement, participation and employee morale. Governments are also deeply involved in training and retraining through creating an appropriate environment, appropriate incentives and supporting infrastructure. However, a more effective integration between these two levels of training provision is becoming urgent, because of the increasing rate of obsolescence of the existing skills base amongst individuals, firms and the wider labour market.

In a situation in which skills go out of date quickly, retraining is important for at least two reasons. First, the existing profiles of skills cannot simply be scrapped. They have to be modified and substituted over a considerable period. Often it is a question of adding to or combining existing skills. Almost always it is a question of importing understanding of some wider objectives of the organization and its changing role. Sometime there is a need to establish entirely new qualification structures. The software skills gap experienced by many firms is being tackled only in part by the new recruitment of young, recently-trained and educated professionals. It is also being resolved by internal re-training of existing engineers, technicians and other personnel within firms. Such people have the advantage of greater familiarity with the firm's products and problems, even though they may lack deep professional training. In the short-run, the re-training and upgrading efforts of firms are essential until there has been an adjustment of long term significance from the formal education system.

Second, the rate of change in IT is such that constant re-training will be necessary even if higher and further education sectors can meet the demand for the output of electronic engineers, software engineers, systems designers, programmers, etc. Life-time re-training is becoming a regular feature of the activity of many firms which are involved in continuous innovation in products and processes and constant renewal of both physical and human capital.

Although much of the re-training will take place at the initiative of firms, many firms are too small, too financially weak, or unwilling to provide it adequately. There is, therefore, an important role for government policy both at the national and European level, in promoting a sufficient level of re-training activity. There are a number of key issues which emerge from the need for government aid in making sure that the general level of re-training activity reaches its optimal level. In particular, there is a need for attention to imbalances and gaps in the provision of re-training.

1. In strategic sectors, such as telecommunications, there are likely to be demographically driven skill bottlenecks over the next 10 years. Sectors such as telecommunications are likely to show substantial and continuing shifts in skill requirements as the demand for more routine jobs supporting network provision decline relative to the growing areas of new telematic services and other valued added services.
2. The re-training strategies in less advanced regions need to reflect current best practice rather than historic practices. So, for instance, there is an opportunity for firms located in such regions to leapfrog obsolete centralized patterns of IT use. The relative lack of inertia created by institutional patterns established under earlier generations of IT may even be turned to a competitive advantage.
3. The formal training system, based as it is upon longstanding and fairly rigid disciplinary boundaries, is often quite slow to reflect the need for managers and workers whose skills span traditional areas of expertise and authority. Thus meeting the need for hybrid managers, who are knowledgeable about IT but are also effective administrators, strategists and entrepreneurs is an area which can only be approached through closer partnership between firms and the training system. It may also require collaboration between firms, as individually they may be unable to provide a sufficient range of experience to support retraining activities. At a most fundamental level, there is also a need for widespread basic

retraining in adult IT literacy and numeracy as part of an overall training policy.
4. There have been actions to recruit women into technical IT-related occupations, which are often motivated by skill shortages. Insufficient attention is often paid to the very real difficulties which women face in working in occupations traditionally regarded as 'men's work'. The opportunities for women to play enhanced roles in 'traditional women's occupations' should also not be ignored. For example, secretaries can use IT to improve office efficiency, and with appropriate training could take on many junior administrative tasks.
5. Retraining in order for workers to take part more effectively in the process of technical change is another area of potential development. Participation in technological change can be important both in terms of workers being able to adapt to new techniques more quickly, and being able to help define more efficient and humane ways of working with the technology.

THE VET SYSTEM

Developments in the 1980s have shown the need for big changes in public education, as well as in industrial training and retraining. Amongst the major issues are:

1. the blurring of the distinction between education and training;
2. the growing role of part-time education and adult education;
3. the rapidly growing demand for certain professions engendered by IT, such as electronic engineers, systems designers, etc;
4. the accompanying demand for computing skills across a wide range of other jobs;
5. the need for a more generally highly educated workforce;
6 the rising importance of inter-personal communication skills;
7 the simultaneous need for educational breadth to be combined with deep professional competence.

The distinction between education and training is blurring as the result of several developments. Learning is no longer viewed as being coterminous with the end of extended adolescence; rather it is a lifelong occupation. Though the responsibility for scientific and technological research and the preparation of highly qualified manpower has never been confined solely to educational institutions of higher learning, these activities are increasingly taking place in industry and other settings outside the education community.

Education and training are less and less the concern of the formal education sector alone. The increasing importance of education qualifications and training as a determinant of labour market authorities has meant that they are provided increasingly by the labour market authorities, employers and others whose main mission has been other than providing education.

These developments imply the need for a re-examination of the fundamental dualism which pervades educational philosophies, that is the dualism between education for the 'citizen' and that for the world of work. Core curriculum needs to cater not so much for an end product but for lifelong learning - initial education is a stepping stone or further education. Particular emphasis should be put on *transferable skills*, including problem solving and entrepreneurial skills as well as developing positive attitudes and values towards later education and training in different settings.

In a number of European countries educational systems do not equip people well either for further education and training or for the labour market. This problem is compounded by the ageing demographic picture, in which the adult learner becomes important, in some cases perhaps more so than the young learner. There are large proportions of older people with low levels of educational attainment. These people may increasingly find their low levels of skills and competence overtaken by rising qualification requirements, while at the same time encountering more difficulties than do more educated workers in updating their qualifications, because of limited basic educational competence.

The market for further education and training for adults assumes greater importance as abrupt and dramatic changes in skills and qualifications requirements, shifts in occupational composition of employment and uncertainty about future developments emphasize the need for frequent retraining during a lifetime career. Meeting this need requires closer co-operation at the policy level in order to allow for and stimulate the building of new networks and partnerships between different providers of education and training, both public and private. It also requires breaking down barriers between authorities making decisions in the traditionally fragmented training domain. The European Commission's Task Force on Human Resources, Education, Training and Youth has been instrumental in breaking down such barriers at the overall European level, and has brought forward a number of cross-disciplinary networks and partnerships. We would like to see actions of this sort becoming more widely adopted.

LABOUR MARKET INSTITUTIONS

The task of the labour market institutions is to help in achieving smooth and efficient functioning of the labour market with the fullest possible utilization of the labour force.   This interest links them with the education authorities on the one hand and with the internal labour markets of firms on the other. Their link with the education system is reinforced by findings of a consistent relationship between the incidence of educational attainment and employment probabilities: adults with the lowest level of attainment consistently face the highest incidence of unemployment and the risk they face seems to be growing.   On the other hand, the employment potential of the economy depends upon how the technologies are used, whether or not they enhance productivity and generate new products and services.

In this perspective the challenges facing the labour market authorities are complex and diverse.   The main constituency of the labour market authorities is made up of the hard to deal with cases: school dropout, long-term unemployed, hard to train individuals, minorities and so on. They aim to respond to a wide-ranging and heterogeneous set of shortfalls in the supply of skills.   Whilst labour market authorities are faced with the responsibility of addressing shortfalls in human resources stemming from weaknesses of the educational system, the enterprise-based training and failures of the labour market, they have little leverage in limiting the nature of the shortfalls they have to address.

Enterprise training often is focused on the group of workers most likely to produce results for the company.   One goal of government policies must be to assume special responsibilities for training those left out of the system and who have the danger of becoming locked into a 'peripheral' work force, characterized by unskilled temporary jobs and recurrent spells of unemployment.   More resources are therefore needed for initiatives at the European level such as the Social Fund. This is part of the broader problem of dualism in the labour market. The implications for VET and for national and European-wide training policies are worth emphasizing.   Both the tertiary and the adult education systems will have an increasing responsibility for assisting these efforts of the labour market authorities by special courses and opportunities.

There is scope for considerable variation in the forms of work organization used in conjunction with a particular technology.   Different combinations of skills may be required to operate a particular technology depending on the way work is organized. But even if the skill requirements associated with a particular technology were to be defined unambiguously, this would not entail a particular form and organization of VET: particular skills can be achieved by means of different patterns of formation: in one country a worker may achieve the necessary skill mainly through training in industry, in another country vocational education may play a greater role. It is only possible to understand the role of VET in the context of national structures of educational provision, methods of work organization and the style and institutional arrangements of industrial relations. These factors tend to reduce the benefits available from economies of scale in relation to curriculum and education developments; from standardization of qualifications between countries; and from diffusion of best practices between countries, which could be achieved by closer co-ordination at the European level.

This argument might seem to indicate that the necessary developments in VET provision could all take place at the national level. But there are clear rules for the European Union. Alongside the creation of the large internal market, one of the principal objectives of European policy should be to diminish current disparities in economic and social well-being across its regions. In the absence of action at European level differences in development and implementation of IT are likely to exacerbate even the present extreme disparities between regions. The existing financial resources available within the EU Regional Fund are from this perspective likely to be insufficient and strongly in need of augmentation. A large single market means also a large variety of regional growth patterns with peripheral areas experiencing possible vicious circles of continuous emigration of highly skilled labour and low development.

Policies for upgrading competitiveness at the periphery of the EU cannot be based on VET alone. Some of the newer members of the European Union, Portugal and Greece in particular, face the problem of poor basic education. This inhibits the catching-up process and the effective use of technologies that would increase their competitive position. In addition the skills need to be matched with patterns of sectoral development and the relationship between inward investment and indigenous growth needs to be taken into account.

Members of the European Union have initiated substantial programmes of VET development to meet emergent demands for improved IT-related competence. These have been paralleled by European Commission programmes such as ESPRIT and RACE, which while primarily concerned to promote development of IT have had training spin-offs. Other initiatives such as COMETT, DELTA and EUROTECHNET have been directly concerned with improving the quality and distribution of IT-related skills and the application of new IT to the development and delivery of education and training. There is, however, a continuing need for the development and improvement of European VET provision to meet internal needs and the challenge from other advanced economies. IT-based competence at all levels of the occupational hierarchy must be developed, from managers to research scientists and engineers, to shopfloor and office workers. There is also a pressing need to develop strategic integration of policies for IT implementation and VET and real dangers that various European policies could be in conflict.

Instruction in the use of IT has been introduced into the curriculum of several member states during the last twenty years, although Denmark ended experimental work in this area in 1985 and investment in it in West Germany fell during the 1980s. An underlying problem is uncertainty about the objectives of such programmes. There are considerable differences between European countries in this respect: for example, France has pursued a strategy of introducing IT as a vehicle for teaching across the whole educational curriculum, while Germany and the Netherlands have tended to confine it to vocational education. The balance of evidence indicates that the French approach is better, but more research is needed to provide a deeper analysis of the relative advantages of each approach. Another area in which progress in the development of training methods leaves much to be desired is in providing training opportunities in respect of the new IT to disadvantaged groups - women, the unemployed adults and ethnic minorities. Whilst some lessons have been learnt about the value of targeted training, the scope of the need dwarfs the resources which have been applied.

It is, therefore, essential to determine clearly the purpose of the inclusion of IT in school curricula. A further stage is to ensure that education and training planners, teachers and trainers gain the necessary competence. Training planners need to understand the implications of IT for the development of training systems: for example the German dual training system is having to adapt as the distinction between school-based and work-place elements of instruction has broken down under the influence of IT. Across Europe, VETs are very varied and there is really no reason to expect or pursue a harmonization in this area. On the other hand, Europe may derive strength from pluralism and variety. However, the benefits of such pluralism will depend upon continued expansion and co-operation between the many initiatives affecting mobility, co-operation, information exchange and comparative research.

Bibliography

ACAS (1988) *Labour Flexibility in Britain: the 1987 ACAS Survey*, Advisory Conciliation and Arbitration Service, London.

Adler, P. (ed.) (1992) *Technology and the Future of Work*, Oxford University Press, Oxford.

Agervold, M. (1990) 'New Technology and Physical and Psychological Stress', F. Butera, V. Di Martino, and E. Kohler (eds), *Technological Development and the Improvement of Living and Working Conditions*, Kogan Page, London.

Alaluf, M. and Stroobant, M. (1987) *Evaluation des Changements Socio-Economique Lies a l'Introduction de Nouvelles Technologies dans l'Industrie (Etudes de Cas)*, Service de Programme de la Politique Scientifique, Brussels.

Albertijn, M., Hanckl, B., and Wijgaerts, D. (1990) 'Technology Agreements and Industrial Relations in Belgium', *New Technology, Work and Employment*, 5(1): 18-30.

Alderman, N., Thwaites, A. and Ball, G. (1987) *New Technology and its Implications for Training in the Engineering Industry*, Final Report to the Engineering Industry Training Board, Centre for Urban and Regional Development Studies, University of Newcastle on Tyne.

Alvey Committee (1982) *A Programme for Advanced Information Technology*, HMSO, London.

APEX (1985) *Job Design and New Technology*, APEX, London.

Appelbaum, E. and Albin, P. (1989) 'Computer Rationalisation and the Transformation of Work: Lessons from the Insurance Industry' Wood, S. (ed.), *The Transformation of Work*, Unwin Hyman, London.

Attlewell, P. (1992) 'Skill and Occupational Changes in U.S. Manufacturing', in P. Adler (ed.), *Technology and the Future of Work*, Oxford University Press, Oxford.

Bachet, D. and Duchemin, I. (1989) *Introduction des Nouvelles Technologies, Concertation et Negociation*, ANACT, Paris.

Bamber, G. (1989) 'Technological Change and Unions', R. Hyman and W. Streeck (eds), *New Technology and Industrial Relations*, Basil Blackwell, Oxford.

Batstone, E. and Gourlay, S. (1986) *Unions, Unemployment and Innovation*, Basil Blackwell, Oxford.

Bean, C. (1985) *Comparative Industrial Relations: an Introduction to Cross-National Perspectives*, Croom Helm, London.

Begg, I. (1989) 'European Integration and Regional Policy', *Oxford Review of Economic Policy*, 5.

Belier, G. (1987) 'L'Evolution de la Negociation Collective dans l'Enterprise en France', Y. Delamotte and G. Spyroupoulos (eds), *Concertation Sociale et Mutations Economiques dans les Pays Sud de l'Europe*, Institut International d'Etudes Sociales, Geneva.

Bélisle, C. and Rosada, E. (1988) *Formation Bureautique 1988*, IRPEACS CNRS, Ecully.

Bell, D. (1974) *The Coming of Post-Industrial Society*, Heinemann, London.

Bell, D. (1980) 'The Information Society', Forester, T. (ed.), *The Microelectronic Revolution*, Blackwell, Oxford.

Belussi, F. (1987) 'Benetton: Information Technology in Production and Distribution: A Case Study of the Innovative Potential of Traditional Sector's', *SPRU Occasional Paper* No. 25, University of Sussex, Brighton.

Bertrand, O. (1985) 'The NIT Revolution and Educational Strategies', *European Journal of Education*, 20: 193-201.

Bertrand, O. and Noyelle, T. (1988a) *Human Resources and Corporate Strategy. Technological Change in Banks and Insurance Companies*, OECD, Paris.

Bertrand, O. and Noyelle, T. (1988b) 'Employment and Skills in Financial Services: a Comparison of Banks and Insurance Companies in Five OECD Countries', *Service Industries Journal*, 8: 7-18.

Bessant, J., (1989) *Microelectronics and Change at Work*, International Labour Office, Geneva.

Bessant, J. and Grunt, M. (1985) *Management and Manufacturing Innovation in the United Kingdom and West Germany*, Gower, Aldershot.

Bessant, J. and Haywood, B. (1987) 'Flexible Skills for Flexible Manufacturing' in P. Brodner (ed.) *Skill Based Automated Manufacturing*, IFAC, Pergamon Press, Oxford.

Bessant, J. and Haywood, B. (1988) 'Islands, Archipelagos and Continents: Progress on the Road to Computer-Integrated Manufacturing' *Research Policy*, 17(6): 349-362.

Beynon, H. and Nichols, T (1977) *Living with Capitalism*, Routledge Kegan Paul, London.

Bieber, D. and Deiss, M. (1990) 'Impacts of New IT Networking in and Between IT-Related Manufacturing and in Selected User Activities, (Automotive and Mechanical Engineering)', report to *Expert Group on Economic Implications of Information Technologies*, Organisation for Economic Cooperation and Development, Paris.

Bird, H. (1990) 'When the Body Takes the Strain', *New Scientist*, 1724(7): 49-52.

Blaazer, C. (1988) 'The Top Jobs That Are Just Waiting For The Right Women', *The Times*, 7th January.

Blauner, R. (1964) *Alienation and Freedom*, University of Chicago Press, Chicago.

Bodet, C. (1989) *Emploi et Aspects Sociaux Lies aux Noveaux Services de Videocommunication et de Telecommunication en France*, Universite Paris VII, Paris.

Bosch, G. (1990) *Retraining - not Redundancy: Innovative Approaches to Industrial Restructuring in Germany and France*, International Institute for Labour Studies, Geneva.

Bradshaw, D. (1990) 'An outfit made of durable fibre', *Financial Times*, 14 June.

Brady, T. (1984) *New Technology and Skills in British Industry*, Manpower Services Commission, Sheffield.

Brady, T. (1990) *SPRU Software Survey*, mimeo, SPRU, University of Sussex, Brighton.

Brady, T. and Senker, P. (1986) 'Economic Incentives and Training: Changing Skill Requirements in Computer Maintenance', *MSC Skill Series No. 6*, Manpower Services Commission, Sheffield.

Braun, F. (1987) 'Vocational Training as a Link between the Schools and the Labour Market: the Dual System in the Federal Republic of Germany', *Comparative Education*, 23: 123-143.

Braverman, H. (1974) *Labor and Monopoly Capital*, Monthly Review Press, New York.

Brunton, A. (1989) 'Review of Electronic Shelf Edge Labelling', *EPoS/EFTPoS 89 Conference Papers*, RMDP, Brighton.

Bucci, M. (1992) *Report on the Access of Young People to Community Programmes in the Field of Education and Training*, Internal Report, EC Task Force Human Resources, Education, Training and Youth, Brussels.

Buchanan, D. and McCalman, J. (1989) *High Performance Work Systems: The Digital Experience*, Routledge, London.

Buitelaar, W. (1989) *Participation in the Management of Occupational Health and Safety Improvement*, RAC/B-Course, mimeo, TNO, Appeldorn.

Burns, J. (1990) 'Operators of Keyboards "Face High Risk of Limb Disorders"' *Financial Times*, 28 February.

Buschhaus, D. (no date) *Vocational Qualifications and Flexible Production in the Industrial Metal-Working and Electrical Engineering Occupations*, Bundesinstitut fur Berufsbildung, Berlin.

Butera, F., Di Martino, V. and Kohler E. (eds) (1990) *Technological Development and the Improvement of Living and Working Conditions*, Kogan Page, London.

CAM (1986) *Nuevas Tecnologias y Empleo en la Comunidad de Madrid*, 5 volumes, Comunidad de Madrid, Madrid.

Campbell, A., Sorge, A. and Warner, M. (1989) *Microelectronic Product Applications in Great Britain and West Germany*, Avebury, Aldershot.

Campbell, A. and Warner, M. (1987) 'New Technology, Innovation and Training: an Empirical Study of British Industry', *New Technology, Work and Employment*, 2: 86-99.

Campbell, A. and Warner, M. (1989) 'Training Strategies and Microelectronics in the Engineering Industries of the UK and West Germany' paper presented to the Training Agency Seminar on *Vocational Education and Intermediate Skills*, Manchester, 21-22 September.

Cane, A. (1990) 'UK Lags Behind the Computer Times', *Financial Times*, 11 July.

Carabana, J. (1988) 'Comprehensive Educational Reforms in Spain: Past and Present', *European Journal of Education*, 23: 213-28.

Castells, M. (1989) *The Informational City*, Blackwell, Oxford.

Castells, M., Barrera, A., Casal, P., Castaño, C., Escario, P., Melero, J. and Nadal, J. (1986) *Nuevas Tecnologias, Economìa y Sociedad en España*, Alianza Editorial, Madrid.

CBS (1988) *Automatiseringsstatistieken particuliere sector*, Staatuitgeverij, Den Haag.

CEC (1984) Supplement on New Technologies and Social Change: Office Automation, *Social Europe*, Commission of the European Communities, Brussels.

CEC (1987a) 'Information Technology and Social Change in Spain and Portugal' *Social Europe* No. 1/87, Commission of the European Communities, Brussels.

CEC (1987b) 'Commission Recommendation of 24 November 1987 on Vocational Training for Women' *Official Journal of the European Communities,* No L 342/35, 4.12.87.

CEC (1988) 'New Technologies and Social Change', *Social Europe* 1/88

CEC (1989a) 'New Technologies in Printing and Publishing' *Social Europe Supplement*, No. 6/89, Commission of the European Communities, Brussels.

CEC (1989b) *The Regions of the Enlarged Community: Third Periodic Report on the Community*, Commission of the European Communities, Brussels.

CEC (1989c) 'Women in Graphics', *Women of Europe Supplement*, No. 30, Commission of the European Communities, Brussels.

CEC (1990a) 'The Labour Market for Information Technology Professionals in Europe, *Social Europe Supplement* 1/90, Commission of the European Communities, Brussels.

CEC (1990b) *Employment in Europe 1990*, Directorate General for Employment, Industrial Relations and Social Affairs, Commission of the European Communities, Brussels.

CEC (1991) *Standing Committee on Employment Situation of Women in the Community*, Commission Staff Working Paper.

CEC (1992a) 'Proposal for a Council Recommendation on Access to Vocational Training', Commission of the European Communities, Brussels.

CEC (1992b) 'The Position of Women on the Labour Market: Trends and Developments in the Twelve Member States of the European Community 1983-1990', *Women of Europe Supplements*, No. 36, Commission of the European Communities, Brussels.

CEC (1993) *EC Educational and Training Programmes 1986-92. Results and Achievements: An Overview*, Commission of the European Communities, Brussels.

Cecchini, P. (ed.) (1988) *The European Challenge: 1992 - the Benefits of a Single Market*, Gower, Aldershot.

CEDEFOP (1985) *Vocational Training in Italy*, CEDEFOP, Berlin.

CEDEFOP (1987) *Vocational Training in Greece*, CEDEFOP, Berlin.

CEDEFOP (1988a) *Training in the Spanish Textile and Clothing Industry - the Situation in Catalonia and the Autonomous Community of Valencia*, CEDEFOP, Berlin.

CEDEFOP (1988b) *Textiles and Training in Portugal*, CEDEFOP, Berlin.

CEDEFOP (1989) *Vocational Training in the Textiles and Clothing Industries in Greece*, CEDEFOP, Berlin.

Cerych, L. (1985) 'Problems Arising from the Use of New Technologies in Education', *European Journal of Education*, 20: 223-32.

Child, J. and Loveridge, R. (1990) *Information Technology in European Services*, Blackwell, Oxford.

Christiansen, D. (1992) 'Female Participation in the Training Programmes of the Task Force Human Resources', unpublished paper presented to the *Social Dialogue Seminar on Women, Training and Equal Opportunities*, Madrid, February.

Christis, J., van Klaveren, M. and Pot, F. (1985) 'Tecnologie-overeenkomsten Vergeleken', Tijdschrift voor Arbeidsvraagstukken, 1(4): 630-675.

CICA/Peat Marwick McLintock (1987) *Building on IT, Construction Industry*, Construction Industry Computing Association and Peat Marwick McLintock, London.

234   *Employment and Technical Change in Europe*

CICA/Peat Marwick McLintock (1990) *Building on IT for the 90s*, Construction Industry Computing Association and Peat Marwick McLintock, London.

Clark, J., McLoughlin, I., Rose, H. and King, R. (1988) *The Process of Technological Change: New Technology and Social Choice in the Workplace*, Cambridge University Press, Cambridge.

Clarke, K. (1991) *Women and Training: A Review*, Equal Opportunities Commission, Manchester.

Cockburn, C. (1985) *Machinery of Dominance: Women, Men and Technical Know-How*, Pluto Press, London.

Cockburn, C. (1986) 'Women and New Technology: Opportunity is Not Enough', K. Purcell, S. Woods, A. Waton and S. Allen (eds), *The Changing Experience of Employment: Restructuring and Recession* Macmillan, London.

Connor, H. and Pearson, R. (1986) *Information Technology Manpower into the 1990s*, Institute of Manpower Studies, Brighton.

Corbett, J. (1987) 'Psychological Study of Advanced Manufacturing Technology: the Concept of Coupling' *Behaviour and Information Technology*, 6(4): 441-453.

Cressey, P. (1990) 'Participation and New Technology', F. Butera, V. Di Martino, and E. Kohler (eds), *Technological Development and the Improvement of Living and Working Conditions*, Kogan Page, London.

Crompton, R. and Jones, G. (1984) *White Collar Proletariat*, Macmillan, London.

Crompton, R. and Sanderson, K. (1990) *Gendered Jobs and Social Change*, Unwin Hyman, London.

Cutler, T., Haslam, C., Williams, J. and Williams, K. (1989) *1992: the Struggle for Europe*, Berg, Oxford.

Daniel, W. (1987) *Workplace Industrial Relations and Technical Change*, Pinter, London.

Deery, S. (1989) 'Determinants of Trade Union Influence over Technological Change' *New Technology, Work and Employment*, 4(2): 117-130.

Della Rocca, G. (1986) 'Trade Union Involvement in the Introduction of New Technology in Europe', paper presented at *Olivetti/TCC Conference on Industrial Relations in the Information Society*, London, December.

Department of Industry and Commerce (1989) *Strategy for the Irish-Owned Electronics Industry*, Dublin.

Deroure, F. (1990) *Accompanying Measures in Women's Training: Vocational Training for Women*, DGV, Commission of the European Communities, Brussels.

Diederen P., Kemp R., Muysken J., and de Wit, G. (1990) *Diffusion of Information Technology in Banking: the Netherlands as an Illustrative Case*, mimeo, MERIT, University of Limburg, Maastricht.

Dodgson, M. and Martin, R. (1987) 'Trade Union Policies on New Technology: Facing the Challenge of the 1980s', *New Technology, Work and Employment*, 2(1):9-18.

Dore, R. (1976) *The Diploma Disease*, Allen and Unwin, London.

Dore, R. (1987) 'Citizenship and Employment in an Age of High Technology', *British Journal of Industrial Relations*, 25: 201-26.

Dore, R. and Sako, M. (1989) *How the Japanese Learn to Work*, Routledge, London.

Dostal, W. (1988) *Beschaftigungswandle in der Druckerei -und Verielfaltigungsindustrie vor dem Hinter technischer*, Anderungen.

Drucker, P. (1983) *Innovation and Entrepreurship: Practice and Principles*, Harper and Row, New York.

Ducatel, K. (1989) 'WIRS Synopsis 2: Part-time Workers', *PICT Research Report*, 12, CURDS, University of Newcastle, Newcastle.

Ducatel, K. and Coombes, M. (1989) 'Contextualising Flexible Accumulation: Linking Labour Market Characteristics to Emerging Spatial Divisions of Labour', paper presented at *Conference on Industrial and Social Change in Western Europe*, Durham, 26-28 September.

Dundas-Grant, V. (1985) 'The Organisation of Vocational, Technical and Technological Education in France', *Comparative Education*, 21: 257-272.

Durkan, J. (1990) 'Indigenous Services', G. Foley and P. Mulreany (eds.), *The Single European Market and the Irish Economy*, IPA: Dublin.

Ebel, K. (1986) 'The Impact of Industrial Robots on the World of Work', *International Labour Review*, 125(1): 39-51.

Ebel, K. (1989) 'Manning the Unmanned Factory', *International Labour Review*, 128(5): 535-551.

Ebel, K. and Ulrich, E. (1987) 'Some Workplace Effects of CAD and CAM', *International Labour Review*, 126(3): 351-370.

Edquist, C. (1988) *The Developments and Diffusion of New Technologies - Determinates and Consequences for Working Life*, mimeo, University of Linköping, Sweden.

Edquist, C. and Jacobsson, S. (1988) *Flexible Automation, The Global Diffusion of New Technology in the Engineering Industry*, Blackwell, Oxford.

EITB (1987) *Economic Monitor*, June, UK Engineering Industry Training Board, London.

Elger, T. (1987) 'Flexible Futures? New Technology and the Contemporary Transformation of Work', *Work, Employment and Society*, 1: 528-40.

Emeriaud, M. and Paponneau, C. (1989) 'Nouveaux Systemes, Nouveaux Metiers', *Revue Française des Telecommunications*, March.

EOLAS (1989), *Electronics Manpower Study: Trends in the Irish Electronic Manufacturing Industry up to 1995*, EOLAS, Dublin.

Equal Opportunities Commission (1993) *Formal Investigation into the Publicly-Funded Vocational Training System in England and Wales*, Equal Opportunities Commission, Manchester.

Esser, J. and Hirsch, J. (1989) 'The Crisis of Fordism and the Dimensions of a "Postfordist" Regional and Urban Structure', *International Journal of Urban and Regional Research*, 13: 417-37.

Essex, S., Callender, C., Rees, T. and Winckler, V. (1986) *New Styles of Training for Women: An Evaluation of South Glamorgan Women's Workshop*, Equal Opportunities Commission, Manchester.

European Foundation (1985) *The Role of the Parties Concerned in the Introduction of New Technology*, European Foundation for the Improvement of Living and Working Conditions, Dublin.

European Round Table of Industrialists (1989) *Reshaping Europe*, European Round Table of Industrialists, Brussels.

Eurostat (1988) 'Full-Time Education in the European Community', *Rapid Reports: Population and Social Conditions*, Eurostat, Luxembourg.

Eurostrategies-Planet-Turu (1989) *Employment Structures and Trends in Telecommunications*, 3 volumes, Report to Commission of the European Communities, Brussels.

Evans, J. (1984) 'Trade Unions and New Technology Agreements in Europe: Negotiating Technological Change' K. Grewlich and F. Pedersen (eds), *Power and Participation in an Information Society*, CEC-FAST, Luxembourg.

Ewers, H., Becker, C. and Frisch, M. (1990) 'The Effects of the Use of Computer Aided Technology in Industrial Enterprises: It's the Context that Counts', Schettkat, R. and Wagner, M. (eds) (1990) *Technological Change and Employment: Innovation in the German Economy*, de Gruyter, Berlin.

Eyraud, F., d'Iribarne, A. and Maurice, M. (1988) 'Des Enterprises Face aux Technologies Flexibles: Une Analyse de la Dynamique du Changement', *Sociologie du Travail*, 1-88: 55-77.

Eyraud, F., Maurice, M., d'Iribarne, A. and Rychener, F. (1984) 'Developpement des Qualifications et Apprentissage par l'Entreprise des Nouvelles Technologies', *Sociologie du Travail*, 4-84, 482-99.

Fasano, C. (1985) 'Beyond Computers - Education', *European Journal of Education*, 20: 257-64.

Federal Minister for Education and Science (1992) *Vocational Training in the Dual System in the Federal Republic of Germany: An Investment in the Future*, Federal Minister for Education and Science, Bonn.

Fenton, J (1989) 'Skills Shortage of Computer Scientists in Industry', paper presented to the *Conference of Professors of Computer Science*, University of Lancaster, July.

Ferner, A. and Hyman, R. (eds) (1992) *Industrial Relations in the New Europe*, Basil Blackwell, London.

Fielder, S., Rees, G. and Rees, T. (1990) 'Regional Restructuring, Services and Women's Employment: Labour Market Change in South Wales', Project Paper No. 3, ESRC Research Programme on the *Institutional Determinants of Adult Training*, Social Research Unit, University of Wales College of Cardiff, Cardiff.

Fielder, S. and Rees, T. (1991) *High Level IT, Training and Women's Employment*, Social Research Unit, School of Social and Administrative Studies, University of Wales College of Cardiff, Cardiff.

Finegold, D. and Soskice, D. (1988) 'The Failure of Training in Britain: An Analysis and Interpretation', *Oxford Review of Economic Policy* 4(3): 46-62.

Forsey, G and Finlay, P. (1989) 'Information Technology Support for Corporate Bank Lending', *The Service Industries Journal*, 9(1), January.

Friedmann, A. (1977) *Industry and Labour: Class Struggle at Work and Monopoly Capitalism*, Macmillan, London.

Friedmann, G. (1955) *Industrial Society: the Emergence of the Human Problems of Automation*, Free Press, Glencoe, Illinois.

Fröhlich, D., Fuchs, D. and Kriger, H.(1990) *New Information Technology and Participation in Europe: the Potential for Social Dialogue*, European Foundation for the Improvement of Living and Working Conditions, Dublin.

Gann, D. (1991) *Technological Change and Construction Skills in the 1990s*, Construction Industry Training Board, London.

Gann, D. (1989) *New Technology, Employment and Operative Skills in Building Services*, mimeo, Science Policy Research Unit, University of Sussex, Brighton.

Gallie, D. (ed.) (1988) *Employment in Britain*, Basil Blackwell, Oxford.

Gallie, D. (1991) 'Patterns of Skill Change: Upskilling, Deskilling or the Polarization of Skills' *Work Employment and Society*, 5(1): 319-351.

Gennard, J. (1987) 'The NGA and the Impact of New Technology' *New Technology, Work and Employment*, 2(2): 126-141.

Gottelmann, G. (1989) *Strategies D'Innovations Technologiques et Politiques Educatives: en France, en Republique Federale d'Allemagne et au Royaume Uni*, UNESCO, Paris.

GRAP (1985) 'Des Robots au Concert' *Annales des Mines-Gerer et Comprendre*, 1.

Graves, D. (1989) 'EPoS - Staff Scheduling - Customer Service', EPoS/EFTPoS 89 Conference Papers, RMDP, Brighton.

Gürtler, J. and Pusse, L. (1988) 'Mittelfristige Entwicklung von Beschäftigung und Arbeitsproduktivität im Kreditgewerbe: Tendenzen und betriebliche Maßnahmen', *Mitteilungen aus der Arbeitsmarkt- und Berufsforschung*, June.

Hall-Sheehy, J. (1988) 'Management Turn-on to Computers', *International Journal of Computing* 1(2): 15-20.

Handke, G. (1982) 'Design and Use of Flexible Manufacturing Systems', K. Rathmill (ed.) Proceedings of the *Second International Conference on Manufacturing Systems*, IFS Publications, Kempston.

Heizmann, J. (1984) 'Work Structuring in Automated Manufacturing Systems, Exemplified by the Use of Industrial Robots for Body Shell Assembly', T. Martin (ed.) *Design at Work in Automated Manufacturing Systems*, Pergamon, Oxford.

Henderickx, F. and Raeymaekers, A.M. (1987) *Evaluatie van de sociale en econonische veranderigen die gepaard gaan met de invoering van nieuwe informatietechnologieën in de industrie (gevel studies)*, Services de Programmation de la Politique Scientifique, Brussels.

Hingel, A. (1990) *Diversity, Equality and Community Cohesion*, FAST Working Paper PD 1/01, mimeo, Commission of the European Community, Brussels.

Hirsch, P. (1989) 'EFTPoS Developments in Europe - Less Publicity, More Progress', *EPoS/EFTPoS 89 Conference Papers*, RMDP, Brighton.

Hoch, H. (1988) *The New Industrial Metalworking Occupations*, Bundesinstitut fur Berufsbildung, Berlin.

Hoch, H. (1988) *The New Industrial Metalworking Occupations*, Bundesinstitut fur Berufsbildung, Berlin.

Höflich-Häberlein, L. and Häbler, H. (1990) 'The Diffusion of New Technologies and their Effects in the Private Service Sector', R. Schettkat and M. Wagner (eds) *Technological Change and Employment, Innovation in the German Economy*, de Gruyter, Berlin.

Hofstede, G. (1980) *Culture's Consequences. International Differences in Work-Related Values*, Sage, Beverly Hills.

Huggett, C. (1988) 'Participation in Practice. A Case Study of the Introduction of New Technology', *Engineering Industry Training Board Research Report No. RC22*, Watford.

Hughes, C. (1989) 'Customer Self-Scanning', *Proceedings of EPoS/EFTPoS '89 Conference*, RMDP, Brighton.

Hutton, S. and Lawrence, P. (1981) *German Engineers: the Anatomy of a Profession*, Clarendon Press, Oxford.

ILO (1986) 'VDUs', *Conditions of Work Digest*, 5(1), International Labour Office, Geneva.

ILO, (1987a) 'Training and Retraining - The Implications of Technological Change' *Report 3, Fourth Regional Conference*, International Labour Office, Geneva, September.

ILO (1987b) *ILO Yearbook*, International Labour Office, Geneva.

ILO (1988) *ILO Yearbook*, International Labour Office, Geneva.

IMS (1986) *Changing Working Patterns*, report to National Economic Development Office and Department of Employment, Institute of Manpower Studies, University of Sussex, Brighton.

IPRA (1991) *Future Skill Needs of the Construction Industries*, report prepared for the Employment Department by IPRA Ltd., Brighton.

Irizarry, R. (1980) 'Over-education and Unemployment in the Third World: the Paradoxes of Dependent Industrialisation', *Comparative Education Review*, 24.

Jarvis, V. and Prais, S. (1989) 'Two Nations of Shopkeepers: Training for Retailing in France and Britain', *National Institute Economic Review*, 128, 58-74.

Jones, B. (1982) 'Destruction or Redistribution of Skills? The Case of Numerical Control', S. Wood (ed.) *The Degradation of Work?*, Hutchinson, London.

Jones, B. and Scott, P. (1987) 'Flexible Manufacturing Systems in Britain and the U.S.A.' *New Technology, Work and Employment*, 2(1): 27-36.

Jurgens, U., Malsch, T. Dohse, K. (1986) *Moderne Zeiten in der Automobilfabrik*, Springer Verlag, Berlin.

Kaplinsky, R. (1984) *Automation: The Technology and Society*, Longman Harlow, London

Keogh, V. (1989) 'The Need for Multi-Skilling in Industry' paper presented at *Multi-Skilling in Maintenance Conference*, London, 18 May.

Kern, H. and Schumann, M. (1984) *Das Ende der Arbeitsteilung? Rationalisierung in der Industriellen Produktion*, Verlag C.H. Beck, Munich.

Kern, H. and Schumann, M. (1987) 'Limits of the Division of Labour: New Production Concepts in West German Industry', Economic and Industrial Democracy, 8: 151-170.

Kern, H. and Schumann, M. (1992) 'New Concepts of Production and The Emergence of the Systems Controller, P. Adler (ed.) *Technology and the Future of Work*, Oxford University Press, Oxford.

Kortteinen, M., Lehto, A.. and Ylöstalo, P. (1987) *Information Technology and Work in Finland*, Tilastokeskus Statistikcentralen, Helsinki.

Krais, B. (1979) *Relationships Between Education and Employment and their Impact on Education and Labour Market Policies*, CEDEFOP, Berlin.

Kristensen, P. (1986) 'Technological Projects and Organizational Changes', paper presented at *New Production Systems. Implications for Work and Training in the Factory of the Future*, Torino, Italy, 2-4 July.

Læssøe, J. and Rasmussen, L. (1989) *Human-Centred Methods*, Institut fur Samfundsfag, Lyngby.

Lane, C. (1985) 'White Collar Workers in the Labour Process: The Case of the Federal Republic of Germany', *Sociological Review*, 33(2), May.

Lane, C. (1987) 'Capitalism or Culture? A Comparative Analysis of the Position in the Labour Process and Labour Market of Lower White-Collar Workers in the Financial Services Sector of Britain and the Federal Republic of Germany', *Work, Employment and Society*, 1: 57-84.

Lane, C. (1988) 'New Technology and Clerical Work' D. Gallie (ed.), *Employment in Britain*, Blackwell, Oxford.

Lane, C. (1989), *Management and Labour in Europe*, Edward Elgar, Aldershot.

Lefebvre, M. (1992) *Evaluation of Women's Involvement in ESF Co-Financed Measures*, Report to DGV of the Commission of the European Communities, Brussels.

Lemaitre, A. and Teyssier, F. (1987) 'Droit du Travail et Automatisation', *CEJEE*, February.

LIBER (1989) *Technological Change, Resources in the Service Sector: The Case of the Netherlands*, University of Maastricht, Limburg.

Lincoln, J. and Kalleberg, A. (1990) *Culture, Control and Commitment*, Cambridge University Press, Cambridge.

Lindley, R. (ed.) (1992) *Women's Employment: Britain in the Single European Market*, Equal Opportunities Commission, Manchester.

Littler, C. (1982) *The Development of the Labour Process in Capitalist Societies*, Heinemann, London.

Lochet, J. and Verdier, E (1987) 'Is There Really a Specific Market for Computer Specialists?', *Training and Employment*, 17.

Locksley, G., Morgan, K. and Thomas, G. (1990) 'Barriers to Growth: Skills and Training in Telematics', *New Technology, Work and Employment*, 5: 5-17.

Long, R. (1987) *New Office Information Technology. Human and Managerial Implications*, Croom Helm, London.

Lovegrove, G. and Hall, W. (1987) 'Where Have All the Girls Gone?' *University Computing* 9: 207-210.

Lutz, B. (1981) 'Education, Employment: Contrasting Evidence from France and the Federal Republic of Germany', *European Journal of Education*, 16:73-86.

Lythe, C. (1991) 'Scotland and European Community Regional Policy in the 1990s' G. Day and G. Rees (eds.), *Regions, Nations and European Integration*, University of Wales Press, Cardiff.

McCandless, H. and Duffy, L. (1989) 'Changing Roles in the High-Tech Office', *Practical Computing*, 39-46, July.

MacNamara, F. (1990) *Women and Training*, MSc Econ Women's Studies (unpublished dissertation), University of Wales College of Cardiff, Cardiff.

Manzanares, J. (1985) *Trabajo y Nuevas Tecnologias*, FUNDESCO, Madrid.

Martin, C. (1989) 'Management Computer Support: Analysing the Top Manager's Perspective on Interactive Systems', *Knowledge-Based Management Support Systems*, Ellis Horwood, Chichester.

Maurice, M. (1990) 'Convergence and/or Societal Effect for the Europe of the Future?', paper presented to the CEDEFOP/Work, Employment and Society Conference, *Employment, Training and European Integration*, University of Bath.

Maurice, M., Sellier, F. and Silvestre, J. (1986) *The Social Foundations of Industrial Power*, MIT Press, London.

Maurice, M., Sorge, A. and Warner, M. (1980) 'Societal Differences in Organizing Manufacturing Units: a Comparison of France, West Germany and Great Britain', *Organization Studies*, 1, 59-86.

Meager, N. (1991) 'TECs: A Revolution in Training and Enterprise or Old Wine in New Bottles?' *Local Economy*, 6(1): 4-20.

Miles, I. with Brady, T., Davies, A., Haddon, L., Jagger, N., Matthews, M., Rush, H. and Wyatt, S. (1990) *Mapping and Measuring the Information Economy*, British Library (ILR Report No. 77), Boston Spa.

Miles, I., and Matthews, M. (1992) 'Information Technology and the Information Economy,' K. Robins (ed.), *Understanding Information: Business, Technology and Geography*, Belhaven, London.

Miles, I., Rush, H., Turner, K. and Bessant, J. (1988) *Information Horizons*, Edward Elgar, Aldershot.

Millward, N. (1986) *Workplace Industrial Relations Survey* (computer file), ESRC Data Archive, Colchester.

Morgan, K. and Sayer, A. (1988) *Microcircuits of Capital*, Polity, Cambridge.

Mumford, E. (1983) *Designing Secretaries*, Manchester Business School, Manchester.

Murphy, P. and Mullan, T. (1989) *Time for Women in IT*, Department of Education, University of Ulster, Jordanstown.

Murray, P. and Wickham, J. (1982) 'Technocratic Ideology and the Reproduction of Inequality: the Case of the Electronics Industry in the Republic of Ireland' G. Day (ed.), *Diversity and Decomposition in the Labour Market*, Gower, Aldershot.

Murray, P. and Wickham, J. (1983) 'Technical Training and Technical Knowledge in an Irish Electronics Factory' G. Winch (ed.), *Information Technology in Manufacturing Processes*, Rossendale, London.

Murray, P. and Wickham, J. (1985) 'Women Workers and Bureaucratic Control in Irish Electronics Factories' H. Newby, J. Bujra, P. Littlewood, G. Rees, and T. Rees (eds.), *Restructuring Capital: Recession and Reorganisation in Industrial Society*, Macmillan, London.

National Board for Science and Technology (1981) *Micro-Electronics: The Implications for Ireland*, NBST, Dublin.

NCC (1987) *Improving the Quality and Diffusion of Software Sector Data in the EEC*, National Centre for Information Technology, London.

NEDC (1989) *Jobs and Technology in the Food and Drink Industry*, National Economic Development Council, London.

NEDC (1991) *What Makes a Supervisor World Class?* Engineering Skills Working Party, National Economic Development Council, London.

NEDO (1983) Policy for the UK Information Technology Industry, National Economic Development Office, London.

NEDO/MSC (1984) *Competence and Competition*, National Economic Development Organisation, London.

Newton, P. (1991) 'Computing: An Ideal Occupation for Women?' in J. Firth-Cozens and M. West (eds), *Women at Work*, Open University Press, Milton Keynes.

Newton, P. and Haslam, S. (1988) 'Girls and Computers in Secondary Schools: a Systems Failure?' paper presented at the *British Psychological Society Annual Conference*, University of Leeds, Leeds.

Nichols, K. (1989) 'A Retailer's View of EFTPoS and the Inaugural Service of EFTPoS UK', *EPoS/EFTPoS 89 Conference Proceedings*, RMDP, Brighton.

Nikolinakos, M. (1989) *Information Technology and Social Change in Europe: Employment and Social Aspects of New Telemedia Services*, Institute for the Study of the Greek Economy, Athens.

Nikolinakos, M. (1990) 'Greece in the EC, The Labour Market for Information Technology Professionals in Europe', *Social Europe*, 1/90.

Northcott, J. Rogers, P., Knetsch, W. and de Lestapis, B. (1985) *Microelectronics in Industry; An International Comparison: Britain, France and Germany*, Policy Studies Institute, London.

Northcott, J. and Walling, A. (1988) *The Impact of Microelectronics: Diffusion, Benefits and Problems in British Industry*, Policy Studies Institute, London.

OECD (1986) *New Information Technologies: a Challenge for Education*, Organisation for Economic Cooperation and Development, Paris.

OECD (1988) *New Technologies in the 1990s: a Socio-Economic Strategy*, Organisation for Economic Cooperation and Development, Paris.

OECD (1989a) *The Internationalisation of Software and Computer Services*, Organisation for Economic Cooperation and Development, Paris.

OECD (1989b) *Government Policies and the Diffusion of Microelectronics*, Organisation for Economic Cooperation and Development, Paris.

OECD (1989c) *Telecommunication Network Based Services: Policy Implications*, Organisation for Economic Cooperation and Development, Paris.

OECD (1989d) *Technology, Flexibility of Manufacturing and Industrial Relations*, Organisation for Economic Cooperation and Development, Paris.

OECD (1990) *Technological Change and Human Resource Development: The Service Sector. Main Trends and Issues*, OECD, Paris.

OECD (1993) *Usage Indicators: A New Foundation for Information Technology Policies*, Organisation for Economic Cooperation and Development, Paris.

OECD/CERI (1986) *New Technology and Human Resource Development in the Automobile Industry*, OECD/CERI General Distribution, Paris.

Oliver, N. and Wilkinson, B. (1988) *The Japanisation of British Industry*, Blackwell, Oxford.

PA Consultants (1992) *An Evaluation of the IRIS Network*, PA Economic Consultants, Cambridge.

Palmer, C. (1988) 'Using IT for Competitive Advantage at Thomson Holidays', *Long Range Planning*, 21(6): 26-29.

Palmer, C. and Ottley, S. (1990) *From Potential to Reality. 'Hybrids' - A Critical Force in the Application of Information Technology in the 1990s*, A Report by the British Computer Society Task Group on 'Hybrids', British Computer Society, London.

Palmer, J. (1989) *1992 and Beyond*, Office for Official Publications of the European Communities, Luxembourg.

Palmer, J. (1991) 'Europe After the Revolutions' M. Kaldor (ed.), *Europe From Below*, Verso, London.

Pate, C. (1989) *Strategies for Survival: Industrial Relations Aspects of New Technology and Restructuring in the British and Swedish Newspaper Industries*, Unpublished D. Phil Thesis.

Pearson, R., Connor, H. and Pole, C. (1988) *The IT Manpower Monitor*, Institute for Manpower Studies, Brighton.

Pelgrum, W, and Plomp, T. (1991) *The Use of Computers in Education Worldwide*, Pergamon Press/International Association for the Evaluation of Educational Achievement, Oxford.

Penn, R. (1990) 'Skilled Maintenance Work at British Telecom: Findings from the Social Change and Economic Life Initiative', *New Technology, Work and Employment*, 5(2).

Penn, R. and Scattergood, H. (1988) 'Continuities and Change in Skilled Work', *British Journal of Sociology*, 39(1).

Perry, R. and Greber, L. (1990) 'Women and Computers: An Introduction', Signs Vol. 16(4): 74-101.

Piganiol, C. (1989) 'Industrial Relations and Enterprise Restructuring in France', *International Labour Review*, 137(5): 525-543.

Piore, M. and Sabel, C. (1984) *The Second Industrial Divide*, Basic Books, New York.

Posthuma, A. (1988) The Internationalization of Clerical Work, SPRU, University of Sussex, Brighton.

Prais, S. (1989) 'How Europe Would See the New British Initiative for Standardising Vocational Qualifications', *National Institute Economic Review*, 129: 52-54.

Prais, S. and Wagner, K. (1988) 'Productivity and Management: the Training of Foremen in Britain and Germany', *National Institute Economic Review*, 123: 34-47.

Quintas, P. (1986) 'Information Technology and Employment in Local Government', *New Technology, Work and Employment*, 1(2).

Rajan, A. (1985) *New Technology and Employment in Insurance, Banking and Building Societies*, Gower, Aldershot.

Rajan, A. (1987) *Services - The Second Industrial Revolution?*, Butterworths, London.

Rajan, A. and Pearson, J. (1986) *UK Occupation and Employment Trends to 1990*, Butterworths, Sevenoaks.

Ray, L. (1991) 'A Thatcher Export Phenomenon ? The Enterprise Culture in Eastern Europe' R. Keat and N. Abercrombie (eds.), *Enterprise Culture*, Routledge, London.

Rees, G. (1990) 'New Information Technologies and Vocational Training In the European Communities: the Challenge of the 1990s' Report for the EC's *Project on Employment and Training in the New Information Technologies in the European Communities*, University of Wales College of Cardiff, Cardiff.

Rees, G., Williamson, H. and Winckler, V. (1989) 'The "New Vocationalism": Further Education and Local Labour Markets', *Journal of Education Policy*, 4: 227-44.

Rees, T. (1992) *Skill Shortages, Women and the New Information Technologies*, Commission of the European Communities, Brussels.

Rees, T. (1993) *Women and the EC Training Programmes*, Report to the European Commission Task Force for Human Resources, Education, Training and Youth, School for Advanced Urban Studies, Bristol.

RMDP (1989) *EPoS in the Major Markets of Western Europe*, RMDP, Brighton.

Rolfe, H. (1986) 'Skill, Deskilling and New Technology in the Non-Manual Labour Process', *New Technology, Work and Employment*, 1(1).

Rorato, G. (1989) 'L'Aspetto Strategico dell'Informazione nella STANDA degli Anni '90' *EPoS/EFTPoS 89 Conference Papers*, RMDP, Brighton.

Rosanvallon, A. (1986) 'Flexible Manufacturing Systems and Work Organization' paper prepared for the EC-Symposium *New Production Systems*, Turin, Italy, 2-4 July 1986.

Rose, M. (1985) 'Universalism, Culturalism and the Aix Group: Promise and Problems of a Societal Approach to Economic Institutions', *European Sociological Review*, 1: 65-83.

Rubery, J. and Fagan, C. (1992) *Occupational Segregation amongst Women and Men in the European Community*, Commission of the European Communities, Brussels.

Ryan, P. (1984) 'Job Training, Employment Practices and the Large Enterprise: the Case of Costly Transferable Skills', P. Osterman (ed.), *Internal Labour Markets*, MIT Press, Boston.

Sabel, C., Herrigel, G., Deeg, R. and Kazis, R. (1989) 'Regional Prosperities Compared: Massachusetts and Baden-Wurttemberg', *Economy and Society*, 18, 374-404.

Schettkat, R. and Wagner, M. (eds) (1990) *Technological Change and Employment: Innovation in the German Economy*, de Gruyter, Berlin.

Schiersmann, C. (ed.) (1988) *Mehr Risiken als Chancen? Frauen und neue Technologien*, Institut Frau und Gesellschaft, Hannover.

Schmehr, H. and Millner, G. (1992) *Skills for a Competitive Europe: a Human Resources Outlook for the 1990s*, Task Force Human Resources Education, Training and Youth, Commission of the European Communities, Brussels.

Schuh, E. (1990) 'Working Conditions in the European Community: Situation and Trends', paper presented at the *Future of Work and Workers' Health*, Karlinska Institute, Sweden, April, 2-4.

Schultz-Wild, R. (1990) *The Application of Information Technology and the Restructuring of Production Work in West Germany*, ISF, Munich.

Schweikert, K. (1982) *Vocational Training of Young Migrants in the Federal Republic of Germany*, CEDEFOP, Berlin.

Scott, A. (1988) 'Flexible Production Systems and Regional Development: the Rise of New Industrial Spaces in North America and Western Europe', *International Journal of Urban and Regional Research*, 12: 171-85.

Senker, J. and Senker, P. (1990) *Technical Change in the 1990s: Implications for Skills, Training and Employment,* Report to the Training Agency, Science Policy Research Unit, University of Sussex, Brighton.

Senker, P. (1990) 'TVEI: evaluation, economic policy and ideology', Hopkins, D. (ed.), *TVEI at the Change of Life,* Multilingual Matters, Clevedon.

Senker, P. and Beesley, M. (1986) 'The Need for Skills in the Factory of the Future' , *New Technology, Work and Employment*, 1(1): 9-17

Senker, P., Townsend, J. and Buckingham, J. (1989) 'Working with Expert Systems: Three Case Studies, *AI and Society*, 3: 103-116.

Sessar-Karpp, E. (1988) 'Computerkurse von Frauen Fur Frauen', C Schiersmann (ed.) *Mehr Risiken als Chancen? Frauen und Neue Technologien*, Institut Frau und Gesellschaft, Hannover.

Shaiken, H. (1984) *Work Transformed: Automation and Labour in the Comuter Age*, Reinhart and Winston, New York.

Simmonds, P. and Senker, P. (1989) *Making More of CAD. A Report on a Longitudinal Study in British Engineering Companies*, Engineering Industry Training Board Research Report RC23, Watford.

Smith, S. (1987) 'Information Technology in Banks: Taylorization or Human-centered Systems?', *Science and Public Policy*, 14(3) June.

Smith, S. and Wield, D. (1987) 'New Technology and Bank Work: Banking on IT as an "Organisational Technology"', R. Finnegan, G. Salaman and K. Thompson (eds), *Information Technology: Social Issues*, Croom Helm, London.

Sorge, A. (1984) *Technological Change, Employment, Qualifications and Training*, CEDEFOP, Berlin.

Sorge, A. and Warner, M. (1986) *Comparative Factory Organisation*, Gower, Aldershot.

Steedman, H. (1987) 'Vocational Training in France and Britain: Office Work', *National Institute Economic Review*, 120: 58-70.

Steedman, H. (1988), 'Vocational Training in France and Britain: Mechanical and Electrical Craftsmen', *National Institute Economic Review*, 126: 57-70.

Steedman, H. and Wagner, K. (1989) 'Productivity, Machinery and Skills: Clothing and Manufacture in Britain and Germany', *National Economic Review*, 128.

Stefanou-Lambropoulou, P. (1987) 'Information Technology and Women's Employment in the Greek Public Sector', *Dyosios Tomeas*, 20, 46-49.

Stevenson, H. (1989) 'Expert Systems in the UK Financial Services Sector: A Symbolic Analysis of the Hype', G. Doukidis, F. Land and G. Miller (eds) *Knowledge-Based Management Support Systems*, John Wiley, Chichester.

Storey, J. (1987) 'The Management of New Office Technology: Choice, Control and Social Structure in the Insurance Industry', *Journal of Management Studies*, 24(1): 43-62, January.

STT (1983) *Microelectronica in beroep enbedrijf, Stichting Toekomstbeeld der Techniek*, Her Kantoor, Den Haag.

Swann, J. (1986) *The Employment Effects of Microelectronics in the UK Services Sector*, Technical Change Centre, London.

Tallard, M. (1989) 'Bargaining Over New Technology: a Comparison of France and West Germany', R. Hyman and W. Streeck (eds), *New Technology and Industrial Relations*, Basil Blackwell, Oxford.

Task Force Human Resources, Education, Training and Youth (1991) *Joint Opinion on Access to Continuing Training*, Commission of the European Communities, Brussels.

Teague, P. (1989) *The European Community: the Social Dimension - Labour Market Policies for 1992*, Kogan Page, London.

Teague, P. and Grahl, J. (1992) *Industrial Relations and European Integration*, Lawrence and Wishart, London.

Thompson, L. (1989) 'New Office Technology and the Changing Role of the Secretary', *Work Research Unit Occasional Paper 44*, London.

Tidd, J. (1991) *Flexible Manufacturing Technologies and International Competitiveness*, Pinter, London.

Treu, T. and Negrelli, S. (1987) 'Worker's Participation and Personnel Management Policies', *International Labour Review*, 126(1): 249-258.

UNIDO, 1989, 'Textile Policy for Developing Countries' *Industry and Development*, 25.

Valavanidis, A. and Sarafopoulos, N. (1989) 'Occupational Health and Safety in Greece: Current Problems and Perspectives', *International Labour Review*, 128(2): 249-258.

Valenduc, G. (1989) *Aspects Economiques et Sociaux du Developpements des Nouveaux Services de Telecommunication en Belgique*, Fondation Travail, Universite Bruxelles, Brussels.

Vickery, G. and Campbell, D. (1989) 'Advanced Manufacturing Technology and the Organisation of Work' *STI Review*, 6:105-146.

Vilkstrup, K. (1988) *Information Technology in Danish Industry, 1987*, Agency of Industry and Trade, Copenhagen.

Vine, R. (1985) *The Impact of Technological Change in the Industrial Democracies: Public Attitudes Towards Information Technology*, Atlantic Institute for International Affairs, Paris.

Wajcman, J. (1991) *Feminism Confronts Technology*, Polity, Oxford.

Walby, S. (ed.) (1988) *Gender Segregation at Work,* Open University Press, Milton Keynes.

Walby, S. (1990) *Theorising Patriarchy,* Blackwell, Oxford.

Warner, M., Wobbe, W. and Brodner, P.(1990) *New Technology and Manufacturing Management: Strategic Choices for Flexible Production Systems*, John Wiley, Chichester.

Watanabe, S. (1987) *Microelectronics, Automation and Employment in the Automobile Industry*, John Wiley, Chichester.

Webster, J. (1990) *Office Automation,* Harvester Press, London.

Wedderburn, K. (1990) *The Social Charter, European Company and Employment Rights: an Outline Agenda*, Institute of Employment Rights, London.

Wellington, J. (1989) *Education for Employment: the Place of Information Technology,* National Foundation for Education Research, Windsor.

Williams, R. and Steward, F. (1985) 'Technology Agreements in Great Britain: a Survey 1977-1983', *Industrial Relations Journal*, 16(3): 58-73.

Williamson, J. (1989) 'European Cellular Telephony: An Overview', in *Pan European-Mobile Communications*, IBC Technical Services, London.

Willman, P. (1986) *New Technology and Industrial Relations: a Review of the Literature*, Department of Employment, London.

Wilson, F. (1988) 'Computer Numerical Control and Constraint' D. Knights and H. Wilmott (eds), *New Technology and the Labour Process*, Macmillan, London.

Wix, P. (1989) *The Impact of IT on Building Design and Construction*, CICC Publications, London.

Women's Technology Scheme (1989) *Annual Report 1989*, Women's Technology Scheme, Liverpool.

Wood, S. (ed.) (1982) *The Degradation of Work*, Hutchinson, London.

Woodward, J. (1958) *Management and Technology*, HMSO, London.

Woodward, J. (1965) *Industrial Organization: Theory and Practice*, Oxford University Press, Oxford.

Yap, C. (1986) *Information Technology in Organisations in the Service Sector*, DPhil Dissertation, University of Cambridge.

Yuchtman-Yaar, E. (1989) 'Economic Culture in Post-Industrial Society', B. Strumpel (ed.) *Industrial Societies After the Stagnation of the 1970s*, de Gruyter, Berlin.

Zuboff, S. (1988) *In the Age of the Smart Machine*, Heinemann, Oxford.

Index